PENGUIN BOOKS

BLACK SWINE IN THE SEWERS OF HAMPSTEAD

Thomas Boyle grew up in eastern Pennsylvania and holds degrees from Cornell and New York University. A professor of English at Brooklyn College, he is the author of the crime novels *Only the Dead Know Brooklyn* and *Post-Mortem Effects*.

Ford Madox Brown's *Work* (1852-65)

❖

Excavations in Heath Street, Hampstead.
"*Work* can be seen as a neurotic attempt to control an
environment which is rapidly getting out of control"

(page 216).

BLACK SWINE IN THE SEWERS OF HAMPSTEAD

Beneath the Surface of Victorian Sensationalism

THOMAS BOYLE

PENGUIN BOOKS

PENGUIN BOOKS
Published by the Penguin Group
Viking Penguin, a division of Penguin Books USA Inc.,
375 Hudson Street, New York, New York 10014, U.S.A.
Penguin Books Ltd, 27 Wrights Lane,
London W8 5TZ, England
Penguin Books Australia Ltd, Ringwood,
Victoria, Australia
Penguin Books Canada Ltd, 2801 John Street,
Markham, Ontario, Canada L3R 1B4
Penguin Books (N.Z.) Ltd, 182–190 Wairau Road,
Auckland 10, New Zealand

Penguin Books Ltd, Registered Offices:
Harmondsworth, Middlesex, England

First published in the United States of America by
Viking Penguin, a division of Penguin Books USA Inc., 1989
Published in Penguin Books 1990

1   3   5   7   9   10   8   6   4   2

Grateful acknowledgment is made for permission to
reprint an excerpt from *Victorian Panorama*:
Paintings of Victorian Life by Christopher Wood.
By permission of Faber and Faber Ltd.

LIBRARY OF CONGRESS CATALOGING IN PUBLICATION DATA
Boyle, Thomas.
Black swine in the sewers of Hampstead: beneath the surface of
Victorian sensationalism/Thomas Boyle.
p.   cm.
ISBN 0 14 01.3975 3
1. English fiction—19th century—History and criticism.
2. Sensationalism in literature.   '3. Detective and mystery stories,
English—History and criticism.   4. Great Britain—Popular culture—
History—19th century.   5. Crime—Great Britain—History—19th
century.   6. Crime in literature.   I. Title.
[PR878.S44B69   1990]
823'.809355—dc20   90–6823

Printed in the United States of America
Set in Garamond #3
Designed by Ellen S. Levine
Frontispiece by Ford Madox Brown courtesy of
Manchester City Art Galleries

To the memories of
Alan Bell Macdonald (1914–1987) and
Gordon Norton Ray (1915–1986),
two gentlemen of great distinction.
This book would never have been completed
without their unstinting generosity and
I deeply regret that neither
lived to see its publication.

❖

Acknowledgments

The National Endowment for the Humanities provided me with a fellowship which enabled me to take time off from teaching, to travel, and to effectively wrap up the research for this manuscript. My wife, Margaret Taylor Boyle, editor and psychologist *par excellence*, saw me through the rest.

Portions of this book, in significantly altered form, have appeared in *Literature and History* and *Tennessee Studies in Literature*.

❖

Contents

CONTENTS

BLACK SWINE IN THE SEWERS OF HAMPSTEAD

Prologue: A Lost Archive of Crime

In the late summer of 1972, my wife and I stopped off in England on the way back to New York from an extended tour of the Continent. In those days, London was one of my favorite ports of call, having well earned—at least in the more youthful and prosperous precincts—its "swinging" reputation as a kind of pleasure dome. But on this particular visit I intended to avoid such distraction. I had to find, or, more precisely, recover a career.

A few years before, I had abandoned a projected doctoral dissertation in English to pursue fame and fortune by writing a novel. This fictional endeavor had not been a success, a fact dramatically underlined by the pile of humbling rejection slips I had accumulated at various *poste-restantes* and American Express offices throughout Europe that summer. Now there seemed to be little choice but to return to the academic thesis so I could at least get the degree which would—I hoped—enable me to hold onto my teaching job.

Actually, in spite of my ambivalence about it, my dissertation topic was rather attractive, certainly not tainted from the start with the usual promise of dull erudition. I had always been a fan of mysteries and thrillers. In graduate school I had read some of the earlier Victorian crime novels—most notably Wilkie Collins's *The Woman in White* and M. E. Braddon's *Lady Audley's Secret,* along with Dickens's later dark studies—and found them not only readable but also, I thought, quite subversive to the Victorian cult of respectability. I had proposed to my university department that for my degree I write a comprehensive survey of a lot of these so-called Sensation novels, with the end in mind of discovering them to constitute an entire genre antagonistic to orthodoxy. It goes without saying here, I hope, that in those days I subscribed to the generally accepted notion of an obsessively prudish Victorian society in which the sensational was quite exceptional, and usually unacknowledged.

It also seemed to me that such a state of literary affairs would suggest that somewhere in that society was a body of knowledge which these writers had used as background material for their tales of adultery, murder, and madness, and which had heretofore gone unremarked by historians and critics.

This brought me to my idea about the newspapers. I knew there were newspapers in the nineteenth century, a lot of them. I knew that there were many notorious murder cases in Victoria's reign, Jack the Ripper being only the most visible. Braddon and Collins and Dickens in their thrillers were working from their own imaginative observations, but there must have been some mother lode of information about illicit life at the time. This source would have contributed significantly to making their novels quite different from what had come before them, more radical, more iconoclastic. Certainly the popular press of the time would be a most likely place to look.

In 1972, the most comprehensive collection of this journalism I knew of was the British Museum Newspaper Library, in an obscure section of London called Colindale. I was determined to find Colindale and wrap up my holiday there, trying to get a head start on the rest of my life by immersing myself in century-old criminal events.

The Northern Line rises above the ground soon after fashionable Hampstead, the furthest north I had previously ventured on the Tube. The view here was of a gloomy wet day, of unprepossessing housing and a lot of waste space. Colindale was two stops from Edgware, the end of the line. I puddle-jumped my way down Colindale Avenue, past working-class houses which gave no impression of having seen better days. The few shops had Asian counterboys, unstocked shelves, and an air of purposelessness.

Reaching the library, I went about my task. It took the usual half day to present credentials, learn the system, the rhythms of request and delivery, the availability, speed, and expense of copying facilities; and the rest of the day to set up. I selected from the card catalogues what I hoped would be a reasonable cross-section of newspapers from years in which they could have been expected to come to the attention of the Sensation novelists.

When I returned next morning, my requests awaiting me in the shape of enormous bound volumes, I attempted to put myself into the mind of a contemporary reader. I imagined myself encountering one newspaper or the other at my breakfast table, hot off the presses; at my pub or club in a leather chair with a glass by my side; at home by the blazing hearth, in a starched collar and a smoking jacket, reading aloud to my respectfully dutiful and obedient wife and family after strolling home from the office by gaslight.

This was not so easy after I started reading, for I found immediately that the mid-Victorian newspaper was sensational to say the least, certainly not supportive of an image of domestic tranquility.

The Times of January 3, 1857, lay open before me. It featured an account of "The Double Murder of Children in Newington"; a lead article on "Robberies and Personal Violence"; an extended rendition of "A Week of Horror." Having consumed these tidbits, I decided to move on to something I assumed would be quite different. *The Miner and Workman's Advocate*—the other end of the journalistic social scale from the august *Times*—featured, on page 3 alone of the January 7, 1865, edition, "The Poisoning of Five Persons at Gresford," "Extraordinary Outrage in Ireland," "Horrible Murder at Aldershot by a Madman," "Steamer Runs Down and Four Men Drowned on the Clyde," "Shocking Child Murder," and "Horrible Death by Fire." Then I moved back in the direction of *The Times,* opening the first volume of *The Daily Telegraph,* 1856, the paper of the rising young middle class. There I found prominently featured: "Singular Death of a Youth from Sanguineous Apoplexy" and "Suicide Through Destitution." Placed, without benefit of a headline, on the bottom of page 2 of this issue was a remarkable item, which I quote in its entirety: "On Thursday, about one o'clock, Sgt. Major Strothers, Fourth

Light Dragoons, stationed at Brighton, who had been unwell for some days, suddenly jumped out of bed, seized a razor, and cut his throat in a dreadful manner. Death was instantaneous. He was much respected by his officers and comrades."

The passage startled me. The staccato matter-of-factness of the prose made the gory tale resonate with a pervasive sense of anxious torment. And it demonstrated in miniature the possibility that the newspapers were indeed the source (or *a* source) of the troubled and subversive tone of the Sensation novels. It also recalled a passage from a scholarly book I had once read, Humphrey House's *The Dickens World.* House, commenting on Dickens as a novelist of social protest, had remarked that "unanswerable disquiet was normal among the very few who were not led into the easy optimism" which typified the 1850s. "Unanswerable disquiet," it seemed to me, must have characterized at least briefly not the very few but the very many who had read about Sgt. Major Strothers that morning. This made the crime columns loom ever larger as significant historical artifacts. I read on in the *Telegraph.*

The longest item in the October 20, 1856, issue seemed to expand on and clarify the issues raised. "Frightful Accident at Surrey Gardens" tells of what had happened the day before at an Evangelistic prayer meeting:

> The attention of the immense audience was attracted by a slight tingling sound, resembling that of a bell, and almost simultaneously cries arose in different parts of the building. "The place is falling!"

> The audience rose *en masse,* as if electrified, and, apparently with one mind, made a rush toward the various places of exit, causing the most fearful confusion and uproar, every person endeavouring to save their own lives at the risk of sacrificing those of their fellow creatures.

> The preacher tried to calm them, saying it was a false alarm, but . . . the pressure from the people in the first gallery was so great that . . . the iron bannisters which were fixed into the stone staircase and surmounted by a thick mahogany rail were torn from their sockets, shivering to atoms the mahogany, and precipitating between 50 and 60 persons down the

side of the staircase onto the crowd below, killing some instantly and fearfully wounding others.

They pressed furiously on, treading furiously on the dead and dying, tearing frantically at each other. Hundreds had their clothes torn literally from their backs. . . . Masses of men and women were driven down and trodden over. . . . One subject only appeared to fill the mind of all and that was self-preservation.

The intensity of the moment, the *sensation* of it all, was neatly captured by the minutely detailed, feverish realism of the writing here. It unabashedly blurred the lines between fiction and fact. This sort of prose in 1972 was being hailed as a "New Journalism," exemplified by major writers like Tom Wolfe, Norman Mailer, and Truman Capote, who willfully inserted imaginative but uncorroborated versions of "truth" into their non-fiction narratives. Also, the image of mankind presented in the Surrey Gardens item was more suited to that of Hobbes or Swift than any "Golden Times" or "Age of Improvement," as this decade has been characterized by eminent modern historians. It seemed to me particularly striking that these Victorian people, whose minds were full of desperate self-interest, were neither mentally ill, like Sergeant Strothers, nor were they destitute and ignorant, like the poor wretches I had previously associated with such stories. They were good, respectable, Bible-reading Christians, indulging their instincts not in the slums of the East End or the industrial squalor of the Midlands but at a suburban prayer meeting.

My vision of the Victorian paterfamilias complacently reading the newspaper to his family was extremely difficult to reconcile with the papers spread out before me. I remembered Dickens's Mr. Podsnap, in *Our Mutual Friend* (1865), who refuses to allow in his house anything which might bring "a blush to the cheek of the young person." Why was it, I wondered, that Podsnap and not Sergeant Strothers remained firmly embedded in our minds as synonymous with "Victorianism"?

We were staying at Bailey's, a hotel in South Kensington which had become during the 1960s a favorite of mine. It was moderately priced and saturated with the sort of atmosphere that is usually identified with England before the wars, a mixture of Victorian and Edwardian. The rooms were commodious but damp, and in all but a few the hall bathroom was shared with other inmates of the gloomy corridors. The service staff was all male, Cockney or Irish, dressed with shabby formality, deferential. There were public lounges off the lobby with velvet ropes at the entrances and high ceilings and thick carpeting, now threadbare in spots, and overstuffed chairs and sofas.

The clientele on my previous visits had most resembled a provincial delegation of the Conservative Party. But now, in 1972, things had changed. Bailey's new patrons seemed to be constituted in large part of people displaced from their homelands by the breakup of the Empire upon which the nineteenth century had declared the sun would never set. On the little verandah of the hotel facing the Gloucester Road Tube stop there sat through the day an entire family from the Indian subcontinent in native dress, as if they were waiting for some providential delivery from the sky. Inside, the lobby was filled with more families. Many of the fathers wore dashikis and djellabas.

On one of the days after I had been reading sensational Victorian newspapers at Colindale, we returned to the hotel and peeked into the public TV lounge. There we found more idle refugees and heard for the first time the terrible news that the Israeli athletes had been taken hostage and then slaughtered at the Olympic Games at Munich. We sat in numbed silence among these strange men with hooded indifferent eyes, watching reruns and updates of the tragic events on the telly. Somehow, the intensity of the reaction I felt—the horror—combined with the weird surroundings in Bailey's to bring me up short. Moment by moment, rational cultural perspectives were being turned topsy-turvy: Tories unseated in Bailey's by the Third World; Nixon cruising to a landslide in the USA, hotbed of counterculture; the spectacle of Germans avenging Jews broadcast around the world by satellite. All of these images combined in bizarre historical juxtaposition. Here I was, trying to reconstruct the history of the nineteenth century in order to rewrite it while the history of my own time (and its communications media) was rewriting itself around me. Today, sixteen years later, I realize I was experiencing first hand the same sense of dislocated desperation a respectable mid-Victorian must have felt as he confronted the disturbing messages broadcast by the crime columns of his newspaper.

Back in New York, I called up my dissertation adviser, Gordon N. Ray, to ask whether I might resume working with him on my degree. Ray had distinguished himself in his career as the definitive biographer of Thackeray as well as editor of his papers; and as chairman of the English Department and vice-chancellor of the University of Illinois. Now he served as president of the John Simon Guggenheim Foundation in New York and Professor of English at NYU. He was also one of America's leading bibliophiles, with a collection of manuscripts, first editions, and illustrated books that was virtually unrivaled.

A much less accomplished and busy professor would have been more than justified in refusing such a prodigal's return, but characteristically, Gordon was at once warm and briskly businesslike. We worked out some strategies and a timetable for my thesis.

I did preliminary work on the crime fiction of the 1860s and went to see Ray a couple of months later. The Guggenheim Foundation headquarters are on one of the top floors of a Park Avenue skyscraper, so visiting there was, for a lowly unpublished Ph.D. candidate, quite a glamorous experience. I followed a private secretary down a corridor lined with books by former Fellows and then into the president's office.

I went over my work with Ray. He approved it. He looked pleased. "Now, I've found something that may interest you," he said. He walked to a sort of anteroom. When he returned, he was carrying two ancient leather suitcases. "I picked these up at an auction recently, thinking of you. Perhaps you would like to peruse them, at your leisure, in private."

He had his secretary escort me to a room down the hall, as I carried the heavy cases. Opening them, I found five thick volumes. Inside each someone had pasted clippings from newspapers. At a glance all the clippings appeared to concern criminal matters. I turned to the front pages and found the holograph title "Various Trials Cut from Newspapers." At the rear of two of the volumes were indexes: Assault, Bigamy, Criminal Conversation, Murder. . . . I turned back to the front again for some reference or indication of their provenance. The only identifying clue was a bookmark of a family crest with the Latin *Nec Tempore Nec Fato* and what I took to be dialect, Gaelic perhaps, *I Beir the B'el,* and the names "Bell Macdonald" and "Rammerscales" in script. I looked at the spines and saw that the volumes spanned the years 1840–61, just the period preceding the height of popularity for the Sensation novel. For more than an hour I pored over headlines, pausing again and again to read thoroughly the compelling stories of brutal and libidinous Victorians. In Volume 3 I found myself confronted with a murder case—a Midlands surgeon had been accused of poisoning at least fourteen people, family and friends, over an extended period of time—which contained at least 100,000 words of coverage. I went back and knocked at Ray's office door.

"It's incredible," I said.

He nodded: "Nine million words worth. Can you use them?"

"You bet!"

"Take them then. They're yours until you're done with them."

In the short run, I knew I had a thesis to write, a degree to earn. But the long haul was different. I felt I had a greater responsibility. Having had a treasure of cultural history bestowed on me, I had to make sense of it, all nine million words, twenty-one years worth of clipping. The source of the volumes would have to be traced, their historical context established; then they would have to be reread through the prisms of newly available historical research and critical theory.

I made a plan. The dissertation could go only so far toward the ultimate goal. I limited the first stage of the project to description and the most obvious and necessary (and tentative) interpretations *vis-à-vis* the Sensation novel.

In a reference book listing British gentry, I found that the papers had probably been clipped by a naval surgeon named William Bell Macdonald, who had in 1837 retired to his position, inherited from a maternal uncle, as Laird of Rammerscales, a manor house in the south of Scotland. His death in 1862 coincided with the end of the clippings in the volumes. I wrote the current laird, Alan Bell Macdonald, and found that the cuttings had indeed been made by his great-grandfather and were sold at auction after World

War I. Six thousand volumes remained in the library the first Macdonald of Rammerscales had established, including more clippings, on assorted subjects. Alan, remarkably friendly and interested in my project, wrote that the size and nature of these latter suggested that the police reports were probably not really a primary interest to his ancestor, who was reputed by family tradition to have spent most of his days in the library translating the Greek classics.

It occurred to me at the time that this official family version of the great-grandfather's scholarly preoccupations—to which, significantly, were attributed his neglect of the estate and a subsequent decline in the value of the property—was, to put the best light on it, naive. Certainly the nine million words of news copy, neatly chronological and well catalogued up to a point, had taken no small effort to assemble. It was an ambitious, painstaking endeavor. I did not get the opportunity to communicate these reservations to Alan Macdonald, however, until I visited Rammerscales many years later. But by that time I had become sufficiently familiar with the late Victorian tendency to ennoble—if not whitewash—the proceedings of the earlier years of the Queen's reign; and it took little effort to demonstrate to the current laird that *Various Trials Cut from Newspapers* had been a major project in the Rammerscales library over the twenty-odd years spanning the middle of the previous century.

But here I am getting ahead of my story. I did write my thesis, adhering to the limitations Ray and I had agreed upon. I received my degree in 1976, "with distinction." In the decade or so since then I have, while achieving a modicum of success with my own crime fiction, dedicated my scholarly labors to better understanding the Victorian background and expanding my acquaintance with the world of the newspapers, so that I would one day be able to provide a more comprehensive explanation of the curious relationship between sensationalism and orthodoxy in the nineteenth century.

1

❖

Bawdy Victorians

Inevitably, the first encounter with Bell Macdonald's clippings induces in today's reader an expression of disbelief, then laughter. The most immediately striking entries are ribald, often hilariously so, suggesting James Joyce or Henry Miller rather than Anthony Trollope or George Eliot. Consider the details and deadpan irony of an item from 1855:

> John Challis, an old man about 60 years of age, dressed in the pastoral garb of a shepherdess of the golden age, and George Campbell, aged 35, who described himself as a lawyer, and appeared completely equipped in female attire of the present day, were placed at the bar before Sir R. W. Carden, charged with being found disguised as women in the Druids'-hall, in Turnagain Lane, an unlicensed dancing room, for the purpose of exciting others to commit an unnatural offense.*

Nor were such revelations restricted to transvestites and other outcasts from orthodox domesticity. The court reporters cast their

---

* There is usually no indication in *Various Trials* of the exact source of the clippings, although they are arranged chronologically, so the date can easily be inferred. I have made a special effort to determine the journal from which a story was cut only in those cases in which the source is essential to the discussion. It should be apparent from what follows, however, that only incidents of very limited provincial interest were so isolated as to conceivably not be relevant to my general argument. There are notes at the back of the book giving the volume and page in Macdonald of each reference.

nets as wide as possible and let them fall, usually without reverence, where they may. For example, the following modest item, which appeared in March 1854, gives us an original perspective on the relationship between respectability and Sensation, with some contemporary eschatology thrown in. The article, called "Melancholy Death of a Fellow of King's College, Cambridge," begins: "On Sunday morning last the death of a Fellow of King's College, Cambridge, took place in a house of ill-fame, under the distressing circumstances detailed below." The "distressing circumstances" were that the deceased and a friend had entered a brothel between 1:00 and 2:00 a.m. He had gone to a room with one of the women, undressed, and either before, during, or after intercourse (this delicate point is left to the reader's imagination) had died of what the doctor referred to as "the bursting of an aneuris of the aorta or large vessel which carries the blood from the heart." The prostitute,

Sarah Chamberlain, who was much affected, and swooned on entering the inquest room, on being restored to consciousness, deposed with much difficulty and amid the deepest manifestations of grief.

The jury returned a verdict that "Deceased died by the visitation of God."

It is a singular fact that the father of the deceased (a surgeon) met his death at the hands of an insane patient whom he was attending professionally, his patient having thrown him with violence from a window in a paroxysm; a brother of the deceased died from the effects of a fall while at college at Oxford; a second brother was drowned; and a sister now surviving was nearly burnt to death.

In the first place, the piece is hilarious. The juxtaposition of "Melancholy" in the headline with the sardonic first sentences and the excessive, if not unlikely, "distressing circumstances detailed below," indicates that the writer is playing on the contradictions between the celibacy required of university fellows and the embarrassing location of the demise of this particular Fellow, and perhaps indulging in a bit of self-satire as well.

In another sense, the recitation of the other sensational deaths in the family reminds one of Steven Marcus's discussion of "pornotopia" in *The Other Victorians*. Here, instead of indefatigable profligacy and perpetual orgasm, we find a universe of violent death. Life, it seems to be saying, is precarious at best, and downright dangerous when one mixes with sex and madness. Especially, the implicit warning continues, if one is a member of the respectable classes. A pattern common to the police reports emerges: A private tragedy is made public in the courtroom. Melodrama ensues. Morbidity and sexuality overlap. The God of the establishment, though mentioned in the obligatory manner, seems ridiculously far away. Surface notions of respectability are implicitly challenged. There is a kind of black humor which, while happily attacking surface piety, also manages to communicate a sense of unease.

This material also qualifies one aspect of Marcus's otherwise masterful study. He assumes that the almost omniscient force he calls the "Victorian official consciousness" had sufficient power to repress information about sexual indiscretion, to keep it so "almost no one was reporting on it." However, these clippings suggest that such scandalous reports were quite commonplace, in spite of being inevitably characterized by headline writers as "extraordinary."

In 1858, for example, a landlady in Camden Town brought a young merchant to court for "indecent and most extraordinary conduct." She deposed that he had let her front parlor because his own house was being painted; left a quantity of clothing, some of it female, as a deposit; and told her that he would not be sleeping there since he was staying with a friend.

The next day he came back and she saw him sitting in an arm chair by the window dressed in female's clothes. He quitted in his ordinary male attire. He was also at the house on Saturday, and also on the previous day (Tuesday), when he came in at ten in the morning, and having put on a lady's dress, with a wreath of roses round his head, he behaved in a manner too disgusting and offensive to particularly describe. She watched him on many occasions between ten and five, and saw him standing near the window, and observed that he was behaving most indecently; he left and returned at ten at

night, when he pulled off his trousers and put on a pair of
ladies drawers, and a white crinoline petticoat.

Other notable cases include that of a young man who walked about
Piccadilly grabbing women by the crotch. He defended himself
on the grounds that, as an artist, he was susceptible to fits of
passion.

And the headlines often manage to emphasize the comic aspects
of the wicked details. The Piccadilly artist's story, for example, is
wryly titled "More Zeal Than Discretion," while the case of a
seventy-seven-year-old woman who accused a male contemporary
with whom she had been drinking gin of attempted rape is headed
"Chacun à Son Goût."

Of course, all that we find in Bell Macdonald's volumes is not
kinky comedy. Much of it we may already know, or have suspected. Mayhew's prostitutes, drifters, and eccentrics are ever
present. The abysmal living conditions in the slums provide a
distressing complement to the stories of child beating and starvation. The cruel oppressiveness of institutional life—from the
hospital to the workhouse to the ragged school; from the courtroom to the prison or asylum—the sort of material which informs
government Blue Books and the protest novels of Mrs. Gaskell
or Charles Reade (not to mention Dickens), is reenacted daily in
newsprint. Nevertheless, as I have said, what strikes the reader
first is what is *not* expected: the steady parade of prosperous and
reputable, yet lascivious, Victorians through these courts, and the
even-handed, even worldly, ways in which they are handled by
judges and reporters alike.

One of the more amusing cases of the period reemphasizes this
point nicely, while taking us further by unexpectedly providing
some insights into the role played by the history of Divorce Law
in Victorian sexuality, as well as public attitudes on such matters.
In the courtroom report, an upholsterer named Lyle brought suit,
in August 1857, against his business partner, a Mr. Herbert, who
had been boarding in his house, for Criminal Conversation. A suit
for Crim. Con.—as adultery was popularly known—was an action
brought by a plaintiff to recover damages from a defendant for
having "seduced and debauched" his wife. Lyle, having become
suspicious of his wife, had hired an unemployed cabinetmaker,

one William Taylor, to observe her conduct with Mr. Herbert. Taylor and Lyle rented a room in the next house, which happened to be adjacent to Mrs. Lyle's bedroom. Taylor, according to his own testimony,

> then bored a hole in the party wall, but this was of no use, and he fixed up an apparatus, with an index attached to it, that would indicate when any person got into the defendant's bed. He could tell by this apparatus whether one, two, three or four persons got into the bed. (A laugh) He called the apparatus an "indicator." (Laughter) On the night of the 18th of June, he was watching, with his ear to the hole, when the "indicator" acted. (A laugh) A lever fell according to the weight. (Laughter) It first informed him that one person got into bed, and then that a second person had done so. (Renewed laughter) He immediately proceeded to the roof, and entered by the trap-door, took the servant by the hand, opened the door of the defendant's bedroom, tore down the curtains, and turned the bullseye upon them. (A roar of laughter) Mr. Herbert and Mrs. Lyle were in bed together. Mr. Lyle was at this time making the best of his way to the place. . . .

Under cross-examination, Taylor acknowledges that he and the wounded husband had been blithely drinking gin-and-water while waiting for the device, which the judge, in his summing up, was to refer to as a "crimconometer," to act; and that after the offending adulterers had been discovered,

> he and the plaintiff and several others went to a public house and had some drink. . . . Believed that after the discovery was made they had a glass of brandy and water all around. (A laugh) After this they all went back to the house. There was gin and water on the table. He stole a bottle of gin from Mr. Herbert's bedroom at the time of discovery. (A roar of laughter) It was Mr. Lyle's gin and he had his authority for taking it. They had pickled salmon, gin and tea, but he could not say whether the meal was supper or breakfast; but it was more like breakfast than supper because it was in the middle of the

night. . . . By witness' advice, Mr. Herbert was allowed to remain in the house all day after the transaction, and he took his boots away in order that he might not leave. (A laugh)

The case is, on one level, pure bedroom farce, and the audience treats it as such. The judge himself, while struggling to maintain decorum, is visibly amused. Nor is he blinded by any prudish moral outrage. With tongue in cheek he finds for the plaintiff, the cuckolded Mr. Lyle, and then awards him damages of one farthing, "the lowest coin in the realm." The newspaper sardonically headlines the piece "A Merry Tale from Croydon." Certainly the very existence of such an account (printed, the piece avers, throughout Britain) suggests a decidedly un-Victorian spirit abroad.

More important, the newspaper calls the attention of its readers to just this point, noting that "a day rarely passes without the unfolding of some curious tale of crime and horror, or of debauchery and dissipation" in the court reports, and that such cases transmit a sobering message:

The grotesque character of the details drew inextinguishable laughter from counsel, jury, and gallery auditors; but, as we have often before had occasion to remark, it is useless to blind our eyes to these disease spots in our system. The case presents a strange aspect of our boasted conjugal life—of that domestic bliss which is vindicated by actions for damages, and watched over by "crimconometers."

It also becomes clear that the writer is not addressing only a sexual issue, but the cash interest which informed it and which had doubly polluted England's "boasted conjugal life." By probing further in *Lyle* v. *Herbert,* we realize that the one-farthing damages represent not only a judge's down-to-earth sense of humor but also a recognition that the Criminal Conversation statute had been debased into a confidence game in which a needy or greedy husband might throw his attractive young wife in the path of an older, richer man and thereby make a profit out of his own cuckoldry. In many such cases, money in pocket, the offended husband and violated wife might live together happily, and prosperously, ever after. This explains Lyle's convivial mood on the discovery of his wife's infidelity.

In fact the Divorce Act, which went into effect January 1, 1858, was passed largely in response to these abuses. In a speech in 1857 in favor of liberalized divorce legislation, the Marquess of Lansdowne lamented "the monstrous assumption that the loss of affections of a wife is to be treated as a loss of ordinary chattel, and is to be compensated in pounds, shillings, and pence." The continuing publication of these cases, he went on, was "that great stigma upon the legislation, the manners, habits and customs of this country," which "is represented in all other countries of the world as an indication for, I will not say degraded, but of the loose, sordid, and selfish principles which prevail in this country."

Nor were all of the Crim. Con. cases so merry as the tale from Croydon. Indeed, many were so lewd and presented such a Swiftian vision of the brutishness of humankind that today's most sensational tabloids would be more likely to bowdlerize them than did the Victorian press. In one such example, a soldier named Ling brought suit against an older fellow officer named Croker. Ling had been stationed in India when his wife took up with Croker. Letters written by each of the men to Mrs. Ling are produced in the trial. The prosecution uses Croker's to portray him—with his own words—as the heavy-breathing lecher. In one *billet-doux,* after offering his paramour a detailed home remedy for an upper respiratory infection, he warms to the task:

Mind and obey this positive order; it will do you all the good in the world, and before long cover your dear little bones with good hard flesh; you will be yourself again; and when we meet, the more ready and willing to do "is moffie." (A phrase in Hindostanee) How I long for the time that will find your sweet little self cuddled up in my monster arms, lip to lip; and slowly emerging from a scene of exquisite delight! What think you about all this; and have you consented to the wish expressed in my last? I am sure you have, dearest. You would not disappoint in even the most disagreeable act, if you hoped that by it I should be for a moment gratified. This is the only thing left to comply with; when I tell you it will be a great satisfaction I am sure you will surrender unconditionally; and on my part, and on the instant, I promise you the most perfect bliss and unconditional indulgence in any way you please, even to a greater extent than that comprised in your last act. Do you recollect it? And how delighted you were at the perceptible result. Next time you shall dispose of it as you fancy; as a further inducement, I will tell you one or two things you are ignorant of.

The wounded husband's missives are in part expurgated, but his coarsely venal scheming is as manifest as Croker's lust. He writes from his tent in India before his estrangement from Mrs. Ling: "There is a Mrs. C—— out in these parts—the only petticoat almost that I have seen since I left home. She is a —— pretty woman. You may remember her husband in India. She lives with any one I believe. Last evening I had her to dinner but found to my disgust that the —— blackguard Smith (his servant) had taken ***."

One wonders what Smith had taken which ruined Ling's rendezvous with Mrs. C; but in any case, after his return to England, and about to pursue his claim as the wounded husband, his particular charm is not diminished:

You see what a —— of a scrape you have got me into with that —— mother of yours. I shall take Mrs. C's advice and burke the whole matter—providing you agree to certain conditions, the only ones upon which I will allow that cursed scoundrel C. to escape. Between you, I care not how, I require that the 250 L. which you have spent be immediately placed to my account at Cox's. Powell's receipt for which must be sent me, and that in two months from this time you place at my disposal the further sum of 300 L. available should I desire it. Solely and entirely upon these terms alone, do I consent to squash the damnatory evidence of your guilt.

In this trial, it is proven that Mrs. Ling had in fact moved in with Croker. As a consequence of such revelations Croker is ordered to pay Ling £1,000 (a sum equivalent to well over $100,000 in today's currency) for having alienated his wife's affection. Ling subsequently was to bring his suit to the still very expensive and generally inaccessible Divorce Court. Mrs. Ling defended herself—one wonders why by this time—by countering that her husband had an affair aboard ship from India to Europe while she was confined with their youngest child, and *before* she had taken up with Croker. She was not able, however, to produce concrete proof of her charges, and Ling was granted his divorce one day after Mr. Lyle of Croydon received a farthing for having contributed the Crimconometer to Victorian progress.

The coming of the Divorce Law a few months after these trials—contrary to the Marquess of Lansdowne's expectations—did nothing to bring to the newspapers a renewed respect for Britain's pretense to sexual restraint. Many more Victorians than had been anticipated rushed to Sir Cresswell's Divorce Court, and the details were published as enthusiastically as had been those in the Crim. Con. proceedings. In 1861, after only three years under the new law, one newspaper editor was able to comment:

It is impossible to look back upon the history of our divorce and matrimonial causes without a sensation of shame and humiliation. Never before in the national annals was there such a catalogue of evil passions and revolting vices—such a chronicle of petty meanness, of crawling lies and subterfuges, of wretched spite, of scandalous collusion, of base and villainous motives. This narrow tribunal of Westminster Hall is the dissecting room of English morality. There the skin is stripped off; there the muscles are laid bare, there the sharp knife severs and keen probe penetrates; there when the ghastly labour is over, we come to the grinning skull and fleshless bones.

It was not only the petitioners in the Divorce and Criminal courts who filled the newspaper columns and suggested to the public and literary establishment the basic instability of the official version of English society. Upper-class *demi-mondaines* might be shrugged off as unfortunate but inevitable leftovers from Regency amorality. Less easily dismissible were events like the public meeting called—and reported widely in the papers—to discuss the "Confessional in Belgravia." At St. James Hall in 1858, before a large all-male crowd, including at least fifty peers, two hundred members of Parliament, and innumerable clergymen, an Anglican curate was charged *in absentia* with luring women—particularly attractive young widows—into a darkened drawing room outfitted with candles and a makeshift altar, donning a surplice and sash, and bidding the women kneel before him and confess the most intimate details of their sexual lives and fantasies, asking "questions . . . so grossly indecent as to be unfit for publication [which] created a great sensation in the meeting." The self-appointed prosecutor justifies bringing the case to a public hall because it is necessary that the "bishops of our Church should see the danger of allowing these clergy once to overstep those bounds which separate . . . the Reformed Protestant Church from the Church of Rome. (Loud cheers) It is like a man who begins dram drinking. He goes on step-by-step and at last ends in *delirium tremens*. These 'holy fathers' have long been in a happy *delirium;* and I think when this case becomes known the *tremens* will begin."

And so the clippings go on, for 1,500 pages. A farmer is sued, a few miles from Thomas Hardy's birthplace, for breach of promise by a destitute laborer's daughter who had borne him a child; he accomplished the seduction in question by constantly and ostentatiously driving his herd of bullocks and sheep past her front porch. Hugh Rowley, son of Lord Longford, "a black sheep of the aristocracy" and devotee of "peg top trousers and Inverness wrappers," sits smugly mute in Divorce Court as his wife provides shocking details of his "cruelty, adultery, and desertion." Then, the divorce having been granted, Rowley sues his now ex-wife for perjury in another court, a charge for which, if convicted, she will go to jail. Had he challenged the truth of her allegations in the divorce proceedings, he would not have been free of an undesirable mate, nor could he have wreaked such a punitive revenge.

2

❖

Seeds of Paradise

The documentation of scandalous exploits in the newspapers of the 1850s and early 1860s strikes more and more of a somber tone as one reads on, however. The dominant mood of the Victorian world of illicit sexuality, it becomes clear, was as often one of insistent and unmistakable pathos as of titillating entertainment. It is a kind of dismal swamp, honeycombed with quicksand and teeming with predators. An 1853 case headlined "The Outrage at the War Office," for example, tells not of a military scandal, but of the critical wounding of a four-year-old girl, stabbed in the "private parts" as she squatted to urinate over a grating at one of the War Office buildings. The housekeeper is charged with inflicting the injury from her quarters below stairs. Acts combining brutality and sex—like this one—from which one can easily infer a variety of symbolic patterns, are, sadly, not exceptional in Bell Macdonald's clippings. They take place, after all, in a world which—beneath the pretense of sanitized respectability—is randomly violent, suffers from inadequate (or nonexistent) hygienic conditions, and in which public relief of bladder and bowels is commonplace. The ultimate sense conveyed here is not "outrage," but doleful resignation. How many other ground-floor and below-stairs habitations were treated as sewers? How many other such defensive-aggressive transactions were taking place—understandably—minute by minute?

Another case from 1857, which follows on the heels of "A Merry

Tale from Croydon" in *Various Trials,* is titled pithily "Ignorance and Depravity" and illuminates this mood further. I quote it in full:

Isaac Rushford, aged forty-two, was indicted at York for feloniously administering a quantity of seeds of paradise to Kitty Littlewood, with intent to procure abortion, at East Ardsley on the 2nd of February last. The prisoner lived in Dewsbury Road, Leeds, and had got a reputation as a wizard. The prosecutrix having been unwell for some time, and the doctors she employed doing her no good, acting on the advice of a neighbour she went with her father to Leeds to consult the prisoner. The prisoner, as the prosecutrix described it, "ruled her planet and gave her some pills." Not improving under his treatment, she sent for him to Sheffield, and the prisoner told her she would never prosper until she went to live at West Ardsley—a place near Leeds and easily accessible. She and her father accordingly went to live at West Ardsley and there the prisoner frequently saw her. At first he gave her some medicine, which he said was for palpitation of the heart. He then told her she would never be well unless she suffered him to have connection with her. This she refused several times. She afterwards re-moved to East Ardsley, and the prisoner continued to attend her, and at length she permitted him to have an improper intercourse with her, on his representation that she never would get well unless she did. On one occasion he gave her something which stupefied her, and it was on that occasion that the intercourse commenced, and it was afterwards continued for some time. At length she became in the family way and the prisoner then brought her a quantity of the seeds of paradise, and told her to make a tea of it, and drink it. She did so, and had a miscarriage on the 26th of March. On another occasion after that the prisoner brought her a bullock's heart and some shoemaker's awls. He burnt the heart, and said the awls were to keep her enemies off. She was to place them under her pillow and wear them in her pocket. He also sent her two pieces of parchment as charms, and said one would get her a young man, and the other was to prevent her being bewitched. She gave him £ 5 for these. The learned counsel objected that there was no proof of the administering of the drug by the prisoner. His lordship overruled this objection and the jury found the prisoner guilty. His lordship said it was quite lamentable to think that such an amount of ignorance should prevail. Such practices must be severely punished. The sentence of the court was that he be imprisoned eighteen calendar months, with hard labour.

No one will deny that Kitty Littlewood and Isaac Rushford, at least as they are presented here, can be characterized as "ignorant" or "depraved." Yet something is missing. There is another level of meaning to these terms, in this setting, which insinuates itself more deeply into the consciousness. The judge's pronouncements, after all, do seem a bit disingenuous in the context of the Victorian courtroom as we have come to know it from these newspapers— a compound, indeed, of hypocrisy and self-delusion. The clichés of the headlines seem consistently misdirected, the product of a society vigorously and self-consciously on guard against "problems" but not at all introspective or self-aware. As the outrage at the War Office might more appropriately be aimed at sanitary conditions and practices, so the judge in this case might better lament the apparent failure of both the educational and legal systems to cope with social realities, including the terrible poverty which is so often apparent. The judge's platitudes seem an attempt to distance himself from the real questions: what has this depressing saga of mean Midlands lodgings and seeds of paradise, of sun-signs and shoemaker's awls, of pills and bullock's hearts, to do with fornication? And what in turn has fornication to do with eighteen months at hard labor? And what has any of this to do with Victorian progress?

One thinks here again of *The Other Victorians* and the way in which these news clippings further illuminate the significance and pervasiveness of the "displacement and denial" which Professor Marcus finds at the heart of both official and illicit Victorian sexual writing. His analysis of a passage describing the Cremorne "Pleasure" Gardens in Chelsea (a notorious haunt of prostitutes and swells) in William Acton's 1858 treatise on prostitution might well apply to many of these court reports:

There is a peculiar confusion; one is never quite certain of the source or location of its intense and frozen sadness. The depression is there in the scene itself, but it is also present in Acton, and not merely as a response to what he is observing but as something he has brought to this event and projects onto it. This inability to separate out satisfactorily what one must call the subjective and objective components of an experience indicates, I think, a dimmed consciousness, and, further, a disinclination to examine the contents or meaning of one's responses.

Marcus makes it clear that this reluctance to look at things with "objectivity" is not necessarily devious or hypocritical—contrary to our suppositions. It is, in Freudian terms, a form of resistance, a defensive *need* to avoid the threatening element which in this case is sexuality. In medical texts and other attempts to "master the subject" (even H. S. Ashbee's "obsessional" attempt to include all the pornographic material ever published in one massive bibliography for the avowed purpose of providing a list of works to avoid), the final effect, however, is not to isolate the subject from further inquiry but "to reproduce on another level and in a symbolic way the original chaos and disorder they were intended to bring under command."

It is here that we find the crucial difference between pornography and official pseudo-science on the one hand, and the police reports on the other. While the latter may themselves be quite disordered (often, apparently, consisting entirely of unedited transcripts), their effect on the reader is not to dim but to undim consciousness, to press for an examination of the meaning of the raw experience on the page. In the most notorious cases, which drew substantial editorial commentary, this tendency is quite overtly stated, even outspoken. Even those cases which are presented without commentary evoke deep feelings of dismay in the face of details which suggest that received beliefs are shallow and have the potential to be exploited for immoral and self-serving ends. Consider this superficially titillating courtroom report from Kingston, which Macdonald clipped in 1855.

A fifteen-year-old "young gentleman" named Elton was accused of "feloniously assaulting" Mary Elizabeth Crawley, seventeen, a servant at the rectory home of his clergyman uncle, with the assistance of two other servants, Elphick, the groom, and Miss Fenn, the cook. The content of Crawley's testimony, at first glance, bears close resemblance to contemporary "fictional" pornography:

> While witness and Fenn were undressing, Elton came in and passed to his own room, and witness locked her door. She and Fenn then went to bed and directly afterwards Elphick came into the room, and unlocked Elton's door, and said to him, "George, you come in and lie on Fenn's side." Witness said that if they did so, she would tell Mr. Sugden (her master, husband of Elton's sister), and Elphick replied, "Oh no, you won't." Elton then came to her bedside. He was undressed and he got into bed. Witness screamed as loud as she could, and the prisoner Fenn put her hand over the mouth, and Elphick held her while Elton committed the assault with which he was charged. . . . Fenn [then] told her it was no use complaining, it was done now, and could not be undone. Elphick then told her than unless she consented to similar treatment a second time she would be sure to be in the family way and Fenn confirmed what he said, [and then] Elphick assaulted her in the same manner Elton had done. This all took place without her consent. . . .

In spite of the bawdy promise of the piece, in the end—once again—we are left with a distinctly sour aftertaste. Crawley's predicament is a tragic indictment of the social context in which she appears to be trapped. It is soon clear that she has been at least the victim of religious bigotry—she is a Catholic—if not sexual ill-usage. She has had no privacy; her biological ignorance is pathetically exploitable. The prosecutor seems more concerned in his histrionic way with the likelihood of such indignities taking place in the house of a clergyman on a Sunday than with the emotional or physical welfare of the girl whose interests he is supposed to represent.

Crawley is at one point subjected to a severe cross-examination by the defense, "the greater portion" of which, the reporter notes, is "not of a character fit for publication." The defense hammers at the point that Crawley, as well as Elphick and Fenn, had been for some time sexually experienced, and that Elton's poor uncle "merely appeared to have the misfortune to be troubled with a parcel of immoral and debauched servants."

The judge's summing up to the jury dwells on two points: first, that "in all such cases a most essential ingredient for the consideration of the jury was the conduct of the woman who complained about the outrage both before and after it occurred"; secondly, he takes pains to assure the public that the arrangement of the bedrooms in the Reverend Sugden's house had in no way contributed to the incidents that had taken place within. The jury, after "a short deliberation," find the young gentleman not guilty.

Whether Crawley's story is true is not the point here. Rather, it is how decidedly unappetizing the story becomes. The girl's position, appearance, and experience cry out for sympathy; yet we find no evidence that these are given serious consideration. But the reader is implicitly asked by the paper's recounting of details to care about *all* of these unfortunate children of Kingston, of England, and instead we see the inexorable closing of ranks against the religious and economic outcast without reference to her human condition. Distrust of orthodoxy, then, is overtaken by outrage. This outrage—if multiplied as it was by a media bombardment of such incidents—must have contributed to an atmosphere of subversive social criticism. And these cases of sexual misconduct were by no means the most outrageous or numerous of unpalatable crimes.

3

❖

Brutal Victorians

Whereas reports of sexual misconduct may be occasions for a wide range of reactions—from humor to outrage—the details of the violence of one person to another evoke more immediate and visceral responses. There is no room for laughter in a courtroom when we hear verbatim the circumstances of a child being beaten to death, and the smile of the cynic is swallowed as grave after grave of murdered bodies is, literally or figuratively, opened. The fact that, as today, most violent crime occurred within families served to intensify this effect in an age which so vocally prided itself on its domestic solidarity. I will present here two reports at some length, because I would like them to be confronted here essentially as the reader of the early 1850s did. That little commentary is necessary is self-evident. Such items—unlike the more "mysterious" murders in the upper ranks of society, which did not proliferate until later in the decade—reappeared through 1862 with depressing consistency. The first, headed simply "Murder by Starvation," appeared in 1853.

An almost unprecedented amount of excitement and alarm has been created at North Common—a hamlet of Gloucestershire, situated about six miles from the city of Bristol—in consequence of the arrest of an agricultural labourer, named John Cornish, and Eliza, his wife, upon a charge of having murdered Mark Cornish, a boy of about eleven years of age, the son of the former, and step-son of the last-named prisoner. The murder was alleged to have been committed by the most horrible of all means—slow starvation; and the condition of the corpse when seen after death was in every way confirmatory of the suspicions entertained; when weighed by the superintendent, found to be only 27 lbs.—the ordinary weight of a full-grown infant of from eighteen months to two years old. The appearance of the corpse was that of a skeleton, having a layer of a thick skin closely drawn over it, for the muscular and fatty development had entirely, or all but entirely, disappeared. The circumference of the thigh at its thickest part below the hip, was only eight inches and a half; that of the calf of the leg six inches, and that of the large muscle of the arm four inches and three quarters. From the information the police have been enabled to gather since the unhappy boy's death, it would appear that his maltreatment by his parents had been for many months a matter of perfect notoriety in the neighbourhood. That it had been known to the board of guardians and the relieving officer, and that the case had been actually three or four times visited by the last-named functionary; and that another child of the same father, aged fourteen years, had been reduced to pretty nearly as wretched a condition. The two ill-used children were the offspring of a first wife of the prisoner John Cornish, who died some eight years ago, shortly after her confinement with an infant since dead. . . . The deceased boy and his sister Jane have been often found by the neighbours picking pig's victuals from vessels, or potato peelings, or crusts of bread, and other cast-off food, wherever they could find it, and eating of it greedily. On one occasion he was found in a pigsty, covered over with straw, in which he had been lying for twenty hours, with no other food with him but a few raw potatoes. At other times he has been found in a carpenter's outhouse, coiled up in the shavings, or at a disused coke-oven in the neighbourhood, seeking warmth by burying himself among the ashes, and he has also been discovered almost frozen by the cold in other and more exposed situations. The neighbours who have been in the habit of going occasionally to his father's house have noticed that while the second [wife's children] daily have partaken of the parents' food, the other children [of the first marriage] have sat in a distant part of the room, and cries, as if of suffering, have also been heard issuing from the boy. Notwithstanding the decaying state of the deceased, no medical aid had been sought for him by his parents. . . .

The summary of the case having been given by the reporter, the testimony of the dead boy's sister is then reproduced:

Mark and her used to pick the potato rinds off the mixen [dunghill, compost heap], and eat them, because their mother-in-law did not give them any victuals; sometimes father had meat, but he never would give them any; all they used to be allowed was sometimes half a round, and sometimes a quarter of a round, sometimes once and sometimes twice a day, never more than twice a day; the only thing they had to drink was cold water, they never had any tea or coffee. The deceased had been pining away ever since Christmas. Both her father and mother used to beat both her and the deceased, sometimes with a stick and sometimes with their hands. They used to beat them very often. Her mother-in-law used to call her a great cat, and great lie-about. She often called Mark (the deceased) a nasty dog, and after he was dead she said it was a good job the Almighty took him. She used to beg a good bit of victuals, and took it home, but she was never allowed to touch it, and if she ate any on the way, she was beat. . . . Latterly her mother had told them to lie in bed till late in the day, as she did not want them in her sight. When they used to get up, they had a half-round of bread. On the Saturday before Mark died, her mother-in-law hit him up against the coal-house door, and her father also struck him the day before he died. On the night before, he asked for some water, and his father took him a cupful. No doctor was sent for. Her father was going for a doctor, when her mother told him it was not good, Mark was dead. When Mark was alive, her father and mother and the other children used to have toast and butter for breakfast. Witness and deceased used to be put to sit on the other side of the room, and her mother used to say to them, "you nasty devils." The witness further stated that she and her brother used to rob the neighbours' gardens. They were hungry, and were obliged to do so.

It is difficult to imagine any reasonably intelligent person in a Victorian household maintaining the complacency which supposedly characterizes that age's notion of itself after reading one such item. Yet comparable cases, as I have indicated, were almost a weekly event in the newspapers. In the 1960s, it has been argued, public apathy toward the Vietnam War was promoted by the callousness produced by the daily television coverage of burning villages and burning babies. Perhaps the newspaper accounts had numbed the sense of outrage of Victorian readers by this sort of overkill. So many descriptions of the emaciated bodies of starved children created in a relatively well-fed reading public a distance and lack of concern about the atrocities. Perhaps, but to the readers of today it seems unlikely, especially when confronted by an account like that of "The Horrible Case of Child Murder" (1854), which is so real and so terrible that it fairly leaps off the page:

Mary Ann Alice Seager, aged 32, wife of a brick-layer, was charged at the Lambeth police-court, on Monday, with the wilful murder of William Seager, her step-son, aged 7 years. . . . The details of the evidence were so revolting that they drew tears from the magistrate as he examined the principal witness, the sister of the deceased, a little girl, 9 years of age, who seemed perfectly cognizant of the nature of an oath, and gave her evidence with a fearfully distinct minuteness. The prisoner, who paced the dock with a theatrical air, and assumed various positions which she intended to be imposing, evidently tried to appear indifferent, but was shaken and unnerved at some portions of the evidence.

Ernest Henman, a tailor, with whom the prisoner and her husband lodged, stated that between four and five on Sunday afternoon the prisoner came home and commenced beating the children. Sounds of violence were continued for a considerable time. Her husband came to the door, and had to knock twice before he was admitted. He left shortly afterwards, and the violence commenced again. Then there was silence for a little, and soon after he heard the prisoner cry out, "My God, what have I done? Give me strength to go through it." He heard her own child Tommy, by a former husband, frequently say to her, "Mother, leave off." The witness then heard sounds of lamenting mingled with cries of "My darling boy."

Harriet Henman, wife to the last witness, corroborated his evidence. She heard sounds of stripes, and vibrations as if a heavy cricket ball was dashed along the floor. There was screaming, which subsided into cries, and then into low moanings, which every moment grew more and more feeble. She heard the prisoner's boy say, "Don't do it again, mother, don't do it again." . . .

Watson, the constable, produced the dress which was saturated with blood. Blood seemed to have squirted on the wall, and there was a good deal on the floor, a part of which was washed.

The chief evidence against the prisoner was that of her step-daughter, Ann Cooper Seager, a little girl only nine years of age, and very intelligent, but looking much younger than she really is. Her appearance excited the greatest commiseration, and contrasted strongly with the healthy and comfortable appearance of her step-mother. The girl having satisfactorily answered the questions put to her relating to the nature of an oath, said, I am nine years of age; that is my mother, pointing to the prisoner, but fearing to look up at her. She was in the room when I came home yesterday. My two brothers were in the room—one is Tommy, who is seven years of age, and Willie (the deceased), who is six years old. When mother came in yesterday she beat my brother William. Billy complained that Tommy hit him, and told father, who hit Tommy. When mother came in Tommy told my mother that Billy had got him in a row. Then mother slapped Billy and put him to bed. He got up again, and sat on the box. Mother knocked him off the box with her fist. Then he got up again, and mother got a strap and strapped him. She beat him on the arm with the strap while he laid on the floor. He got up again from off the floor and undressed himself. He had his clothes on when he was put into bed the first time.

When he got up again she hit him with her hands. She hit him on the side of the head twice. Then my mother put him in a tub of water. He was naked. She hit him once on the arm and once on the temple while he was in the water. His nose was pouring blood when she hit him. He could hardly stand up. She hit him several times in the tub, and his nose poured out with blood all the time he was in the water. He could not get out of the water. He was lifted out. My brother Tommy wiped him and put him to bed. Willie got up again, and mother told him to rub a tin tray a little while. Then my mother took him up by his feet and shook him a long time. Then my mother took him up again, I think it was by his hair, and threw him across the room. He fell upon the boards. She took him up again and threw him on a box and kicked him. I don't know on what part of his body she kicked him. She took him up and threw him on the chair on his back, and his head was hanging down, and she said to me, now you may take and do what you like with him. I said, Willie get up from the chair, and let me wash you, and he could not get up. Then my mother threw me down and kicked me over the eye and made this wound, and kicked my face. . . .

My brother Willie was in bed then. My mother told him to get up and wipe his forehead, but he could not get up. Because he did not get up my mother kicked him down. He was sitting up in bed and could not move, and because he couldn't she took him out of the bed, and kicked him, and made a neat lump on the forehead as big as a walnut. She did that with her foot. She kicked him about half-a-dozen times. She kicked him once on the forehead, and once on the chest, and once on the side. I don't know anywhere else. She took him by his hair, and threw him right across the room, and he fell down on the floor, and could not move. My mother took Billy up from off the floor and was going to throw him down again, but he was dead then, and she said, "Oh, Billy, I do love you." Mother called out, "Give me some warm water, and go and fetch four pennyworth of brandy." My brother Tommy poured it in Billy's mouth and he could not swallow it. Then mother said to me, "Oh I shall be hung; mind he fell down against the tin box." Then, sir, she wrapped him in a sheet and took him to the hospital. Before going out mother said, "Be quiet, the people of the house are listening."

MR. INGHAM *(to the prisoner)*: Have you any question to ask of this witness?

PRISONER: Yes. Look at me, Annie. Look at your dear mother.

The child turned half way round, and then averted her glance, turning her eyes on the magistrate, as if she felt confidence only in him.

PRISONER: Is she not allowed to look at me?

MR. INGHAM: You see she will not do so. Ask her what you choose through me.

PRISONER: Ask her who has tutored her in this tale. She has been in custody of Mr. and Mrs. Henman all night, and she could not remember all she has told unless she was well tutored.

MR. INGHAM: Did any one teach you to say anything, child?

WITNESS: No, sir, no one; I have told the truth.

PRISONER: May God forgive you, Annie, as I hope he will forgive me, for a third of what you have said is not true.

The painfully graphic statement of the child was heard with breathless silence, and her father, who was in the back of the court, appeared like a man demented.

There were no scenes like this in any novel—Sensation or otherwise—of the nineteenth century. Besides the obvious light these pieces shed on the public's exposure to reports of bestial behavior, and my hypothesis that they played a central role in bringing about self-awareness, some interesting connections to the literature of the times are suggested. First of all, Dickens has often been criticized for his excessive sentimentality about the deprivation of, and cruelty to, children, particularly those of the poor. In real life, we see, by the reactions of the magistrate and the courtroom audience, there were similar public cathartic effects. Dickens's own childhood deprivations are often credited for this aspect of his work. Certainly, this is true, but we can also see that, even without his blacking-factory experience, he had ample evidence—not requiring research—of the maltreatment of children, at least for his later works. Next, the conventional approach of studies of the

Victorian age is to attribute to government Blue Books and tours of slums and factories by eminent citizens the revelations of the squalor of the poor which led to legislative reform. Certainly, again, the role of the newspapers must be given greater consideration—and not entirely in terms of overt editorial statements. The crime columns indeed provided sufficient evidence—without commentary—that there were two Englands, but also that poverty and passion revealed a brutal strain in the English people of all classes which was at odds with the notion of a superior Anglo-Saxon breed or, for that matter, any conception of man as ranking near the angels in the hierarchical scale of creation. Moreover, new light is shed here, I believe, on Dickens's impassioned and self-destructive public readings, in the late sixties, of the scene from *Oliver Twist* in which Bill Sykes murders Nancy. Obviously, there was a fascination with the details of violence of repressed passion, which characterized not only Dickens's work in later years but the entire mid-Victorian culture so far as it is reflected in its newspapers. Publicly respectable and authoritarian, devoted to "moderation," the age was at the same time obsessed with the unspeakable and unrestrainable excitations of the human organism. Like Dickens's villain Bradley Headstone, in *Our Mutual Friend,* society in these accounts often appears to be teetering, privately, on the brink of madness, while presenting to the outside world an image of buttoned-up respectability.

4

❖

Sensuality and Slavery

Lest it be inferred from these two newspaper reports that sensational journalism was focused only on the agricultural and urban lower classes, it must be emphasized that, especially from 1850 on, barbarous behavior among the buttoned-up and respectable was generally reported as well. One of the most notable early instances concerned the December 1850 testimony of Jane Wilbred, a servant, against her master and mistress, Mr. and Mrs. George Sloane, for cruelty. Sloane was an attorney and director of the Church of England Assurance Institution, with a house in Pump Court, Temple.

> Mr. Sloane often beat me; sometimes in the morning early and sometimes in the daytime. Mrs. Sloane used to beat me because I wore my shift sleeves over my arms and shoulders in the morning; and when I cried Mr. Sloane used to beat me for crying. Mr. Sloane called me round to the bedside one morning and beat me on the hands with a shoe. My mistress would not let me wear my shift on my shoulders and neck in the morning, and, because I wore it to keep me warm, she used to beat me on the back with a shoe. She would not let me wear anything on my neck, or any part of my body above the waist; so that, from the waist upwards, I was obliged to go about the house exposed, in the presence of Mr. Sloane. . . . (Sensation)

Beatings and enforced nudity were not the only indignities to which the girl submitted. Her situation had come to light when she was admitted to a charity hospital, covered with bruises, and, according to the physician who treated her, in "a most frightful state of emaciation and debility." There were "marks of vermin" all over her body. She weighed, without clothing, 59½ pounds. Moreover, she goes on when recalled to the stand:

There was no watercloset of any kind in the chambers belonging to Mr. Sloane. There was only one chamber utensil for the use of Mrs. Sloane, Miss Devaux and myself, which was kept in a pan under the kitchen table. I was only allowed to use it once a day. I sometimes used it at night, and when she found it out in the morning she told me she would make me eat the contents. (Great sensation.) I was generally locked in my bedroom all night, so that I should not use the chamber utensil. When she told me she would make me eat the contents she used to try and do so. (Prolonged hissing.) She has made me eat it more than once, and when I struggled to prevent her, and it dropped on the floor, she picked it up and put it in my mouth. (Sensation.) When I have not been able to get to the chamber utensil at all during the day I have dirtied the floor, but I could not help it. My mistress on one occasion got a piece of turnip and cut a hole in it and filled it with some of the dirt, and forced it down my throat by means of a large iron tablespoon. (Great sensation.) Mr. Sloane was not present when she at first attempted it, but he was when she succeeded in pushing it down my throat. He stood behind me, so as to keep me close in front of my mistress while she put it into my mouth. (Sensation.) He beat me on that occasion with a shoe because I refused to do as my mistress wanted, and he beat me again after it. . . .

After the servant's day in court, an angry mob awaited the Sloanes, stoning them and chasing them home. The two defendants were ultimately convicted and sentenced to two years hard labor for their treatment of Jane Wilbred. It was generally believed that the depth and breadth of the news coverage of the trial had incited the public to retributory action and, no doubt, had influenced the judge.

The courtroom reports then had the power to influence both citizenry and officialdom. The reactions of the crowd and the judge may not have been exactly unique or absolutely new, but the detailed news coverage of the Sloanes' treatment of Jane Wilbred reinforces what I inferred when I first confronted Bell Macdonald's *Various Trials Cut from Newspapers.* Something was changing in the *Zeitgeist* at midcentury. That something seemed inextricably tied up with the development of the popular press. A key word in this evolution was "Sensation"—"Sensation" as it referred to the much-vilified Sensation novels and Sensation dramas, of course; but, even more elementally, the use of the term "Sensation" in the newspaper reports to indicate an emotional tremor in the courtroom (in response to such testimony as Jane Wilbred's) which was an unhappy combination of electricity and dread.

The forcing of human feces into the servant's mouth may also have significant implications, since similar incidents recur throughout the *Trials.* The nature of the act itself, not to mention the audience's outrage, may have represented in the simplest terms an understandably intolerable fear which was more general than we today can readily imagine. J. H. Plumb, having read Marcus and sexual memoirs such as *My Secret Life,* believes that what these works make particularly manifest (as, perhaps more intensely, do the newspapers) is that one can only understand the deep-set and evangelical nature of the Victorian ideology of respectability if one understands the gross reality which it set itself in opposition to. Indeed, one can see the "hypocrisy" and "prudery" in this light as justifiable acts of defensive self-preservation (in some ways parallel to the violent aggression of the housekeeper at the War Office). Plumb, noting that "poverty and destitution were always so close to Victorian men and women that they easily became the victims of those members of the propertied class who wished to debauch them," writes that, in part as a result of this fact of life, "the Victorian youth was presented with endless opportunity for sexual indulgences," while at the same time the newly prosperous middle classes were desperately afraid of sliding back into the slough where sensuality (a form of bestiality in this reading) and slavery were often synonymous.

One of the primary areas in which the popular press was asserting itself, then, was as a daily reminder to many reputable Victorians that the past they were trying to forget was ever present. In fact the graphic and voluminously detailed nature of this coverage may well have made crime and sexuality appear to these estimable citizens of the new industrial urban age as more ominous—and certainly less comprehensible—than it had been when it resided with them under the same metaphorical roof in more "primitive" times. Implicit in this observation is the suggestion that the self-esteem which accompanied the relatively democratic prosperity of the nineteenth century was foundering on a paradox: the same technology—in the form of a more efficient and expansive news media—which gave the age wealth, literacy, and leisure now provided its people with the opportunity to be iconoclastic about the ideals to which they had so arduously aspired.

5

❖

Newgate to Newspapers:
Establishing a System

There are potential problems built into working with such materials as these news clippings. It is suspect, at least, to attempt to characterize a twenty-three-year period—even in the most qualified way—on the basis of journalistic accounts which were as often as not aimed at the baser elements of the populace; which were certainly factually unreliable in part; and which appeared as the work of one man, an amateurish editorial project of dubious consistency, one full of gaps (particularly in regard to the specific sources of individual stories), and of virtually unmanageable proportions.

Let us then begin by considering the facts. First, there are the clippings themselves. These five volumes are bound in boards 12½ inches by 7½ inches across. Gilt letters on the spines give the dates, ostensibly included in the contents. For example, Volume I is declared to cover the years 1840–50, but the first item is actually from November 1839, when Bell Macdonald was thirty-two years old and had been master of Rammerscales for two years. It contains 386 pages of newsprint and a holograph index in ink which gives the names, alphabetically, of the principals in each case and the sort of crime with which each was charged. There is at the end an appended clipping from an 1812 poisoning case in the local county, Dumfriesshire.

The second volume is marked 1850–1853. After the last entry from the period, in December 1852, there is an added update of a case which had run intermittently through the volume. It is 1859, and Kirwan, an Irish wife killer who had been transported to Bermuda in lieu of the death sentence, has become eligible for parole. The writer expresses general outrage at the prospect of the man returning to the British Isles. There is a complete index here, also, for the 364 pages of cuttings, including another antique story from 1801.

In Volume 3, January 1853 to the end of 1856, there are 411 pages, of which only the first 56 are covered by an index. The fourth volume runs from January 1857 to the end of 1858, with 386 unindexed pages. The spine of the last volume indicates that it runs from 1859 to 1861, but the last dateline is February 24, 1862. It has 439 pages.

What does this information tell us? For one thing, it shows that the first fourteen years of clipping yielded only 750 pages of fully indexed stories, while the last nine years produced 1,236 pages, with a mere 56 indexed. It is easy to infer that Macdonald found himself confronted with considerably more crime coverage in the later years, and that this added burden of newsprint caused him to give up on the meticulous indexing of the earlier volumes. Moreover, the impression the reader gets is of a body of journalism in which editorializing on crime—and commentary about the *reporting* of crime as a more-or-less separate phenomenon from the crime itself—rises dramatically after the second volume and continues to do so until the sixties. As to content, this commentary is largely hostile to complacency—and the facts in the stories tend more and more to suggest that deterioration in the social fiber often occurs where things have the greatest appearance of propriety. The poisoner is the doctor; the woman who stabs to death her six children is the former wet nurse to the Prince of Wales.

These impressions are corroborated and illuminated not only by a thorough review of official library holdings of midcentury periodicals (as the rest of this book amply illustrates), but also by reading more recent "secondary" books and articles which deal with the historical development of journalism during the period. The years when Bell Macdonald was assembling his cuttings were the formative years in modern news reportage. Technological innovations such as the telegraph and the railroad came into their own in the 1840s and changed forever the nature of the reporter's profession. News came in more quickly on the wire and was distributed more quickly, cheaply, efficiently, and widely by train. Provincial dailies and weeklies grew where there had been sporadic editions or none at all. In the 1850s there were legal changes as well. Various "taxes on knowledge"—in the form of Stamp duties, paper duties, and enforced distinctions between "news" and "opinion" papers—were eliminated by Parliament. This brought cheaper news and more copy to readers.

This democratization process cleared the way for a more openly critical press. The debacle of the Crimean War in 1854 reinforced this tendency when reports of atrocities and ineptitude were telegraphed back to England by the first recorded "special correspondent," W. H. Russell of *The Times,* and aroused indignation in the general population, an indignation which translated into a general iconoclasm.

The reader of these clippings, therefore, is provided with a unique angle of vision on the growth of the newspaper industry in Britain. In the forties and early fifties, one finds papers which are generally expensive, short on print, full of stale news, and given to supporting the strictures of established beliefs. After 1854–55 we find cheap papers, hotter news, and subversive editorializing.

There are many statistics to support the various aspects of this interpretation. One will do to give a taste of the enormity of the basic conditions of this revolution. Before 1855, *The Times* dominated the few other small-circulation dailies in London, and most of the handful of provincial papers appeared only weekly. *The Daily Telegraph,* the first penny daily, made its appearance in 1856, and only five years later led *The Times* (now at threepence) by 141,200 to 65,000 in circulation. No matter how striking any such evidence is, however, it is of course necessary to make a step-by-step analysis of the contents of these papers to determine the quality of these countercultural attitudes—or lack of them—and also to put to a finer test any chronological hypotheses. It is, in short, essential to look at crime reportage in the years from 1800 to midcentury before subjecting Macdonald's clippings to a truly meaningful analysis.

Richard Altick's *Victorian Studies in Scarlet* (1970) provides a summary of the popular literature of violent crime in England from Elizabethan times:

> Then [around 1600], and in the two succeeding centuries, occasional homicides, pathetic or merely horrifying, were recounted in broadsheets, along with such other newsworthy events as military and naval victories, ceremonial observances, fearful calamities, and curiosities such as ghostly apparitions and freak animals, human or barnyard. From Defoe's era in the early eighteenth century, likewise, Grub Street authors scratched for a living by concocting catchpenny biographies, part fact, part pure invention, which narrated the careers of eminent criminals. Collections of such biographies along with accounts of the malefactors' trials and their ensuing executions, found a ready sale among the literate part of the population. The most famous was *The Newgate Calendar,* first issued in 1773 and repeatedly enlarged in the early years of the next century.

At the beginning of the nineteenth century, "intelligence of the latest murders was still being brought to the masses chiefly in the form of half-penny or penny broadsheets." So the bulky volumes named after London's most notorious prison, along with the cheap sheets hawked on street corners, dominated the non-fiction crime market until the periodical press began to take an ascendant interest in such matters. This interest intensified, Altick believes, largely because of the vacuum left by the decline in war news after Waterloo (1815); and it was symbolized by "the avidity with which the press fell on the Thurtell case in 1823–24. . . ."

Altick happens to be one of our leading authorities on nineteenth-century popular culture, so it makes sense here to follow him in these first stages of our pursuit of perspective on crime reportage by examining close up first *The Newgate Calendar* and then news writing on the Thurtell case.

The four volumes of *The Newgate Calendar* put together in London by Andrew Knapp and William Baldwin, between 1824 and 1828, are described on the title pages as "interesting memoirs of the most notorious characters who have been convicted of outrages on the laws of England since the commencement of the eighteenth century with occasional anecdotes and observations, speeches, confessions, and last exclamations of sufferers." A typical early-nineteenth-century "memoir" is that of "Luke Heath, Executed for Murder." We are given about three double-column 9 inch by 5 inch pages describing how Heath, a respectable farmer's son, impregnated his girl friend, then murdered her with a pitchfork, depositing the body in a pond. When suspicion fell on him, he ran away and was not apprehended for two years. When he was discovered in another county working as a farm servant, he was returned to Gloucester, tried, and convicted.

This account—and indeed all the accounts in Knapp and Baldwin, from the eighteenth and nineteenth centuries—is distinguished chiefly by its bland conventionality. It tiptoes around the sort of unappetizing details the newspapers were to revel in. Even the simple recounting of the facts of the case is tainted with a certain complacent reassurance. Luke Heath, just before he was hanged, confessed to his crime and "appeared truly penitent." The summary of the issues raised by the murder represents the kind of moralizing which would not be out of place in a Fundamentalist sermon:

> We have thought it our duty, frequently, to remark upon the evil consequences of excessive drinking, as we find it, too often, the immediate cause of many of those crimes which bring ruin upon families, and disgrace and ignominious death to individuals. Yet, fraught as intoxication is with evil, we still hesitate to pronounce it as productive of crime in its consequence as that demoralizing vice—seduction. The case we are about to detail saves us from the necessity of comment, as it fearfully illustrates the fatal tendency of this too common sin; and holds out an important lesson to the youth of both sexes, in which they may learn that forbidden enjoyments, and honourable fidelity, are as opposite to each other as light and darkness.

The *Calendar*'s pronouncements on fleshly and psychological matters are no more enlightened than the sex manuals of the time.

In unhallowed love, the birth of enjoyment is the death of the passion; and the woman who complies with the lover's importunities soon witnesses a termination of his attentions. Heath and his mistress soon repented of their criminal intercourse; for appearances were beginning openly to declare that she was about to become a dishonoured mother. Their meetings were no longer attended with impatient rapture. Reproach was all on one side, and repentance on the other, while the intervals were spent in fruitless conjectures about what should be done. No doubt she requested of him to blot disgrace from her character by marriage, and the sequel seems to imply that he must have consented.

An examination of *The Newgate Calendar* then shows that it functioned for its readers as a reassuring set of parables which illustrated virtue rewarded and immorality punished.

This is true even of the Thurtell case, which happens to be one of the last crimes included in Knapp and Baldwin's fourth volume. John Thurtell, well-born gambler and rogue with aristocratic connections, had enlisted a couple of sporting colleagues named Hunt and Probert to lure one William Weare, whom they suspected of carrying large amounts of cash and jewels, to a remote cottage in Watford in Hertfordshire.

There they bungled the job a number of times before Thurtell finally managed to bash in poor Weare's head and slit his throat in a country lane. Sadly for the perpetrators, they found that their victim was carrying little of value and they were still faced with the problem of disposing of the body. They placed Weare under a hedge for a time; moved him temporarily to Probert's pond; then carried him in a sack, draped across a horse's back, to a neighbor's pond where they left him in what they hoped would be his final resting place. Alas, it was not to be so. In the meantime the conspirators were observed combing the bushes for additional bounty and the bloody weapon was discovered by a passer-by. After a few days' delay by confused authorities, one of Thurtell's pals confessed and the three were arrested. It was, by the standards of the most sensational cases of the fifties, an unexceptional crime, but there is no question that it had a resounding effect on the contemporary public. *The Newgate Calendar,* while dispensing its customary dosage of moralizing, allows itself to indulge in some rare hyperbole in the almost unprecedented twenty-two pages of print it allots to Thurtell:

> For cold-blooded villainy in the mode of its conception and planning, and in the cold ferocity of its perpetration, this murder stands almost alone; and the sensation it created throughout the country was such, that no recent atrocity can be at all compared with it. To the vice of gaming, and its associations with boxers and blacklegs, this tragical event owed its origin. . . .

6

❖

A Pre-Victoria Media Murder

A close look at the treatment of Thurtell—from October 1823 until the end of the year—in such prominent London papers as *The Morning Chronicle, The Times, The Morning Herald,* and *The Weekly Observer* provides many insights into the state of the art of crime reporting and that of journalism in general in this period.

The most obvious characteristics of these 160-year-old sheets is that they were expensive and short. Each cost sevenpence, and each had four pages, whereas the papers of 1861 usually cost a penny or two and had eight pages. In 1823, moreover, the news tended to be more local and less immediate than in the years after 1855 when urgent communiqués, often international in scope, were commonplace. These qualities of course reinforce the sense of the revolutionary impact of the telegraph and the railroads in the 1840s.

Still, there are similarities as well as differences between the twenties and the fifties. All of the papers except *The Morning Herald* give a lot of space to police reports, often with a humorous slant. For example, the October 24, 1823, edition of *The Times* devotes two of its four pages to advertising. The remainder is divided in the following manner: one column of foreign news; one of London Council reports and sundry items from around town; a couple of letters and birth and death announcements; and then the rest of the paper is occupied with police reports.

Over the week of reportage which followed—and before the

discovery of Thurtell's foul deed—this pattern is maintained, except for a flurry of interest in Arctic expeditions. The headlines give some flavor: "Mad Dogs"; "Hardened Rogues"; "Child Stealing"; "Fatal and Melancholy Accident"; and so forth.

The Morning Chronicle of October 23 has a slightly different format, devoting only page 1 to advertisements and all of page 4 to crime. In addition, an editorial beginning on page 2 reveals public awareness of, as well as certain attitudes to, matters which in other ages might be considered unprintable, if not unspeakable. A respectable tradesman has been accused of indecent exposure by a woman pedestrian. There are no extenuating circumstances, according to the prosecutrix: the man could not have been merely urinating on a wall because he stood openly at curbside "shaking himself" at her. The man is sentenced to a jail term. The *Chronicle* is having none of it. As far as the paper is concerned, there is more evidence of a general inclination to deceit among the crowded population than there is of the offense in question: "Persons who swear to acts of indecency may swear to all and sundry with the most complete immunity."

On October 31, a Friday, Thurtell's story breaks . . . but it is already a week after the commission of the crime, six days after the weapon was found, and two days after the arrest. *The Morning Chronicle* begins its coverage of a "Most Horrible Murder Near Watford" on page 3:

On Friday Night last, a murder was committed at a place about six miles from the town of Watford, Herts, which for coldblooded villainy in the mode of bringing it about, and the diabolical ferocity which accompanied its perpetration, has seldom been equalled. Half the county of Hertford has been for the last three days in a state of agitation upon the subject and nothing can exceed the anxiety evinced by all classes for the discovery of the perpetrators. This, we are happy to say, is now in a fair way of being brought to light and the circumstances which have led to it afford another striking proof that

> "——*murder, though it hath no tongue*
> *Doth speak with most miraculous organ.*"

This introductory passage symbolized many of the singular attributes of crime reportage in the 1820s. The most striking of these features was the general state of editorial disarray. In the first place, this initial report on Weare's murder is obviously based on hearsay and conjecture. And although Thurtell was arrested within a day and brought to trial within six weeks, clumsy and inaccurate reporting continues to characterize the coverage through the conviction and execution of the accused, and even the lengthy accounts of the slow decomposition of Thurtell's corpse as it lay being dissected in accordance with the court's sentence at St. Bartholomew's Hospital (where Palmer, the Rugeley poisoner, was to study surgery a couple of decades later). Another example of the primitive state of development in the news-gathering industry is that the reports were slow, very slow. Watford is only a few miles further northeast from Colindale. Gill's Hill Lane, the site of the murder—this case was known to contemporaries as the Gill's Hill Tragedy—still exists and, indeed, can be easily located on the Master Atlas of Greater London, amid golf courses and suburban development, in the village of Radlett, not far from Watford. But the time it took to be reported suggests that the news had to travel under sail from a distant port.

Next, there is a pronounced resemblance between the language of *The Morning Chronicle* report and that of *The Newgate Calendar*. The terms "coldblooded villainy," "ferocity," and "perpetration," along with the claims for the uniqueness of the "sensation" the crime has caused, are in fact identical. One may infer that the *Newgate* writer—published in 1828—has merely borrowed his prose from *The Morning Chronicle* of 1823. But it is not so simple. In fact the first reports of the "atrocity" in *The Times* are identical to those in *The Morning Chronicle;* and the Sunday piece which appears in the November 2 *Weekly Observer* is identical to the first two. At least the *Observer* is creative enough to invent a new—and more decorous—headline: "The Murder of W. Weare, Esq. of Lyons Inn, Strand." In any case the papers, apparently without compunction, went on borrowing or outright plagiarizing not only copy but plates of illustrations from one another.

What this suggests—besides a certain looseness in application of the principles of copyright law—is the absence of any cogent system or convenient transport by which London reporters were rushed to the counties. Nor were professional stringers available, or reachable, in these outlying districts to cover the case from their home base.

Other elements which suggest the relative novelty of attempting rapid, mass coverage of a crime are the general disregard for the rights of the accused. Thurtell and his cronies are regularly referred to in both headlines and body copy as "the murderers," and Thurtell's deposition was released to the papers over the objections of his counsel. Moreover, there is the conspicuous absence of the detailed—and often disgusting—forensic reports which papers in later decades published *in toto*. The entire situation suggests not only primitive reporting methods but primitive technology, shoddy legal discipline, and even crude laboratory procedures and inefficient record keeping on the part of the authorities.

It is, in short, a different world from the world of Bell Macdonald's later clippings. Nowhere is the atmosphere of this world better conveyed than in the famous interview conducted with Thurtell by the best-selling novelist Pierce Egan for *The Times* (and reprinted in the relatively unsensational *Morning Herald*). Egan's report begins:

> He [Thurtell] advanced toward me with a cheerful step and smiling countenance. Mr. Wilson, the governor, was present. I never saw Thurtell look better; in fact, his personal appearance was altogether considerably improved. He was fashionably attired in a blue coat with gilt buttons, a yellow waistcoat and dark trousers. His irons, which are rather heavy, were tied up with a silk handkerchief. His shirt and handkerchief white as snow; the pin tastefully displayed; and his collar and wrist-bands corresponding with the style of the present period.

In this interview the intimacy Egan—and, presumably, his readers—shares with Thurtell, the well-known gentleman gambler, is strongly felt. This phenomenon accounts for what *The Times* refers to as the "ferment of the public mind" over what (as Altick puts it) was in fact "a run-of-the-mill affair." The literate upper and middle classes who could afford the sevenpence for the paper experienced the frisson which accompanies the revelation that a person one has known—or *could* have known—is a murderer or master criminal. Thurtell was the son of a prosperous merchant, was well known to all who consorted with sporting life, and had, at the time of the murder, already become famous in some circles because of prose sketches of him by William Hazlitt and George Borrow. It is actually a small world, a provincial one. It harkens back to a past when England was knowable and its people knew their place. When they don't—as in the case of Thurtell, who had descended from the respectable to the "fancy"—eternal verities (much like those of *The Newgate Calendar*) provide support. As the November 6 *Morning Chronicle* has it: "It will be instructive to the public to view the rapid transitions that take place from gaming to robbery; from professions of friendship among villains, to their betraying and murdering one another—from the hazard table to the gaol—and from the scene of drunken revelry to the place of execution." If the later editions of *The Newgate Calendar* seem to have borrowed their language from the papers, the papers seem to have borrowed their moralizing from the *Calendar*.

Nevertheless, there *are* signs of modernization. The papers themselves report unanimously that this scandalous story is something new. They respond clumsily at first, but soon become inventive. By November there are urgent headlines ("Received by Express last night") and by December *The Weekly Observer* in particular has begun to devote more and more space to illustrations and bolder headlines related to the crime. Entire sections are devoted to "Letters to the Editor" (many from respectable citizens disavowing rumors that they had once kept company with Thurtell). And then there is the curious editorial in *The Morning Chronicle* of Wednesday, December 17, which suggests that the newspapers themselves have begun to occupy center stage with the murderers in the controversy.

In this piece the writer tells us that one of the more startling byproducts of the murder of Weare by Thurtell and his cronies is the spate of charges made against the press as it has reported on the case. The papers have been charged with undermining any chance the accused might have had to a fair trial, and with blackening Britain's image, at home and abroad. In response to this, the *Chronicle* man recalls that the issue of the relationship between news coverage of crime and the tainting of the sceptred isle had been raised as long ago as a half century before, in 1772, by a Londoner named Johnson in a ninety-three-page monograph, "News and Newswriters."

Johnson, we are told, accused the papers of his day of being "a national reproach—for they bring a charge against us of no less a nature than national depravity. . . . Every species of guilt, every mode of extravagance, every method of gambling, and every possible way of subverting order and setting the laws at defiance, are daily intimated, comforted, and propagated by our newswriters." Foreigners will conclude from the police reports that "one half the nation is supported by robbing the other half." Not only are crimes "unquestionably multiplied by the circulation of newspapers . . . " but a "paper without murders and robberies, and rapes and incest, and bestiality and sodomy, and sacrilege, and incendiary letters and forgeries, and executions and duels, and suicides, is said to be void of news:—*For such are the melancholy themes that, a corrupted and forsaken people are gaping after.*" (My italics.) Johnson, the *Chronicle* tells us, concludes with a passionate (and violent) advocacy of heavy censorship.

The Morning Chronicle writer allows that it is consoling in 1823 to know that journalists of the past were even more despised than he. And yet, the editorial goes on, "the abused and calumniated newspapers, so far from being the cause of crime or immorality, are in reality most efficient aids to justice, and powerful restraints on evil men."

But here the burden of his argument veers off in another direction, one peculiarly characteristic not so much of the later newspapers as of the establishment voices which took up the cause *against* newspaper sensationalism in following decades. The editorialist decides to wield the cudgel of statistics against his critics. He cites evidence garnered from a recent report of a committee in the House of Commons that "during the time of the activity of the Press, atrocious crimes had decreased in the rate of three, if not four, to one," and that newspaper publication of all details of all stages of judicial proceedings was the cause of the drop in the crime rate. He goes further, bringing in the usual favorable contrasts with other cultures. He claims that in England between 1810 and 1818 there were fewer than twenty murder convictions per year, and—while admitting that the "materials for comparison with the other countries of Europe are but scanty"—does not hesitate to attribute one thousand homicides a year to Naples alone; over five hundred in 1817 to France; and seven to the city of Hanover in Prussia, which—he then cleverly calculates—in proportion to England's population, would translate to more than eighty. He deliberately, he tells us, excludes from his consideration Spain, "where the church door is always open to receive the murderer, and where full scope is given to all the worst passions of our nature."

What does this commentary on the Thurtell case tell us today about the news climate of 1823?

First of all, it shows that the reporting of crime was not new; neither was negative criticism of the cultural effects of such publication. What was new in 1823, however, were those elements of quantity of coverage and distribution which naturally accompanied the rising phenomenon of the popular press. (It should be noted here that Mr. Johnson in 1772 had to publish his own monograph from St. Paul's Churchyard in order to even discuss the subject of newspaper sensationalism.) The journalists of 1823 on the other hand, while largely defensive, had begun to treat the topic as quite appropriate to the daily paper. What I am suggesting here is that the inclination to report on crime and sexuality is at least as old as the first news broadcast—in whatever form that took. (Hamlet, remember, refers to the "play within the play" as one of "the abstract and brief chronicles of the time" and that play is, in effect, a murder report.) In the transition from the still largely agricultural economy of the eighteenth century to the industrial nineteenth, we inevitably find more people gathering in cities and more people in quest of news, the livelier the better. William Wordsworth himself decried this phenomenon at the peak of his career at the turn of the century, and it is only logical to infer that, as the urbanization process snowballed, the news reports experienced parallel growth. The eruption of the Thurtell case on the public consciousness—or one like it—would probably have happened even if there had been no Napoleonic Wars nor any dearth of news following them. The cozy small world which is represented in so many of these reports, along with their editorial clumsiness, but reveals the relatively early stage of development of print journalism at the time; not that newspapers (or popular writing in general) ever lacked sensationalism.

The defensiveness—the pat moralizing, the shameless chauvinism, the scrambling for statistics to manipulate for ideological ends—which we find in the *Chronicle* editorial raises another, parallel issue. It certainly seems that the modernization process which we all know so well, the passage from a feudal to an industrial society, also introduced a new sense of identity to the "civilized" countries, and that this is dramatically reflected in the crime columns of the newspapers. This identity is both national and historical: between each line we infer "We are English and we are living in the nineteenth century." What this means is less easy to pin down than what the lead writer hopes it does not mean. That is, all of this marshaling of irrational, biased argumentation (on both the anti-sensationalism and pro-sensationalism sides) is directed against the ominous suggestion that, in spite of progress, the Englishman of the age is as unenlightened and susceptible to bestial urges as he has ever been. Thurtell—as a case in point—was (or had been) a gentleman. He was *one of us*. And yet he is not only a homicidal thief, but an inept homicidal thief. And the most telling paradox is that the very "progress" which has enabled the criminal's story to be told so thoroughly and so speedily has also managed to undermine the notion of human advancement. In the same line, the bogus misleading "statistics" presented reflect the nineteenth century's reverence for certain immutable laws based on new scientific methodology, a need to fix things as one would like them to be, a fear of change. The problem is, of course, that the science is unscientific.

It is important to keep these hypothetical interpretations in mind as we move on a couple of decades, into the world of Volume 1 of Bell Macdonald's clippings. Here we find much more extended, and outspoken, manifestations of the peculiarly defensive-aggressive postures which would become—to posterity—corollaries of the Victorian official consciousness.

7

❖

Bell Macdonald's 1840s

The first volume of Macdonald's *Various Trials* runs from 1839 until 1850. During those years—in and out of Macdonald—the preeminent murder cases involved the respective investigations, trials, convictions, and executions of one Daniel Good in 1842 and of a married couple named Frederick and Maria Manning in 1849. Good, a London coachman, was accused of murdering his mistress, sawing up her body, burning the head and limbs, and burying the trunk under a pile of hay in a stable. Although, as in so many of these cases, the evidence against him was largely circumstantial, he was readily convicted and condemned to death. This, one presumes, effectively quieted the fears raised by his fifteen days on the run. One of Macdonald's columns provides a summary of Good's situation and illustrates Victorian morality at its most pietistic:

> One fact of Good's history (and it holds equally as to all the murderers that have been recently executed) is that he never had in his youth any religious instruction, and that he was awfully, utterly ignorant. A fearful idea this furnishes of that rank evil whence spring such fatal fruit. . . . Had the training of religious education spread in early days its sacred influence over his mind, the tears that we find burst forth occasionally may have been indications of that better nature which, in the most abandoned, never wholly dies. . . . Had this wretched

man been taught in his young days to value his Sundays rightly, the last of them would not have been spent in gloomy anticipation of a frightful doom.

The protagonist of the later case, Mrs. Manning, was the former Maria Roux, a Swiss-born maid who married an English husband, a railway guard. They invited to dinner an Irish lover of hers, murdered him, and buried his body under the kitchen floor. Then, dividing his cash and bonds, they went their separate ways. As Maria was eventually caught in Edinburgh, so her husband was apprehended on the island of Jersey. He confessed, pinning the blame on Maria. Especially since Mrs. Manning was a foreigner, the occasion of their hanging inspired considerable chauvinistic self-satisfaction in the press. One paper crowed that the

crime for which they suffered was committed on the 9th of August, and between the act and its punishment three months and three days have elapsed, thus affording another great proof, if such were wanted, that justice in this country pursues its victims with footsteps swift and sure, and that, though deeds of violence and blood may be concocted with the greatest premeditation, they can rarely escape the detection and punishment of even an earthly tribunal.

We see in these two commentaries—as we do throughout Macdonald's first volume—both a refinement of process and a hardening of position. The editorial on Good is quite a slick exemplar of the complacent faith in the rake's or harlot's "progress." The remarks on the Mannings are notable for their assertive identification of the worldly advancement of British institutions with the perfection of the Supreme Being. At the same time—in spite of this polished aggression—we are still reminded that these remain among the earliest types of modern newspapers. Compared to the post-1855 cases, the coverage of any cross-section of papers and magazines is relatively limited. There are also fewer clippings in Macdonald's collection. Moreover, there lies beneath each editorial the implicit assumption that the lowly birth of the criminals (and this is enhanced, in Mrs. Manning's case, by her being a foreigner) disassociates them to a degree from the real British populace, so well-to-do, God-fearing, and respectable. The fact that new British technology, the telegraph, had helped track them down made loyalists of Victorianism all the more triumphant.

So Macdonald's clippings from the 1840s are the product of a more sophisticated news-gathering apparatus; they include writing which is more professional—that is, self-assured, neither clubby nor hysterical. There is also an intensification of the orthodox Victorian ethos. But the columns remain significantly different from those of the next decade, still representing not dramatic change but a transitional stage in the development of the news media. A brief consideration of the attention devoted to Good in 1842 and the Mannings in 1849 in the *Illustrated London News* provides a neat profile of this evolution.

In fact, the *Illustrated London News* is in a general way representative of the direction taken by the press in the middle decades of the nineteenth century. Founded in 1842, not long before Good's arrest, the *ILN* devotes its Preface to the first volume to the potentially rich contribution to society offered by the illustrated weekly. This Preface itself embodies the sense of novelty and self-satisfied enthusiasm expressed in so many documents of the age: "[W]e discovered and opened up the world as connected with News, and the quick-sighted and sound-judging British public peopled it at once." On their coverage of Victoria's visit to Scotland that year, they are equally contented:

> Scott might carry Elizabeth to Kenilworth through the regions of his fine imagination, backed and supported by books, and we may take *cum grano salis* the Antiquarian and the Poet's word, but the year two thousand will be ten times better assured of all the splendid realities of our own Victoria's visit to the native land of the Northern Magician who enshrined in fiction the glories of Queen Bess. This volume is a work that history *must* keep.

Whether a picture news magazine such as *ILN* will prove in the twenty-first century more valuable to posterity than Scott's novels is not our business here to judge, but there is no doubt that *ILN* neatly traces one aspect of the growth of crime reporting in the 1840s.

In the 1842 volume, only one column—accompanied by an engraving of the convicted murderer's head—is devoted to Daniel Good before another brief item on his hanging. It is apologetic:

> It is not our intention to disfigure the pages of the "Illustrated News" with engravings, especially connected with crime and its consequences; we do not profess to be of the "raw head and bloody bones" school, nor do we desire to encourage the tastes of such as are only gratified by pictorial representations of murders and murderers . . . but he [Good] has only a few hours to live and disciples of Lavater [the phrenologist] may want to get a look at him.

By 1849, the *Illustrated London News* has altered its editorial resistance to crime. No fewer than twelve different articles—most illustrated and full of equal portions of naturalistic detail and conjecture—appear that year on the Mannings' "Bermondsey Murder." The September 1 issue devotes its entire lead article to the case, and in so doing raises most of the paradoxical issues—and doubts—which were to inform the full-blown cultural controversy over sensationalism in the next two decades:

> The most inattentive observer of the daily drama of life, as portrayed in the public journals, must have been painfully impressed by the recent frequency of murders in England. There is scarcely any kind of atrocity which has not been afforded by our criminal annals within the last few years. Such crimes as those committed by Rush [a Norfolk farmer who, threatened with eviction, shot and killed his landlord in 1849] and by the Mannings—the latter, in its cold-blooded hideousness, even surpassing in accumulated horror the fearful tragedy of Stanfield Hall—make Englishmen blush that such things should occur in the bosom of a civilization that boasts to be so advanced as ours. Amidst the shame we feel, there is, however, the consolation which some of our daily contemporaries have endeavoured to administer, that such deeds do not go unpunished—that detection is sure to dog the footsteps of crime—that the guilty wretch, flying on the wings of steam thirty miles an hour, is tracked by a swifter messenger—and

that the lightning itself, by the wondrous agency of the electric telegraph, conveys to the remotest parts of the kingdom an account of his crime, a description of his person, and an incentive to the officers of justice, in the shape of a promised reward, for his capture and conviction. The case of Tawell [a prosperous businessman and ex-convict who poisoned his former mistress with prussic acid in 1845] was one exemplification of the benefits conferred by science in the apprehension and speedy punishment of a great criminal. That of Mrs. Manning, a woman in comparison with whose blackness of guilt the memory of Tawell appears white, is a still greater warning to future criminals of the folly of crime and the certainty of punishment. We willingly accord to the police the high merit of the keenest intelligence and the most admirable activity in managing the arrest of Mr. and Mrs. Manning, and would extend our praise to every department of the Government that has been instrumental in rendering impossible the escape of such criminals. So far, the Law and its officers, the State and its servants, have conferred a high benefit upon society, and done much, not merely to punish present offenders—the least part of the duty of the State—but to deter from, and prevent the commission of such crime in future—a duty far higher and more important. It is upon this latter point, that, dismissing the case of the Mannings, and leaving it to the high tribunal of offended justice, we think it desirable that the attention of public men should be drawn to another kind of murders, still more common in England, which the law might do much to prevent altogether. We allude to cases of poisoning, which our assize reports prove to be very greatly on the increase, and for the commission of which the defective state of our law and police regulations unhappily affords too many facilities. It is recorded that in the days of the infamous Italian poisoners, La Spara and La Tophania, "ladies put poison bottles on their dressing-tables as openly, and used them with as little scruple upon others, as modern dames use lavender-water or *eau de Cologne* upon themselves." We have not reached such a point of depravity as this. The crime of poisoning is no longer practised by the rich, the powerful, and the educated, as in times gone by. It has, however, descended to the multitude; and the women of England of the lowest and most ignorant class are proved to be addicted to this crime, for the sake of pecuniary profit, to an extent which is sufficient to throw disgrace upon the national character in the eyes of all Europe. We need not allude more particularly to individual cases, in which wives have poisoned their husbands, and mothers their grown-up sons and daughters, as well as their young babes, in order to draw the miserable sums due for their burials from the burial clubs. The cases are too notorious; and it is but too probable that many such cases are never brought to light at all. It is in the prevention of these crimes that the law might very obviously be employed with the greatest certainty and advantage. The sale of poison is too open in England; the difficulties in the way of procuring it are not sufficiently great.

There is ambivalence in this piece—the writer can't seem to decide if things are getting better or worse—and it is a prophetic ambivalence. The most sensational murders of the next decade were indeed to be poisonings, although only one of the alleged perpetrators was a woman and all of the accused were from the well-off respectable classes. And all of these—William Palmer in 1856; Madeline Smith in 1857; and Thomas Smethurst in 1859—were reported by the press in such quantity and with such a profusion of subversive detail about English respectability in general that they more than fulfilled the gloomiest imaginings of the *ILN* editorialist.

Not only did these latter cases reveal sordid and upsetting insights into the behavior of inhabitants of slums and high-rent districts alike, but the inconclusiveness, or defectiveness, of law-enforcement procedures became increasingly apparent. The news media began to occupy a more significant place in the spirit of the times. This "low" culture of popular journalism began to bring to bear a radical intelligence on the same concerns which obsessed the "high" culture of poetry, criticism, and science. Indeed, it is arguable that the newspapers provided much of the inspiration and subject matter for many of these more eminently "respectable" intellectual endeavors.

8

❖

The Devil in Patent
Leather Boots

Bell Macdonald's clippings from the mid-1850s onward are emblematic of radical cultural change. Here there are many cases,
moreover, which have continued to resonate through popular culture—in film scripts and novels and non-fiction accounts—for over
a century. There is Madeline Smith, the genteel daughter of a
Glasgow architect, who was accused in 1857 of murdering her
French lover by poisoning his cocoa. Although the Scottish verdict
was "not proven," the presentation (and subsequent publication
in newspapers) of Miss Smith's graphically passionate correspondence from the evidence effectively condemned her among her
respectable Glaswegian peers. She fled, first to London, where she
became a member of the Bohemian Rossetti circle, and then to
Brooklyn, New York, where she died in obscurity and poverty in
1928 at the age of ninety-three. There is the case of Dr. Thomas
Smethurst in 1859. He was accused of terminating a bigamous
second marriage—and his illicit wife's pregnancy and life—with
arsenic. The prosecutor's case was,. not uncharacteristically, bungled, but Smethurst was later, at least, convicted of bigamy and
sent to prison. Bell Macdonald clipped virtually every available
piece of print on these cases, including the entire trial transcripts
and the floods of letters to the editor which the issues raised in
court provoked.

Still, every other criminal prosecution is overshadowed by the
first sensational trial of the period, that of William Palmer, a

churchgoing surgeon and member of the preeminent family of a provincial Midlands town. Palmer was officially charged with only one murder, but was alleged—throughout the widely reported investigation, which dragged on from late 1855 until his trial and execution in June 1856—to have done away with at least fourteen people, including his wife and brother. In this half-year alone, Bell Macdonald managed to clip enough words on Palmer to fill a Victorian novel.

The coverage of the Palmer case represents a significant departure from what came before, and not only in terms of the unprecedented quantity of newsprint devoted to it. What is initially striking, at least to me, is the relative neatness of the earlier cases. The gruesome events at Gill's Hill in 1827, in Good's stable in 1842, or at Bermondsey in 1849, were rather quickly resolved. The suspects were rounded up, tried, and executed with little hesitation on the part of the authorities or any apparent vacillation or soul searching on the part of commentators or the public. Palmer's guilt, on the other hand, like that of his successors in the headlines, Smith and Smethurst, was never "ensured." And although he did not have the good fortune of the lady from Glasgow or the bigamous London physician in escaping the gallows, his execution produced in the public more uncertainty and disquiet than self-congratulation. In contrast to the exotic villains of the popular Gothic fiction of the late eighteenth century, or a Regency rake like Thurtell, or an uneducated "brute" like Good, or a foreign temptress like Maria Manning, Palmer was neither easily categorized nor dismissed as an alien creature by the official consciousness. He was at once a communicant at the altar of nineteenth-century "progress"—a man of family, of property, of science, of religion—and a gambler and womanizer.

There is the possibility that most of what I have written so far about the historical significance of the Palmer case is suspect. It could have been mere coincidence that such a trial came along when it did, also coincidental that cases like Smith's and Smethurst's followed, and that the Palmer craze tells us less about the evolution of the news media than it does about legal procedures. For the moment, however, let us allow these arguments to remain moot, to be evaluated when the reporting on the trial is given detailed attention below. What is undeniable is the incremental change of tone which accompanied the outpouring of unsettling data about Palmer that the investigation and trial provided. We find in the papers a growing inclination on the part of commentators to irreverence; the accoutrements of respectability and technology evoke not respect or complacency, but cold irony. As James Hannay remarked in a special "Letter from Britain" to the *New York Daily Tribune* after Palmer's hanging: "The nineteenth century, in spite of its enlightenment, can do a little in the way of villains; and when such a one as Mr. P. arrives, it appears to have a glimmering that the devil is still extant, will travel by rail as readily as by old coach, and hides his hoofs, jauntily, in patent leather."

Of course, the Palmer case has been written about before. A number of volumes appeared soon after the trial; Robert Graves took it on as the basis for his novel *They Hanged My Saintly Billy* in 1957; and Altick gives it due consideration. But it has never been dealt with specifically as a media phenomenon. Let us then look at the story as it broke in the newspapers and consider it as a representative case of a new journalism, and also as an inspiration for a kind of radical counterculture.

The broad outlines of the Palmer case are, as I have already suggested, familiar to connoisseurs of crime. Still, a brief setting of the stage can do no harm.

A coroner's inquest was held in January 1856 to investigate the mysterious circumstances surrounding the death, two months before, of the gentleman-horseplayer John Parsons Cook in a hotel room in provincial Rugeley, in Staffordshire, in the English Midlands. As a result of this convening, William Palmer, a Rugeley surgeon and Cook's comrade "on the turf," was arrested for having poisoned Cook with strychnine. There were the subsequent revelations: of Palmer's debts and his efforts to avoid the payment of them—Cook, as one of his creditors, had a pocketful of money, and his betting book and the money were missing after his death; of Palmer's penchant for taking out life-insurance policies on friends and relatives who died soon afterwards. There was the exhumation of the bodies of Palmer's wife and brother, and his indictment for having poisoned them; then his bankruptcy and plea of guilty to forging his mother's name in order to acquire money. In any event, Palmer won a change of venue for his trial from his local district to London because of the impossibility—largely due to newspaper coverage—of gaining a fair trial from a jury selected from an enraged and biased pool of his Midlands peers. So he was tried in London, then returned to Stafford, county seat for Rugeley, to be executed.

In Macdonald's clippings, the first items concerning Palmer are brief notes on the allegations regarding Cook and the upcoming inquest. With the inquest, however, the papers soon could not get enough of the case. Macdonald's columns report the proceedings verbatim, beginning with the first person to take the stand: a friend of the deceased who had been present at the death. This was William Henry Jones, a friend and doctor, who had been summoned by Palmer in a letter informing him that Cook had a "bilious attack" at a local inn, after his horse, Polestar, had won a race at Shrewsbury:

I came to Rugeley . . . and found Mr. Cook in bed. . . . I then examined him in the presence of Mr. Palmer, and found that his pulse was natural and slow, and his tongue nice and clean. I made the remark that it was hardly the tongue of a bilious diarrhea attack, when Mr. Palmer said, "You should have seen his tongue before." It was proposed . . . that the morphine pills [just prescribed by Palmer] should be repeated, as on the previous night, and it was suggested by Mr. Palmer that Mr. Cook should not know what the pills contained, as he strongly objected to them on the previous night because they made him so ill. . . . Almost immediately after he had swallowed the pills he vomited, and I and Mr. Palmer searched the vessel for the pills, but could not detect them. A few minutes before twelve o'clock I went to his bed room, and at his suggestion slept in that room. . . . I suppose I had not been in bed more than a quarter of an hour or twenty minutes when he suddenly jumped up in bed, uttering these words, "Doctor, get up: I am going to be ill; ring the bell for Mr. Palmer." I went to him and pulled the bell, and he called out to the chambermaid, "Fetch Mr. Palmer directly." Mr. Palmer came in the space of two minutes, making the remark that he thought he had never dressed so quickly in his life. (Mr. Palmer lives opposite the Talbot Arms, where Mr. Cook was stopping.) I believe Mr. Palmer gave him two pills, which he brought with him, and which he told me contained ammonia. I could not see from Mr. Palmer's appearance whether he had been in bed. Immediately after taking the pills he uttered loud screams, and threw himself back on the bed in very strong convulsions. He then requested to be raised up, saying, "I shall be suffocated." We endeavoured to raise him up, but he was so stiffened out with spasms that it was impossible to do so. When he found we could not raise him he said, "turn me over," and I turned him over on his right side. I listened to the action of his heart, which I found to gradually cease, and in a few minutes he died. I never heard of his having a fit before. I have never seen symptoms so strong before. They were symptoms of convulsions and tetanus—every muscle of the body stiffened. I cannot say what was the cause of the convulsions. My impression at the time was that it was from over excitement.

In response to questions from the jury, Jones concludes: "I believe the jaw was fixed and closed. His body was stretched out, and resting on his head and heels. I never knew any one keep ammonia pills made up."

Jones's testimony is followed in the clippings by the testimony of a sequence of doctors who either had attended Cook during his illness or participated in the postmortem. After the doctors' "scientific" testimony, the chambermaid at the Talbot Arms is quoted at comparable length. She dwells on how Cook was "sitting up in bed, beating the bed clothes with his hands," and how he

looked very wild with his eyes, and his head was moving about convulsively. He said to Mr. Palmer, who was soon there, "Oh doctor, I shall die." To which he replied, "Oh no, my lad, you won't." Mr. Palmer then went and fetched two pills and some mixture of a dark thick kind in a wineglass. It smelt like opium. He took the pills first, and then the draught, and vomited it back immediately. We looked for the pills but neither I nor Mr. Palmer could find them. I remained with him until three o'clock. He asked me to rub his hands. They were stretched out and quite stiff, and were cold and moist.

The juxtaposition of the views, professional and domestic, as it were, is effective in involving the reader's technical curiosity and sympathy. The mixture results not only in horror and outrage but in a strange sort of intimacy with the subjects involved. Ugly as many of these details are, their ultimate effect on the reader is more pedestrian than theatrical. The potential for shock is muted by the quotidian reality of the bedpan. Palmer comes through more as an exemplar of the banality of evil—standing by with reassuring calm as poor Cook beats the sheets in a frenzy—than as the familiar mustache-twirling villain of melodrama. (This quality is enhanced by the illustrations run by some of the papers; Palmer was chubby-cheeked, benign, and slightly stupid-looking. Dickens himself commented in a letter on Palmer's ordinariness. Attending a race meeting, he thought he could see Palmer's face in each of the assembled bettors.) Two tentative insights which will be considered in detail in a later chapter can be gathered from this observation: that Palmer—by virtue of the very familiarity of his image to the public—created a more threatening figure than any semi-fictional grotesque, "the stranger beside me," as it were; and that this aspect of domestic realism strongly influenced the development of criminal fiction in the years following the case.

This is not to suggest that the latitude of Palmer's wickedness was in any way played down by the papers. Several of his cronies "on the turf" can be found bearing witness in court and in print to his financial machinations as well as to bawdy evenings spent carousing in hotels during race meetings. Rugeley chemists acquaint the public with the general availability of poisons (Palmer, as a surgeon, made a habit of regularly purchasing them in quantity). Other Rugeley characters attest to his attempts—sometimes comical—to insure lives under false pretenses: in one case, he attempted to insure, for £25,000, the life of his stable boy, whom he referred to in the application, co-signed by Cook, as "a gentleman of good property and possessed of a capital cellar of wine." And evidence is given of his plot to interfere with Cook's postmortem.

The revelations of the depths of his depravity are even more glaring. He had involved his innocent wife Anne in a scheme to swindle his own mother, and when the wife died suddenly, it transpired that he had recently insured her life for £13,000. His relationship with his brother, Walter, as revealed at the later inquest on *his* death, is particularly gruesome. According to Thomas Walkenden, a self-described corn agent, Walter Palmer "was continually drinking."

I was with him the morning on which he died. I went with him to Wolverhampton on the second day of the races there. He was very much in liquor when we started. We returned to Stafford about half past six the same evening. When we were on the racecourse he drank a few glasses of gin and water. I saw him have two. I left him on one occasion for about ten minutes on the course. He bet the price of a new hat with a man on the course on one of the races, but no money. . . . I had a mutton chop provided for him at Wolverhampton, but I don't think he ate more than an ounce of it, and that was all the solid food he had that day. He went to bed that night at ten o'clock, having his usual companion, the gin bottle with him. He called me up once or twice during the night, and when I went to him he said he was bad, and wanted some drink. I gave him some gin and water on each occasion. . . . He rose that morning about ten o'clock. He was certainly not sober when he got up. It was his general habit to say when he got up of a morning, "Come, let us have another 'tot,'" and I used to replenish his glass. . . . In an hour or an hour and a half afterwards he might have three or four glasses of gin and water. I was with him just before his death, when he was taken ill. He was taken unwell when sitting in an easy chair in the front room. He said to me, "Help me to the sofa, for I feel very ill," which I did. His brother William was then present, having arrived about half or three quarters of an hour before. He had nothing to drink while his brother William was there to my knowledge. When he was taken to the sofa he was sick, which he had frequently been before. I think I was with him the whole of the time that his brother was present, except when, on his being sick, I went to the kitchen to fetch a basin, and I was not more than a minute absent. . . .

After he was attacked his face became very black; the perspiration stood on his countenance like peas, and his head hung over the head of the sofa. I ran to the kitchen for William Palmer immediately, and told him to come and see the state of his brother.

Walter died soon afterwards.

There are a number of points to be made about the effects of such testimony. First of all, it has its literary qualities. The successive witnesses lend the story a peculiar sort of verisimilitude. That is, their very idiosyncrasies—which would disqualify them as official voices of reason—tend to make them more believable. When Walkenden comments that Walter Palmer's "perspiration stood on his countenance like peas," we may be dealing with a Biblical extravagance of phrasing, but the language is at the same time authentically colloquial, convincing. Our witness is a real person too. The sense of audience identification is intense.

Moreover, the content of the testimony has uses conventionally associated with fiction writing. Not only are we given painful insights into the alcoholism which plagued much of Victorian Britain (more effectively—or realistically, if you will—than Dickens's somewhat sentimental portrait of Jenny Wren's father in *Our Mutual Friend,* 1864–65), but the narratives of witnesses engage the reader as well in a page-turner of a story. Each twist of this particular plot adds to an extraordinarily bleak portrait of human nature and English society. The prosecution is using Walkenden here to advance its argument that the witness had been in fact a "bottleholder" for Walter, paid by William for his lethal duties. In other words, Walkenden had been hired by William, who held a life-insurance policy on Walter's life, to kill his charge with the gin which the good doctor supplied by the barrelful.

The case had other novelties. It provided the general public with an advanced course in legal medicine, not to mention, as many contemporaries noted, a do-it-yourself handbook for the aspiring poisoner. The testimony of Dr. Alfred Taylor, the London expert who participated in the inquests of Cook and Anne and Walter Palmer, is a telling case in point, as it was in the trial itself. As a matter of fact, it was Taylor who set the rather high scientific tone of the first inquest. At one point, he speaks of Cook's internal organs as perceived through his magnifying glass:

There was a brownish-coloured bilious-looking liquid adhering to the surface of the lining membrane of the stomach. There was no appearance of ulceration, perforation, or other disease. . . . There was no smell of opium, of prussic acid, nor of spirits, nor of henbane, nor, indeed, of any poison. . . . In the intestines and stomach there was nothing to indicate the cause of death . . . there was only a slight trace of antimony on the parts examined, and there was no trace of any other substance. . . .

Taylor concludes, after a lengthy and detailed summary,

We have no evidence before us to enable us to form a judgment as to the circumstances under which it [tartar emetic, or antimony], was taken by or administered to the deceased, or to enable us to say in this case whether it was or was not the cause of death; therefore, the result is, that we found antimony in the body, which must have been taken while living, but there was no cause of death. Dr. Rees, who made the analysis with me, fully concurs in these conclusions.

Following this thorough but indecisive beginning, Taylor returns to the stand after the dramatic testimony of the chambermaid. Asked to give an opinion on the cause of death, he replies that he believed "the pills administered [to Cook] on Monday night and Tuesday night contained strychnine." For this somewhat unexpected conclusion he gives two reasons: strychnine's speedy absorption rate in the human body; and Cook's corpse being "drawn up like a bow."

The apparent contradiction in the doctor's testimony was ignored by the inquest jury (which agreed with his final conclusion of death from strychnine), but it did not pass unnoticed in the months to come. In fact, Taylor's incompetence was to share with Palmer's roguery in casting an aura of distrust on the entire medical profession, another challenge to Victorian self-confidence. The point here, however, is that everyone, jury and readers alike, was being requested to digest and analyze medical testimony with which even the country's leading experts had difficulty. The compilers of *Notable British Trials,* as a matter of fact, had to edit the medical testimony in the transcript of the trial because it was "a little too much for the erudition of the shorthand writer." A spirit of scientific interest and questioning, however morbid, was abroad and the newspapers aimed to satisfy it.

In the following weeks, Taylor's entire report on the bodies of Anne and Walter Palmer was published, broken down by the contents of the three white jars in which the remains had arrived at the lab: one for the stomach, one for the intestines and a kidney, and the third for the liver, spleen, heart, and right lung. In addition, there was a "packet containing part of the lining of the shell, placed on the lid" on the third jar. After statements on the general condition of the contents of the jars and packet, the "chemical analysis, directed to the detection of mineral and vegetable poisons," was printed in full. The conclusion: Anne Palmer had died of poisoning by frequent small doses of tartar emetic, or antimony. At the risk of belaboring a point, it must be emphasized that this was not a private report for the court, nor did it appear in a specialized magazine; it appeared in daily newspapers which were read in pubs and households throughout the nation.

Not that specialized magazines and other journals ignored the case. Soon publications as disparate as *The Medical Times and Gazette* and Dickens's popular, very domestic weekly, *Household Words,* were publishing lengthy explanations of tartar emetic and strychnine. It is equally significant that Bell Macdonald, who, in spite of his training as a surgeon, previously had shown no predilection—at least in *Various Trials*—for scientific reading added *The Medical Times and Gazette* to his resources.

The Palmer case embodied, then, in virtually all its aspects, the implicit subversion of orthodoxy found in crime reporting. It also was reaching more readers from more varied backgrounds or interests than ever before. And it did so with a vengeance. The notes on the autopsies performed on the exhumed bodies of Anne and Walter Palmer in the commercial room of the Talbot Arms had to be particularly unsettling, not to say revolting:

> The coffin of Mrs. Palmer, made of oak, was first opened. Having been buried a long time, the gaseous exhalations being able to escape through the porous wood, the corpse was comparatively dry, and the smell educed endurable. On the re-

moval of the outer coffin a hole was bored in the leaden receptacle in which Walter Palmer's body was confined, and instantly a most sickening and noxious effluvium escaped, which permeated the entire building, affected parties at the other end of the inn, and produced a sickening effect on all in the immediate vicinity of the coffin. Subsequently the leaden lid was removed, and the spectacle presented by the body was absolutely frightful. The cheeks were so terribly distended as to extend to either side of the coffin; one eye was opened, and the mouth partially so, presenting the appearance of a horrible grin and grimace. Each limb was also swollen to prodigious proportions, and the sight was revolting in the extreme. Nearly all the jurors were afflicted with vomiting and fainting. After the reinterment of the corpses considerable time had elapsed before fumigations could make the house at all bearable; even a week afterwards the close room in which the bodies were opened strongly smelt of the disgusting odour and it was found necessary to have the walls scraped and repapered, the doors and woodwork repainted, and a portion of the floor on which foul matter had dropped from the coffin of the male deceased relaid, it being found impossible by planing to divest the boards of the noxious stain and stench.

It is tempting now to look back at the ruined room in the Talbot Arms as emblematic of the age: an ever-widening stain on the self-image; a strenuous, even desperate, effort to remove the unwanted—and unexpected—blemish. In either case, the effort was fruitless. Indeed, there was virtually nothing which emerged from these proceedings, however well intentioned, which had a cleansing effect.

One of the jurors in the Cook inquest—a member of the Rugeley bourgeoisie—was discovered conducting his own private search for evidence against Palmer. The accounts of testimony and legitimate results of investigative reporting in the papers were interlaced with unsubstantiated and speculative items. Assertions were published that Palmer had poisoned more than sixteen people; that his wife had exclaimed, on her deathbed, to the housekeeper: "Is that wretch in the house? He's murdered me"; and that Palmer had once owned a horse named Strychnine "which figured rather mysteriously on the turf." And there were ineffectual attempts at whitewash. One paper claimed:

> Although it did not officially transpire, it may be stated that the result of Professor Taylor's analysis proves that both Mrs. Palmer (the mother of the accused) and Mr. Walter Palmer (his brother) died from the effects of a slow but certain poison, administered with great tact and knowledge of its effects. What that poison was is not stated; but this fact is known: that it was neither arsenic nor strychnine.
>
> Dr. Taylor's report, the general outline of which is known to the authorities, will prove that the system of poisoning which has been added in reference to the persons whose cases are under examination, is one of the most remarkable that has ever been brought to light in this country; and it is hoped that the detection which has now taken place may lead to such a scientific investigation as will prevent the repetition of such atrocious crimes, or will, at all events, show that they cannot be committed as they appear to have been in past times, without fear of discovery.

The item is simply a fantasy, and an embarrassing one, inviting criticism of the establishment, not support. It was well known that Palmer's lusty, doting mother was by no means dead and, of all the alleged victims, Walter Palmer was least likely to have been poisoned. Moreover, Taylor's testimony had been, in fact, singularly confused and inconclusive. Any assumption—by this time—that his written report would be otherwise, that it actually would be so potent as to diminish, if not put an end to, the increasingly fashionable crime of poisoning, is wish-fulfillment of the most egregious sort. This strained self-satisfaction looks back to the commentary published on the speedy trial and execution of the Mannings in 1849, not to the crumbling of official dogma which was taking place on all fronts of the Palmer case, nor to the uncertain future which loomed ahead. The exhaustive detail of the reports was a natural adversary to the official consciousness on the one hand; on the other, the contradictory nature of many of the reports themselves made presumptive "truth" or any system of fixed beliefs all the more illusory.

At any rate, by the end of January 1856, when the jury at the coroner's inquest on the death of Palmer's wife came to a verdict of "wilful murder," the most immediate emotional effect of the gruesome details and speculative reports on the public was palpable. The verdict, we are told in one report, "appeared to give great satisfaction to the court, and, as soon as the foreman had delivered the verdict, there were manifestations of applause which the police was unable to suppress."

Such demonstrations of public feeling certainly provided support for the contention of Palmer's lawyers that he could not have a "fair and impartial trial at Stafford, Warwick, or in any of the Midland counties, owing to the prejudice which exists," particularly because "there were upwards of thirty newspapers represented by various reporters" at the inquests into the deaths of Anne and Walter Palmer, and "numerous paragraphs have appeared . . . unfavourable to the said William Palmer."

The petition was granted, one of the rare changes of venue in English legal history at that time. More to the point, it is probable that it was the first change of venue granted because of newspaper coverage. So the trial was moved to London. It is unlikely that the move had any effect, however, since the newspapers had saturated their readers far beyond the borders of Staffordshire. What can be said with some sureness is that, ironically, the first change of venue by reason of newspaper coverage had been preceded in London by the same coverage, like the man who went to Samarra to flee Death. There can be no doubt that the newspapers had become subjects of their own coverage, active agents, as it were, in the tale they told.

There are two inescapable inferences to be drawn by the reader of the coverage of this trial, which go beyond any raised social conscience or parliamentary innovation: that the society described is dissolute and perverse; and that it is administered and watched over by an incompetent and corrupt authority.

Palmer, of course, had been trained as a surgeon, and the notion of a medical man using his professional expertise to murder people instead of save lives was, to put it mildly, disquieting. The presence of other medical men in the case who were *not* accused of murder was hardly more reassuring. Dr. Bamford, who certified Cook's death as having been the result of apoplexy, was a doddering eighty-two year old, and it was soon discovered that Palmer had used him as a tool to legitimize dubious circumstances in a number of other deaths. (Anne Palmer's death he had attributed to "English Cholera.") And Dr. Taylor's eminence began to fall under the shadow of fallibility. One of the papers pointed out, "notwithstanding the positive opinion on the part of Taylor (who, in this instance, spoke as a physiologist, and not as a chemist, and, of course, only from what he heard in evidence), that the organs which would have been particularly affected in case of death from strychnine—viz. the brain and spinal marrow—by some bungling on the part of the medical man who performed the first post mortem (a surgeon's assistant) had not been examined at all." As a consequence, "two first-rate anatomists and physiologists" were brought in for a second opinion and concluded that "both the nerves and spinal marrow have an appearance inconsistent with poisoning by strychnine." Therefore, "it was an utter impossibility to form a correct diagnosis of the cause of death; and it is suggested that the opinion of Dr. Taylor must have been too hastily given; otherwise he would have paused in proving murder, and having previously required an examination of the organs likely to be affected by the poison, whose administration he sought to establish."

Not only do we have here an excellent example of the sort of scientific exercise in deduction to which the general public was being exposed, but also the beginning of Taylor's downfall. Professor of Medical Jurisprudence at Guy's Hospital and author of a well-known treatise on poisons and forensic medicine, he was regarded as the leading specialist in his field. Yet he had to admit, under cross-examination at the London trial, that he had written a book about strychnine but had never personally observed its effects. The result outside the trial was a great controversy. Medical schools were in a furor and large meetings were held to protest a verdict based on Taylor's evidence.

This was but the beginning of Taylor's descent into disrepute. His testimony in the 1859 trial of Dr. Thomas Smethurst, when Smethurst was accused of poisoning his pregnant wife, was demonstrated to be based on the faulty analysis of arsenic which had come from Taylor's own laboratory supplies rather than Mrs. Smethurst's stomach. Bell Macdonald collected dozens of letters to *The Daily Telegraph* which indicate that the paper had mounted a campaign against Smethurst's subsequent conviction. One of the clippings holds forth vigorously on the subject:

> What species of figure has the "infallible" Dr. Taylor the Toxicologist who hung Palmer, who will hang Smethurst, made by his dogmatical yet contradictory evidence? . . . The Doctor seems to have brought his arsenic along with him when he came to seek for it; and he was compelled to acknowledge his most grievous error and blunder when his much vaunted copper gauze boiled away in the potassium.
>
> From the trial of Smethurst, the dogmatical value of scientific evidence will sensibly decline. . . . It may be false; it may be as murderous as the deed it professes to discover. If Dr. Taylor blunders once, why not a hundred times? . . . In the interests of human justice we might demand that in future, and in trial for murder, some confirmatory evidence of fact should be requisite to support scientific suppositions. . . .
>
> We do trust . . . that, for the credit of English justice, Dr. Alfred Taylor will not in future be called upon to follow the subtle tracks of poison; otherwise modern toxicology will eclipse middle-age witchcraft in the atrocity of its superstition and the ignorance of its cruelty.

"Dogmatical yet contradictory" is a phrase which effectively characterizes the uncomfortable role into which orthodoxy is generally cast in the later volumes of Macdonald's archive. This is most obvious in regard to those in the medical profession who during the period were using their pseudo-scientific "knowledge" to exercise repressive control over patients, particularly—as Marcus has shown—in the area of sexuality. The reports on Palmer undermined this position. Not only was the shadow of doubt cast on forensic studies, but physicians representing both defense and prosecution were demonstrated to be corrupt, foolish, murderous, scheming, profligate, incompetent, and confused. Of course, this aura of disrepute was not reserved for doctors. The coroner and postmaster of Rugeley were tainted by Palmer's conspiratorial brush as he contrived to elude suspicion. Much of the Staffordshire sporting middle class was associated with his tippling and habitual wenching. Rumors of his old mother's licentiousness found their way into print. And it was alleged that the good doctor had impregnated his housemaid on the night of his wife's death. Nothing was left sacred.

The word "sacred" is not inappropriate here. The extent to which the Victorian establishment liked to see such matters as respectability, scientific progress, and religion as inextricably bound up together cannot be overstated. To question the stability of one was to question the stability of all. The universe was supposed to be a neat and tidy place, presided over by one Christian deity, infused by "immutable" laws which promised healthy forward movement in all matters—from population control to the preservation of the social order to ensuring those who qualified as respectable a happily celestial afterlife. There was of course a terrible underlying contradiction to this mind-set: change, which implied movement, was at the same time based on the maintenance of a fixed, hierarchical system. The "progress" that was so happily trumpeted was grounded in the status quo.

The mass media treatment of crime which was inspired by the Palmer case in turn inspired a reaction in many ways comparable to the "convulsions of the national mind" brought on three years later by the publication of Darwin's *Origin of Species*. Crime reporting, as we have seen above, had been a threat to British complacency for some time; so too had been discoveries in evolutionary biology. Neither the reporting on the Palmer case nor Darwin's book materialized out of the blue. Each was in its way a logical development of what had come before. But each was a landmark as well, bringing into focus—concretizing, if you will—certain realizations. Chief among these was the rediscovery of an old truth that mankind, to paraphrase Tennyson in *In Memoriam,* had not yet worked out the beast.

9

❖

A Very Special Correspondence

I. THE GRAVES ARE OPENED

As this subversive strain worked its way to the surface, it is reasonable to assume, a substantial journalistic counterculture must have existed in London. Clearly, there were reporters, anonymous and now-forgotten, who confronted on a daily basis a darker, more lascivious society than anything recorded in Mayhew or Dickens. And they were writing about it. With the rise of the Special Correspondent this writing became at once more subjective and more ambitious; more literary, if you will. As it happens, Bell Macdonald clipped an entire special correspondence on the Palmer case which consists of the most overtly and distinctively iconoclastic writing in the Rammerscales collection, and even—it is arguable—in mid-Victorian literature in general. In Macdonald's volumes the source of the pieces is unidentified, but I was able to determine later that they came from *The Leader,* a London weekly. There are four lengthy articles, two from Rugeley in January when Palmer was first indicted and two from Stafford in June when he was hanged, each under the byline "From our Special Correspondent."

The most salient quality of these pieces, in addition to their unmistakable literary merit, is the fact that whatever dismal hints about the state of Britain—spiritual and physical—can be inferred by the attentive reader from the more commonplace daily and weekly news reportage of crime in the 1850s is here explicitly, even flagrantly, broadcast to the British public. Not only is the news given a subversive interpretation for contemporary readers, but the correspondent presents his exegesis in a style at once personal, irreverent, socially comprehensive, and irresistibly lively. While *The Leader* is by no means an exemplary popular newspaper—with a highbrow staff led by George Henry Lewes (who is best remembered now as George Eliot's lover, but at the time had achieved eminence with his 1855 *Life of Goethe* and by introducing Comte's Positivism in Britain) and an elite progressive readership—it seems to me that, in the context of all the other papers, this remarkable coverage is only a logical extension of what was being communicated at all levels of society. I only regret in using it that I am not able to quote the series in its entirety.

From the outset, the Special Correspondent makes clear that he is not interested in "mere reporting of fact." Under the dateline "Rugeley, January 16, 1856," he writes:

Let us imagine a sensible and intelligent Parisian, weary of the eternal chatter and the saunter along the Boulevards, forming the sage resolution of setting up his household gods in the right little, tight little island, famous throughout the world as the peculiar shrine of the domestic affections, of solid comfort and genuine worth. Let him cast his eyes over the length and breadth of the land. Let him survey its bold mountains and smiling valleys, its populous towns and sweet rural villages. Much would be beheld worthy of admiration as a traveller and a cosmopolite, but little pause would he make ere taking up his abode in the pleasant vale watered by the winding Trent. This would be his harbour of refuge from the vanities and vexations of a frivolous or malicious world. This would be to him the promised land—a land flowing with milk and honey. Here, if anywhere, he might hope to exhume the simple virtues hitherto buried in the dull dribblings of pastoral rhapsodies. Here he would expect to find a true manly race, softened by the gentle influences of home, and equally free from the brutal impulses of a barbarous and the calculating selfishness of a too refined state of society.

Alighting at the Rugeley station, he would walk with a buoyant step between well-kept hedges, fencing in "meadows trim, with daisies pied," until, halting for a moment on a bridge that spans a broad canal, his eye would alight upon a substantial redbrick house with its bowwindows looking out upon a lawn sloping down to the water. A small court, filled with Portugal laurels, evincing the genuine Dutch taste for regular forms, separates the house from the road. At the back may be seen what was once a timberyard of some pretensions, where still a few rows of planks attest the presence of a sawpit, and where a wheezy-looking crane enjoys the repose due to a long and faithful servitude. Adjoining these grounds a spacious but densely-peopled churchyard contains whole generations of men who, after slumbering through life, now sleep in death. The pious doggerels commemorating the ungrammatical sorrows of the survivors are already half obliterated by time's "effacing fingers," while two noble arches, clad with ivy, tell by their very ruins how earnest were the men of afore time when they sought to glorify their Creator. On the opposite side of the road now stands a more modern church, fitted for a numerous congregation, and not displeasing to the eye. Here, too, a rapidly filling enclosure proves that the bills of mortality fall due even in the cheerful valley of the Trent: is not the medical profession largely represented in Rugeley?

Behind this edifice our imaginary traveller would behold a tomb, in front of which the gravel had been recently disturbed. Had he stood here a few days since, he would have seen the spade and the pick-axe busily at work, a curious crowd standing around, and the glazed hats of the police conspicuous above all. These were not mourners. Their countenances, where capable of other expression than vacancy, denoted indignation rather than grief.

This is serious satire, comparable to the best novels. Its direction is unmistakable—it is an intricate and virulently ironic attack on prevailing conceptions of domestic life and respectability.

At this point, the correspondent has only begun to introduce the Palmers of Rugeley. But his posture is clearly established. The "right little, tight little island . . . shrine of the domestic affections, of solid comfort and genuine worth" is not at all what it is "famous throughout the world for," but something quite the opposite. That he chooses the device of an imagined French tourist visiting

Rugeley is ironically appropriate since the ethos of France had so often been looked upon in the nineteenth century as the decadent opposite of Britain's domestic solidity. Nor is it only the conflict between the town's exterior tranquility and inner evil which he insists on. Provincial existence in general is attacked: "whole generations of men who, after slumbering through life, now sleep in death." There is an element of literary parody in his deliberately archaic diction which serves to undermine any reverence for a simple rustic past as well. He comments, caustically, on the eighteenth-century graveyard poets while echoing their tone: "The pious doggerels commemorating the ungrammatical sorrows of the survivors are already half obliterated by time's 'effacing fingers.' " In fact no article of faith about British virtue—past, present, or future—is left untarnished. William Palmer himself is introduced as a model of English hypocrisy, an icon of deceit:

> His personal appearance, if not heroic, was by no means disagreeable. His stout, compact form, light complexion, florid hue, and easy smile, bespoke the genuine English yeoman, healthy and good-humoured. To the poor he was kind and considerate. Among the humble fry of clerks, apprentices, innkeepers, and small dealers, he was extremely popular, for he could always guide them in laying their bets upon horses, and freely imparted any certain knowledge he possessed. There is not a chambermaid or waitress within thirty miles, who does not speak of him as "a nice, pleasant sort of gentleman."

But, of course, the writer continues, Palmer's relationships with these people were not "platonic or angelic." He had given many "pledges of fortune": illegitimate children. Even his "passion for the turf" evokes snide social commentary: "Not that anyone would blame him for his good old English tastes. Is not the turf the keystone of the British Constitution? It is the last Conservative element in the land."

Following the introduction of Palmer, we are treated once again to the lively cavalcade of his alleged crimes. Then the correspondent provides us with some timeless sociology, which also takes a cut at the heart of middle-class respectability. Although Palmer's activities had for some time been considered suspicious, we are told, it took an outsider, Cook's stepfather, to bring him to court. "In Rugeley itself the Palmer interest was omnipotent. A family that numbers in its members a clergyman, a surgeon, and a lawyer would anywhere require as cautious handling as a hedge-hog. In Rugeley, no man would venture on such a hazardous encounter." The correspondent's perception, in fact, is of an entire social fabric which constitutes a conspiracy of ignorance and corruption. This is particularly manifest in his observations at the inquest held on the deaths of Anne and Walter Palmer: The little coroner is "ferrety," and "a slow penman." The jurymen have "open countenances and lips well apart, of average provincial misunderstanding, and no doubt as weighty as any twenty-three men in the kingdom chosen at random." A "well-known barrister of the Oxford Circuit" has "hair in front bristling up like a cockatoo's crest, that behind wondrously short and curiously cropped; over-all boots not too polished, coming up above the knee; a grey coat demanding nerve to wear; barnacles on nose; a square grin taking liberties with the lips, and exhibiting moss-grown teeth; and a very plain face under a very rough hat." The police are "pompous and fussy, and looking as if they were about to burst out of their uniforms." The reporters are "busily plying the pen, and feeding the insatiate maw of the public." Insurance company representatives are "very indignant about this case, though they must always know that when a man insures his neighbour's life, he is laying the odds on that neighbour's death." The audience is "filled with the local chaw-bacons, who stand for hours 'obstruction's apathy,' occasionally snoring on their legs, laughing consumedly when Mr. Lawyer pokes fun at a witness, cheering riotously when the jurymen splutter out noisy nonsense about their impartiality and fearlessness in the cause of justice, but looking blank and chop-fallen whenever a hitch occurs in the prosecution."

So, the correspondent concludes: "Imagine our Frenchman in such an assembly as this. Truly, he will deem himself a Rip Van Winkle sleeping backwards. He will seem to himself to have gone back four centuries, and to have awakened up among the *manants* of 1450."

Herein lie many of the virtues of the writer. He is fearlessly irreverent; no established value or institution escapes his acerbic wit. He has a marvelous eye for social detail, as well as historical perspective: one thing the respectable Englishman did not want was to be tainted with medieval primitivism. His grasp of the ridiculous is sure. His perceptions of group psychology are sharp. And, as in all good satire, the seriousness underlying the mockery is never far from the surface. A man's life is at stake and the entire provincial legal system is being thrown into disrepute. The angry indignation of the correspondent is at all times strongly felt. In a later report from Rugeley's singular inquest, held at the Talbot Arms, he writes of the coroner's assertion of innocence of the charge of graft: "His red hair bristled as he spoke, rubescent flames flashed from those pinky eyes, and the mantle of the immortal Pecksniff visibly descended upon the shoulders of the much injured but long-suffering little man." In response, the "jurors roared applause, the chaw-bacons joined in chorus, and the Town-hall trembled to its foundations, like the mighty Olympus when great Jove shakes his ambrosial locks."

The intricacy of this satire should not be overlooked. The educated English revere the Greek and Roman classics, so—in the best mock-heroic traditions—the local bumpkins are identified with the gods at Olympus. The novel-reading middle class is familiar with Dickens's Pecksniff from *Martin Chuzzlewit,* who represents, in Angus Wilson's words, "Victorian concern for morality overblown, gone to seed, run rampant," and is told that one of their own guardians of the law is no less foolish and no less hypocritical. The overall tone in fact does not so much look back to Pope's controlled neoclassical satire or Dickens's tolerably bourgeois grotesques. Rather, we hear an anticipation of the freewheeling nihilistic 1920s, of Mencken's scathing denunciations of the "booboisie."

The correspondent's description, though by no means subdued, of Palmer's wife, her family, and her education, is admirable in its humanity, impressive in its psychology, and justifiably sardonic about the education of Victorian ladies. One can see in it a pointed, and hilarious, rejection of the basic tenets of Podsnappery. Born Anne Thornton, she had been the illegitimate daughter of a retired colonel and his housekeeper. The officer drank, and the mistress frequently dragged him home from the pub. Amid such scenes as these, under the care of such parents, did the gentle and delicate Anne pass her infancy and childhood. One night her father was found lying dead upon the floor—a recently discharged pistol by his side. From that hour her mother shuddered at darkness. She would sit up all night, and only laid down when the dawn was breaking. Dr. Knight, the young lady's guardian, no doubt did all that could be demanded from an affectionate zeal. No doubt Miss Thornton learned to strum the "battle of Prague" on the piano, and was equally skilled in the niceties of Oriental tinting. No doubt she waltzed to perfection, and gracefully kicked through the evolutions of the lately imported polka. No doubt she was curious in embroidery, and in the knitting of silk purses and hair watch-guards. No doubt, also, she knew something of English history, the geographical position of metropolitan towns, the rule of three in arithmetic, enough French to decipher "Charles XII," and the various denominations of stitch from "herringbone" upwards. All this she may have learned, and much more—in short, everything that pertains to a "genteel education." But, in all human probability, she had been taught no social duty, nothing that could fit her for the realities of life.

Returning to the hypothetical French traveler, at the end of his first day in Rugeley, the correspondent summarizes the sensational happenings and draws some sober conclusions about England:

But, mark all the incidents of this case . . . perhaps four legitimate children hastened out of the world by their father: perhaps three illegitimate children similarly treated: probably a friend poisoned by this same man five years ago: certainly an intimate ally poisoned two months ago: the coroner compromised: the postmaster suspended: the telegraph clerk committing an irregularity: the chaplain of the gaol completely fascinated by the poisoner . . . and last, though not least, Rugeley discovered and handed down to posterity in the annals of crime. By this time our domestic Frenchman must be preparing to return to the rattling dominoes, the eternal chatter, and the saunter on the boulevards, quite ready to renounce English comfort and an English home provided he may be allowed to finish his useless but harmless existence in his beloved Paris; and there, having lived without regret, die without pleasure.

The reader of these pages then is being taken behind the scenes and beneath the respectable surface of the social and legal establishment to an extent that could not have been imagined a decade before. It is as if we were to reread the entire catalogue of stories like that of the Cambridge Fellow who died in the arms of the whore in a brothel through the eyes of one of the laughing spectators in the gallery at the inquest.

II. THE HANGING

Following Palmer's trial and conviction for Cook's death in June, *The Leader*'s Special Correspondent repaired (with what seemed like half the country) to Stafford to witness the execution. After beginning on the somewhat clever, detached note he had tried and largely discarded in January—"Paris danced on the edge of a volcano; Rugeley proposes to eat drink and be merry on the eve of an execution"—he finds himself, literally, in the midst of the throng and abandons this attitude. On June 12 he casts about for surface details: sixty beds taken at a pound apiece at the "Dodo"; fifty thousand visitors expected overnight; hundreds of policemen stationed at key points and forming a cordon around the gallows; only *The Times* granted permission to report from inside the gate near the scaffold. On June 14, as the bloodthirsty throngs arrive, the detail becomes more concrete, betrays a grimmer reality:

Throughout the whole of yesterday the town of Stafford wore the aspect of a great festal holiday. With every train—and they were incessant—a long line of visitors poured into the streets. All night long the clatter of heavy shoes was heard on the ever-pointed swan's-egg pebbles that stand proxy for pavement. Some came in carriages and carts, very many by rail, but still more on foot. From Derby, and Manchester, and Liverpool, from Birmingham, Wolverhampton, and Tamworth, from Chester, Shrewsbury, and Worcester, hundreds upon hundreds were ever arriving. But the Potteries and "the black country" poured forth their thousands, for at most of the neighbouring works the operatives had claimed a holiday. Comparatively few persons retired to rest that night, and even these were too excited to sleep. The majority whiled away the hours as best they could, listening to the discord of wandering minstrels, rattling the dice-box or indulging in potations deep. So early as two in the morning the more determined sightseers took up their posts, and bravely stood out "the pelting of the pitiless rain" through six long weary hours. Very haggard and wan was their appearance, especially of those who came from Potteries. Thin, stunted, emaciated creatures, with cavernous cheeks, hungry jaws and vacant expression of the eye. Nor is the shoemaking population of Stafford more stalwart or prepossessing. But never did a more orderly crowd assemble to witness the extreme penalty of the law. Scarcely any women disgraced themselves by being present, excepting a few respectably dressed females on the scaffolds erected at every point which commanded a view of the horrid spectacle.

The juxtapositions are especially effective here. The similarity between the wasted appearance of the industrial poor and the occasion they have chosen for their revelry is strikingly poignant. In contrast, the figure of the condemned man, the "villain," looms larger and more alive. In Stafford, the correspondent reports, "he had obliged many, offended none. To the small tradesman, the groom, the ostler, the female domestic, he was invariably kind, gentle, and lavish." A recent evening at the Cremorne in London, the notorious haunt of prostitutes, is recalled in the earlier report from Stafford:

> Round and round the platform circulated the monotonous throng, as if working on a moral treadmill. And their aspects were gloomy, like revellers in the regions of sorrow. Sadly your correspondent gazed on the careworn grubs, who, crawling in the artificial light of coloured lamps, deemed themselves butterflies disporting in the rays of the sun, and mistook the

smell of gin for the aroma of flowers. Then a perambulant siren approached him.

"Why so grave tonight? You look as if you were going to be hanged with William Palmer."

"So say I. I am sorry for him poor fellow. I knew him well."

"You knew him? Come. Tell me all about him. What can I offer you?"

"Well! I don't mind a glass of brandy-and-water; but I can't tell you much, except that he was a very nice gentleman, and quite a man of honour."

"What made you think so?"

"Oh, he used to come to a house where I was a barmaid, down the Walworth Road. He used to order a private parlour. Sometimes a thin, light-haired young gentleman came to see him; and one or two others."

"Well! but what had that to do with his honour? Everybody pays for his room and his beer not because he must."

"Yes; but one day he said to me, 'Mary,' says he, 'I'll lay you 15 to 1 in half-crowns that such a horse wins.' 'Anything you please, sir,' says I. So said, so done. I thought no more about it, till one day he comes in all smiling like, and counts out fifteen half-crowns, one by one; and, says he, 'Mary, you have won the bet. There's your money.' Now, that's what I call honourable, and you won't make me believe he ever did no murder."

The woman herself is believable although her story sounds apocryphal. The correspondent has realized, in a literary way, the implied promise of other newspapers and that of the less elegant and less outspokenly subversive work of pioneer social researchers like Henry Mayhew. He has a theme, he has characters, he has a broad social canvas on which to paint them. The treadmill lives of the prostitutes and glum pleasure seekers is captured poignantly (in a passage almost identical to one Marcus quotes from William Acton's 1858 study of prostitution), and the confusion of the smell of gin with that of flowers is an apt metaphor for the attitudes of the age being revealed to us. In much the same way, we are being told, the Victorians confused respectability with rottenness. Many were, after all, drunk on respectability.

This brings us back to Palmer himself. The earlier transcripts from the inquest had suggested the banality of his evil rather than melodrama. As the investigation developed into the trial and the trial into the execution, the accused became even more subtle and enigmatic a villain, not less, and this serves to place an even greater distance between him and the murderers who preceded him in the British consciousness as arch villains. There was no small amount of sympathy for him, as in the case of the Cremorne woman, and most of what he did (and did not do) during the months preceding his demise contributed further to a sense of ambiguity. He is forever the shadowy and perversely benevolent figure in the corner of Cook's room at the Talbot Arms. Palmer refused to appear at the first inquest. He went on a hunger strike when imprisoned. He did appear—in what was taken to be an heroic gesture—in court when his mother was sued for loans he had taken in her name to testify that he and his wife had committed a forgery and were thus solely responsible. He chose not to testify at his trial. Before leaving his cell for the gallows, he made one final, totally ambiguous, statement: "I am innocent of poisoning Cook by strychnine." Did this mean he *had* poisoned others? Or that he poisoned Cook by some other means? In any case, *The Leader*'s correspondent adapts a different tone of voice during Palmer's last hours, one both urgent and reflective. He manages to exploit both the journalist's prerogative in writing for deadline and the novelist's license to amplify atmospherics. The result is no longer irreverence, but a fearsome sense of impending doom. On the afternoon before the execution, he writes: "Time presses, while matter hourly accumulates. It is impossible to preserve any sort of method. All that can be done is to jot down each particular as it rises on recollection." The subject has become immediate. It is happening now. And the correspondent, flawed and human, is becoming overwhelmed.

The bond of fragile mortality, which the once jolly prisoner shares with journalist and reader alike, is emphasized. Also, fore-shadowing is used to intensify the dramatic effect of the moment itself when it comes:

Walking slowly to the gate, the prisoner will ascend the steps of the drop—a movable machine attached to iron hooks in the solid masonry on either side of the gateway. And when the chaplain shall have pronounced the awful warning, "In the midst of life we are in death," the bolt will be drawn, the drop will fall, and a ghastly corpse will be all that remains of William Palmer. . . . Within ten minutes after the first tolling of the bell all will be over. An hour afterwards the body will be cut down, and buried within the prison walls, enclosed neither in coffin nor shell. A quantity of quick lime and a few buckets of water will be thrown in upon the felon's corpse, the earth rapidly shovelled in, and the place smoothed down to the ordinary level, so that, within a short time, not a vestige will remain of the murderer Palmer. He will have been obliterated, physically annihilated.

In terms of social history, the correspondent's change of attitude reflects, at least in part, the ambivalence of the age about public executions and the notion of capital punishment itself. It is also artful and didactic in manner of presentation. That is, the correspondent is building to a climax and conclusion, and these effects also communicate a sense of community or identity with the prisoner. The frightening mixture of good and evil in Palmer's nature demonstrates the flimsiness of the line separating these elements and, thus, the vulnerability of any received notion of the sameness of "respectability" and "goodness."

At this point in the narration, the Special Correspondent leaves behind any pretention to objectivity. In spite of the occasional bathos in these passages, the writing has undeniable power, recalling Dickens at his most impassioned:

The door of the cell was thrown open: the prisoner set out on his long exile. An ornamental iron staircase of at least a dozen steps leads down to the basement storey. Down these he tripped as lightly as would a schoolboy escaping to the playground. The distance he had to traverse was not less than a hundred and fifty yards. With a jaunty step he made the "running"—as he himself would have said—and reached the foot of the ladder two or three minutes before the appointed time. All this time the chaplain read aloud the impressive service for the Burial of the Dead; but his voice faltered and his frame quivered emotion. And now every head is uncovered, from every lip escapes a stifled exclamation; and then the ear throbs with the unnatural silence. On the center of the drop, right beneath the beam, there stands William Palmer, erect and unmoved. His face, indeed, is ashy pale, but there is a smile upon his lips. Is it defiance? Or rather is it not the shadow of his ancient civility—a trick those lying lips have not yet forgotten? The eyes look puzzled, as if uncertain whether to regard the strange scene as a reality or a frightful phantasma. At each corner of the scaffold stands an official, clothed in black, and bearing a long wand in his hand. The chaplain at the foot of the ladder prays audibly for the departing sinner. The bell tolls on, sad, but inexorable. The people bend forward with throbbing hearts and straining eyes, and deem each minute an hour. The pigeons on the chimney-top plume their feathers, or murmur soft amorous notes—too low in the scale of creation to practice fraud, forgery, seduction, murder, and the other pastimes incidental to beings endowed with reason.

And now the hangman grasps the rope—Palmer bends his head—the noose is slipped over—his face grows yet more ghastly—his throat throbs spasmodically—he moves his neck round, as a man with a tight collar—the hangman is hurrying off the drop—he suddenly bethinks him of the cap—turns back—clutches at the criminal's right hand, as if asking for pardon—"God bless you, goodby," says the prisoner, in a low, distinct voice—the cap or white bag, is pulled over his head—the peak blows out from his chin by the violent and rapid respiration—another second, the bolt is drawn, down falls the drop with a slight crash—the arms are thrown up from the elbow, with the hands clenched—the body whirls round—the hangman from below seizes the legs—one escapes from his grasp, and by a mighty spasm is once drawn up—the chest thrice heaves convulsively—the hangman looses his hold—the body again whirls round, then becomes steady, and hangs a dull, grey, shapeless mass, facing the newly risen sun.

The reader is forced to draw a breath after confronting this scene. However gimmicky and histrionic, it works. And what it works at is a very interesting question. There is in effect an over-lapping between technique and message here. The writer has not only employed a heavy-handed foreshadowing, but exploits the change from past tense to present to underline urgency; telegraphs (as we say today) the symbolism of the pigeons; and is not above resorting, quite literally, to a certain heavy breathing—or spas-modically rapid respiration—in his language. Yet these techniques do have serious applications, and it is here that we begin to detect the connections between crime journalism, the popular fiction of the 1860s, and the quite serious meaning which the Victorians gave to the terms "sensation" or "sensationalism," words which we tend to trivialize today. The final effect of this description of Palmer's hanging is identical to that attributed a few years later by Margaret Oliphant (a popular novelist herself, she was the regular book reviewer for the influential *Blackwood's Edinburgh Magazine*) to Wilkie Collins's *The Woman in White,* the first Sen-sation novel, which made its serial appearance in the same month as the publication of *Origin of Species:* "[The] sensation is again indisputable. The reader's nerves are affected like the [narrator's]. He feels the thrill . . . an ominous painful mystery. He, too, is chilled by a confused and unexplained alarm."

What is most immediately clear here is that Oliphant, a serious and highly respected critic, is by no means taking Collins's "sen-sation" lightly. Her remarks echo a concern which resounds throughout contemporary criticism—the relative merit of arts which appeal to the "nerves," as does the Special Correspondent, as opposed to "reason." That which does speak to the nerves is "ominous" and "painful," perhaps because it is considered "unexplainable."

Of course, responses like Oliphant's to sensationalism can seem at least slightly disingenuous. While the correspondent in Staf-fordshire may be capable of melodrama, his irony seems quite rational, even understandable, especially in light of the mid-nineteenth-century debate over the social and metaphysical im-plications of the evolutionary theory which came to be known as Darwinism. The correspondent is quite explicit in his caustic mes-sage about the relative positions—at the moment Palmer confronts his Maker—of man and pigeons on the "scale of creation." The inferior beasts not "endowed with reason" are, therefore, too "low" to practice such crimes as those committed by the eminent physician.

As we move ahead into the worlds of mid-Victorian fiction and criticism, we shall see how this message, in various and sundry forms, became a staple of journalism and popular literature, while an overheated and defensive set of critical responses—what amounted to a defensive warding off of "mystery," in the criminal as well as metaphysical sense—sprang up like antibodies all around it wherever it appeared. This reactionary stance is what has come down to us as conventional Victorianism.

That this version does not tell the whole story is obvious enough in *The Leader*'s coverage of Palmer—particularly when, having escaped the hypnotic environs of the scaffold, the Special Correspondent applies himself to a summary review of Palmer's career:

> The death of every one of these persons was a gain to him, either immediate or prospective. He had a motive for their removal and they were removed. Besides these criminal offences, he was guilty of the baseness of accusing his dead wife, murdered by his own hands, of forging the name of her mother-in-law, though avowedly for his sole benefit; and he certainly connived at the prostitution of his own mother. On the other hand, he was a very civil-spoken gentleman. He had a smile and a shilling for every groom, ostler, chambermaid and waitress in the country. He was a regular attendant at church, made notes of the sermon, subscribed to charities and missionary objects, and took the Sacrament. And, had he been a free man at the time, would no doubt have addressed His Grace the Archbishop of Canterbury on the impropriety of allowing innocent recreation on the Sabbath.

Here we see a kind of summing up of the general themes which emerge from the Bell Macdonald clippings. The emphasis on "gain" recalls, particularly, the venality revealed in the multitude of adultery and divorce cases clipped by Macdonald in which marital relations are clearly revealed to be defined by financial considerations. The fine play on "innocent recreation on the Sabbath" suggests a reversal in attitude since the trial of Daniel Good in the previous decade when conventional religious instruction was conceived as a social panacea. It is also a sly commentary on the contemporary parliamentary debate over "blue laws" which denied workingmen forms of entertainment on their day off. Palmer's case (to paraphrase James Hannay) had shown that the devil was a nineteenth-century phenomenon, enjoying—and ridiculing by his very existence—Victorian progress by riding the railroads and wearing patent leather boots.

The issues raised by the Special Correspondent are perhaps not always so profound as that in which he points out the contradictory positions of man and beast in a hierarchical universe, but they are all the more accessible for their relative simplicity. In the earlier of the last two passages the writer speaks sardonically of Palmer's "ancient civility" and, in the concluding passage, of how he was "a very civil-spoken gentleman." These perceptions are closer in spirit to twentieth-century uncertainty, if not nihilism, than to any religious dogma. ("Whither had the spirit fled in that brief interval?" asks the correspondent when the execution is accomplished.) The writer clearly wants his reader to see the public hanging of Palmer as a symbol of the beginning of the breakdown of the ideology of respectability.

10

❖

Adventures of a Scholar-Detective

The selection, arrangement, and interpretation of the matter of the preceding chapters is the end result of a long process which was neither smooth nor particularly linear in its execution. The more I delved into one subject or the other, the more I realized that many of the answers I sought would not be found in the history of journalism or technology or literature alone, but rather in the interplay of those disciplines—among themselves and within the often disorderly context of rapid cultural change. Moreover, although the original cultural context was specifically mid-Victorian and British, influences external to the period and place in question kept coming to my attention with considerable force.

These influences were often inextricably tied up with the method and manner of my research, with my own experience. I had become a kind of participant-observer as I attempted to reread the past in light of the present.

In any case, it had become manifest that I could not present the material I discovered as effectively as I wanted if I did not allow the process I followed—the criminal investigation, as it were—to become clearly articulated, with its many twists and turns. In order to recount this process, I return to the day not long after I was handed the clippings in Ray's office—when I first encountered the lines penned by the Special Correspondent from Rugeley: January 16, 1856: "Let us imagine a sensible and intelligent Parisian. . . ." As soon as I had managed to skim this entry, I knew I had encountered something special, something I wanted to give isolated attention in my study. But it was particularly difficult—if not ir-responsible—to focus on such a subjective, brashly personal, ec-centric collection of prose pieces when I had no idea who had written them, let alone where they had appeared. It had up to then seemed to me quite reasonable to suggest generalizations based on arguably representative clippings from Macdonald's enor-mous enterprise; but here I was faced with something which, while sharing many qualities with the clippings around it, was also far too idiosyncratic to lump with the mass. Before going any further I had to find out where the special correspondence on William Palmer had first been printed and, if humanly possible, the name and background of the author.

I began by doing what any sensible neophyte would do. I con-sulted bibliographies, scanned the card catalogue in the library, and, of course, sought the advice of established Victorianists. This was a frustrating process. I knew only the date, the crime, and the likelihood that the paper was a weekly. I was at the point of poring over indexes of books on Palmer, on crime, and on the history of journalism, for a miracle when a brash possibility occurred to me. Why not write directly to Colindale? I did, explaining my predic-ament, adding to the dateline of the columns the first sentence of each. Almost immediately—by return mail it seemed—and for no charge the British Library staff had found my paper: *The Leader*. How they managed this I shall probably never know. There were many likely candidates. For example, *Lloyd's* and *Reynolds'* news-papers were printed weekly (and the dates suggested weekly printing), were taken by Macdonald, and were certainly more crime-oriented than *The Leader*. But at Colindale, they found the right paper for me, and I was launched.

Now I was able to focus my U.S. investigation. Next, I wanted to ascertain the identity of the Special Correspondent. I found in a guide to doctoral dissertations that a thesis had been written on *The Leader* at Yale in 1957, a copy of which was kept there. The *Union List of Serials* informed me that the Yale University Library also held an incomplete set of the short-lived (1850–57) weekly in question. So it made sense to travel to New Haven and try to kill two birds with one stone. The dissertation, however, offered no specific clue as to the authorship of the pieces. In fact, like the other works available on nineteenth-century journalism, it basically ignored crime reporting. Since it seemed to me that the subject of crime and the reportage of crime was everywhere, I looked in all types of work produced during the mid-Victorian period; the absence of these topics in later studies suggested that a revisionist history had been at work, and for a long time—at least since the end of the nineteenth century. I concluded my visit to Yale by looking over the 1855 and 1856 volumes of *The Leader* but found only one allusion to the man who covered the Palmer case. In the January 26, 1856, issue—where the first dateline from Rugeley had appeared—there was a brief item in the editorial complimenting the Special Correspondent as "that true novelist." I made a note of this and headed back to New York.

Back in the Reading Room of the New York Public Library, I found in a 1911 book called *Masters of English Journalism,* by T. H. S. Escott, an allusion to one Edward Whitty as a man whose "bright extemporaneous flippancies lightened, at *The Leader* office, the conversation which, if habitually irreverent in its tone, was often turned by [G. H.] Lewes, [Herbert] Spencer, and [E. F.] Piggott to lofty themes." His writings there were "pieces of literary impressionism that today form a feature in every journal." I also discovered that Whitty's most extensive productions for *The Leader,* a series of parliamentary reports, had been collected in 1906 into volume form. I found the volume. The editor of this maintains that Whitty, "a thoroughly independent critic" and "satirist of the highest order," had "brought into existence a style of newspaper correspondence unknown to the journalism of the time," the publication of which "must have indeed called for some courage" on the part of his publisher. I also found that in 1857 Whitty had produced a novel called *Friends of Bohemia,* and that he had had a child in 1856. I went back to *The Leader* itself. In a September 1856 issue I found an announcement of the birth of a child to one of the paper's correspondents, the budding novelist Edward Whitty. I was closing in on my quarry.

I read Whitty's novel and I read his parliamentary reports. Although in my judgment his skills as a descriptive writer and as a social ironist were best realized in his coverage of Palmer (or, rather, that the Rugeley murders had provided him with more congenial canvas on which to impose his vision), there was no question that the works had been written by the same man. Professor Ray and the other eminent scholars we consulted agreed.

Unfortunately for Whitty, with the Rugeley correspondence and *Friends of Bohemia,* his career had peaked. Never a man to indulge himself in moderation, his research into fast-lane London society for the novel seems to have put him over the edge. Charitable friends were finally able to persuade him to dry out on a temperance ship bound for Australia. The irrepressible iconoclast, however, managed to gain access to the large supply of spirits kept by the ship's doctor and he died as a result, soon after landing Down Under, in 1860.

Another quest, with a quite unexpected climax, was even more stirring. In the fall of 1984 I found myself bound for Scotland on the train from Euston Station to Glasgow. The train makes a local stop at the tiny village of Lockerbie. There Alan Macdonald, Laird of Rammerscales, then a youthful seventy, met me. I found Alan to have a noble bearing and a wit at once incisive and self-deprecating. He was fond not only of literature and sport but the pleasures of the table. He and his wife Rhona served me venison shot on the property and a lovely 1966 claret, gave me my own suite, and allowed me the run of the house. Rammerscales was not the castle in the Highlands I had once envisioned, but it was impressive enough: a Georgian red sandstone cube, fortresslike, with views from its perch at the top of the hill across the meadowlands of Annandale to the English border. The Macdonalds own two thousand acres there, a combination of ancient exotic forest land and tenanted pastures. The house itself is shielded from view by Rammerscales Wood, which stands out—from the highway— among the surrounding agricultural countryside like a spiky punk haircut, a sculpted entity unto itself. For the first time I actually visualized Shakespeare's image of Burnham Wood coming to Dunsinane.

My favorite room at Rammerscales was the Long Gallery, which Bell Macdonald had converted into his library and which stands pretty much as it was when he was clipping trials from newspapers. In that magnificent chamber, extending through the entire 54-foot depth of the south side of the house, I inspected the other collections of clippings (relieved to find that there was nothing consequential to my own work that would alter my hypotheses) and the many rare volumes which reflect his interest in classics and philology. But there were also unexpected treasures. For example, I found a bound set of the *Illustrated London News*. This was in itself valuable, since I had some leisure to skim in a random way pages otherwise available only in research libraries—not for taking home—which then had to be requested, and promptly returned, a volume or so at a time. As I was doing this, however, I was actually regretting that Macdonald had not collected instead the *Illustrated London Times*, which was less accessible in American libraries and which was supposed to have featured the most extensive illustrated coverage of William Palmer and his Staffordshire milieu. Then as I was handling the 1856 volume of the *Illustrated News*, feeling inside the back cover a strange sort of lump, I opened it up to find that Bell Macdonald had pasted the entire *Illustrated Times* coverage of Palmer into his *Illustrated News*. It seemed for a moment that the old crime buff had, 130 years before, anticipated the arrival someday of a visiting scholar and ensured that the guest would not be disappointed in his quest for the last words and pictures on Victorian crime. When I told Alan of my discovery, lamenting that I did not have time to digest the material fully (with an eye to making the modest suggestion that perhaps I might find photocopying services in some nearby town to duplicate these pages and take them with me), he happily and readily volunteered to carry any material I required on the car ferry with him when, in October, he and Rhona closed up Rammerscales for the winter and moved to their second home in the Ardèche Mountains of France, above the Rhône Valley. Then I, living a couple of hours drive to the south, would be able to visit them in my car and carry the books off with me, free to peruse them at my leisure through the spring. I left Dumfriesshire in the glow of an extraordinary new transatlantic, cross-generational friendship.

Perhaps my most serendipitous discovery dates from the same fellowship year when I was delving as deep and wide as I could into the nineteenth century. I was sitting in the windowless office space I had rented just outside Aix-en-Provence, reading Peter Gay's *Education of the Senses*. At two points in his text, Gay alludes to the *Saturday Review*, "that vigorously written and ferociously contentious London weekly, [which] argued from its founding in 1855 that while social mendacity deserved the moralist's whip, the evidence for decency, piety, and truthfulness among the middling orders was creditable, even impressive. . . ." Each time, Gay is referring to situations (in 1856 and 1858) in which the *Saturday Review* rebuked the English press for its "long accounts of crime and criminals" because these often pretended to be unmasking hypocrisy when in fact they were indulging "the lowest appetites of human nature."

I lingered over these references to the *Saturday Review*'s scuffle with the popular press. They would be worth reading in their entirety—and from a fresh point of view—when I returned to Colindale in February 1985.

London provided a fitting objective correlative for the murkily enigmatic business I was continuing to confront there. At the time of my first visit to Rammerscales, in September, I had also done my reading at Colindale on the Thurtell case. Colindale was neither as empty nor as decayed as it had been twelve years before. The Asian merchants seemed to have multiplied and taken on a rich vigor with numbers. The pub at the bottom of the hill was crowded at lunchtime with workmen having a pint and listening to American country and western on the jukebox. There was a Greek gyro shop around the corner whose proprietor came from the borough of Queens, New York City. The little houses were being reno- vated. Gentrification was moving up the Northern Line. London was changing, but it was still London all the same: still a hub of Empire, even if the Empire were fragmented and destabilized in its more official aspects. This interaction of change within no- change (and vice versa) provided a cautionary image as I attempted to make conclusive judgments on the London of 130 years before. I often that year thought of the 1844 map of London hanging in my study back in the United States. It is a map on which much of what we consider essential London today—Pimlico, South Ken- sington, Earls Court, Camden Town, Kentish Town—is blank, barely inhabited, as of course are Hampstead and Colindale. And I was now learning that the period of Macdonald's clipping was the era in which many of the blank spaces were filled in. So as London was becoming "civilized" in the 1840s and 1850s, more and more readers were confronted with a mirror image of savagery, of the decline of civilization.

In February, the weather was an impediment. There were bliz-

zards and black ice. The tabloid headlines proclaimed endless series of multiple deaths on fogbound motorways. On the hills of
Hampstead, near my hotel, one could see pedestrians—many el-
derly—sprawled on the frozen pavements. Nevertheless, for reasons barely fathomable to me today, on my first morning I set out
to walk at least part of the way to Colindale, eschewing the Northern Line.

I trudged up Heath Street to the North End Road, Hampstead
Heath on my right, Jack Straw's Castle—a pub associated vaguely
in my mind with a notorious revolt or with highwaymen, most
likely both—on my left. By the time I was barely out of Hampstead
proper the precarious footing and biting cold, though I was decked
out in Alpine garb, made me indifferent to the fact that I was
passing the house where Evelyn Waugh had spent his early days
or the one where Sigmund Freud had spent his last. The weather
had made me indifferent to history. In this gloomy mood it seemed
likely that the *Saturday Review* would present to me but another
vague and irrational diatribe about the otherworldliness of crime
and carnality to proper English society. It could wait for another
day. But at Golders Green I fortified myself with coffee and salt
beef; pushed through a demonstration of Hasidic men against an
Israeli bank, thinking perhaps I was back in Brooklyn; and took
the Tube the rest of the way, through Brent and Hendon Central,
to Colindale. There I found more—much more—than I had bar-
gained for.

The *Saturday Review* piece from 1856 was not just about "circumstantial reports of revolting murder trials," as Peter Gay had
it; it was about the William Palmer case. And it was not merely
about the general coverage of the Palmer case; it was quite specifically directed to the special correspondence which had been
published in *The Leader*. And it makes quite clear that, in the
judgment of the *Saturday Review* at any rate, *The Leader* reports
are omens that newspaper sensationalism has become a significant
cultural force to contend with. The columns on Palmer are described as "a kind of artistic Newgate Calendar," which suggests
that "the orderly surface of society is but an external covering,
and that it serves only as a cloak for bruises, wounds, and putre-
fying sores." It likens the correspondent's rendering of Palmer's
death to "one of those detailed descriptions by which Dickens and

Victor Hugo have debauched the public mind," and asserts that "actually to witness the execution would . . . have a far less injurious effect" than reading about it in *The Leader*. The *Saturday Review* writer is driven even to the sort of sarcasm Edward Whitty would have appreciated: "We wonder that a contemporary does not expatiate on the advantages of a Palmer scholarship in Toxology at St. Bartholomew's Hospital. . . ."

This discovery warmed my entire being. Here was an ardent representative of the Victorian official consciousness overtly expressing the precise set of reactions to Whitty's reports that I had inferred he would. Moreover, the *Saturday Review* had added some new food for thought about the meaning of all this to its readers. There were the allusions to the threat of bestiality—suggesting even more strongly that the war between Science and Religion was being waged behind every closed door of the imagination; it was the subtext to virtually every topic. The hostile reference to Dickens rekindled in my mind not just that I too had thought of his work while reading Whitty, but the extent to which the Inimitable Boz had come—particularly after a realistic novel of urban crime and upper-class corruption such as *Bleak House* in 1853— to represent not the security of the bourgeois English hearth but its enemy. Paired with this was the curious yoking in "artistic Newgate Calendar," which implied a comparison between "art" and subversion, since—as we have seen—the *Calendar* itself was oppressively moralistic, no matter how criminal its subject matter. Then there was the question of history, to which once again but in another fashion I was losing my indifference. Here was the sense that the Victorian age was not only "new" and "progressive" but that these epithets had built into them a separation from a licentious past.

Nevertheless, I was no longer struck by this insulating historical position in the same way as when I had first confronted it. When the critic asserts that it is not the job of the newspapers to bring attention to the devil in patent leather boots or the place of the pigeons on the scale of creation, but to "sobriety, outward decency, self-restraint in a thousand forms, spreading over the surface of society," and that vices are now less common and "some virtues more common, than in times of greater license," I thought not of hypocrisy or complacency but of J. H. Plumb's point that the odious Victorian prudery could be seen sympathetically as well, as a kind of fearful defense—pathetic and understandable—against the terrible conditions of the past from which the new middle class was emerging. Finally I had to ponder further the profound impact of newspaper journalism. The *Saturday Review* writer was no Podsnap, no simple Philistine, and yet he was willing to go so far as to suggest that the publication of Whitty's prose was more injurious to the tender and innocent than actually witnessing Palmer's hanging. Even to a greater degree than I imagined, the correspondence about the good doctor from Rugeley was a kamikaze attack on a particularly fragile new order; and writings like those in the *Saturday Review* were covert pleas to allow the battered official consciousness time and space to regroup.

11

❖

"Morbid Depression Alternating with Excitement"

I moved on to the next *Saturday Review* piece which Gay had cited—from a couple of years after the Palmer scandal, June 26, 1858. I had no higher hopes than I had nurtured while trudging from Heath Street to Golders Green. After all, one stroke of good fortune such as I had experienced in rediscovering Whitty's pernicious influence was sufficient for the entire trip. Besides, it had to be admitted that it was not all that remarkable that a case of the magnitude of the Rugeley poisonings would turn up in this context. It defined the term *cause célèbre*. So when I found that the *Saturday Review* had chosen the general coverage of Mrs. Robinson's divorce trial as the target of an even greater salvo of outrage than Whitty's columns, I was more than pleased. I had always wanted to write about this case for its fascination but had held back because of the superficially unrepresentative and inconclusive nature of its appearance in Macdonald's clippings. And, after all, unlike Thurtell, Good, the Mannings, Palmer, Smith, Smethurst, et al., the Robinson case, so far as I could tell, had been almost forgotten by written history.

The Robinson affair was the most bizarre case to come out of the "dissecting room of English morality" in the first years of the Divorce Court. Mrs. Robinson was accused by her husband of committing adultery with the family hydrotherapist. In *Various Trials* the prosecution begins by summarizing the respectably banal early stages of the Robinsons' marital history:

The marriage took place in February, 1844, Mrs. Robinson being then the widow of a Mr. Dansey, and possessed of between £400 and £500 a-year, which was settled upon her to her separate use. They resided after their marriage at Blackheath, Edinburgh, Boulogne, and Reading. During their residence at Edinburgh in 1850 they became acquainted with Mr. Lane, who was then studying for the law. He afterwards married a daughter of Lady Drysdale, and set up a hydropathic establishment at Moor-park, well known as Sir William Temple's residence. Mr. and Mrs. Robinson in 1854 were living at Reading, and their acquaintance with Dr. Lane was renewed. Mrs. Robinson visited Moor-park from time to time, but her husband had no idea that his wife was unchaste. In 1857, however, during an illness of Mrs. Robinson, he made a discovery which opened his eyes. He discovered a diary written by his wife containing an extraordinary narrative of her impure conduct.

After objections of Lane's attorney are overruled the prosecution reads extracts from the diaries which, in three large volumes, covered the years 1850 to 1855. The most significant passages describe a visit Mrs. Robinson made to Moor Park in 1854. They testify to the "preponderance of amativeness [a phrenological term suggesting a propensity to sexual passion] in her character," as, in an earlier entry, she had described herself:

OCT. 7, SUNDAY—Fine sunny, warm, genial day, almost like the former month. Dr. Lane asked me to walk with him, but I thought he meant only politeness; and I went to the nursery and stayed with my little pets more than an hour. He met me there at last, reproached me for not coming, and bade me come away. I still lingered, but at last joined him, and he led me away and alone to our private haunts, taking a wider range, and a more secluded path. At last I asked to rest, and we sat on a plaid; and read *Athenaeums* chatting meanwhile. There was something unusual in his manner, something softer than usual in his tone and eye, but I knew not what it proceeded from, and chatted gaily, leading the conversation—talking of Goethe, women's dress, and of what was becoming and suitable. We walked on and again seated ourselves in a glade of surprising beauty. The sun shone warmly down upon us, the fern, yellow and brown, was stretched away beneath us, fine old trees in groups adorned the near ground, and far away gleamed the blue hills. I gave myself up to enjoyment. I leaned back against some firm, dry heather bushes, and laughed and remarked as I rarely did in that presence. All at once, just as I was joking my companion on his want of memory, he leaned over me, and exclaimed, "If you say that again, I will kiss you." You may believe I made no opposition, for had I not dreamed of him and of this full many a time before. What followed I hardly remember—passionate kisses, whispered words, confessions of the past. Oh, God! I never hoped to see this hour, or to have any part of my love returned. Yet so it was. He was nervous, and confused, and eager as myself. At last we raised ourselves and walked on happy, fearful, almost silent. We sauntered, not heeding where, to a grove of pines, and there looked over another view beautiful as that on this side, but wilder.

Later, on the same day, they find themselves together again, in the library:

How the evening passed I know not. It was full of passionate excitement, long and clinging kisses, and nervous sensations, not unaccompanied with dread of intrusion. Yet bliss predominated. He was particularly gentle, soothing my agitation, and never for any instant forgetting the gentleman and the kindly friend. . . . I tried to raise my drooping head, but in vain; and, at last, in absolute dread of any one breaking in, he advised me to go. I smoothed my tumbled hair, and in a few moments found myself in the drawing-room, at half-past 9. Fortunately, only a few of the guests were there. No one had a right to question my absence or appearance. At last, after occupying myself with a book of autographs and chatting with Mr. S——, Dr. and Mrs.—— came into the room together, and soon after Lady D——. What an escape I had had! What a calm appearance I could now make! General conversation followed. I turned to listen, and Dr. Lane repeated to Miss B. some of the finest odes of *Byron*. When they went I rose too, and was gliding away, when Dr. L—— gave me a warm shake—so warm that it crushed my fingers with the rings, so that I felt it for an hour. Alas! I slept little that night, waking, rising, longing, dreaming—and slowly came the morn.

On the next day she writes:

Lane joined me at the foot of the stairs, and we sauntered out together, walking all round the grounds and by the water, yet saying little to one another; for both were weary and feeble. I named my not having slept; he said he was in pain, and could hardly get on at all. Both were agitated, confused, and nervous, and I asked him how it was he acted as he did on Sunday. At last I proposed leaving the grounds (as the air was hot and moist), and getting a breeze on the hill. We climbed it slowly, and rested among the dry fern. I shall not say what followed. He rose more composed and cheerful, and we went home quickly, fearing its being too late.

Two days after this brief encounter, they walk again over the "usual circuit." This time, however, they devote themselves "with the utmost confidence" to conversation:

I entreated him to believe that since my marriage I had never before in the smallest degree transgressed. He consoled me for what I had done, and conjured me to forgive myself. He said he had always liked me, and had thought with pity of my being thrown away, as my husband was evidently unsuited to me, and was, as he could see plainly, violent tempered and unamiable. Then we spoke of his early age, 31, the sweet unsuspicious character of his wife, rather than pain whom he would cut off his right hand.

The "fictive" element in the case is apparent here. This is not simply in the sense that the prose is melodramatic and derivative and therefore may be a figment of Mrs. R's imagination, but rather that there are other possibilities—that the adultery *did* take place but that Mrs. Robinson's understandable subjectivity, and perhaps her penchant for French novels, has allowed her to reshape the events to the extent that they function at some remove from "reality." Perhaps she was merely a failed novelist herself. This is not to suggest that her imagery is incapable of persuasive directness:

We drove off, Alfred soon taking his place on the box. I never spent so blessed an hour as the one that followed, full of such bliss that I could willingly have died not to wake out of it again. All former times were adverted to and explained. He had not refrained on past occasions from a display of his true feelings without much pain, and from prudential motives. I reminded him of my lines from *Paul and Virginia,* and owned they were addressed to him. I shall not relate all that passed; suffice it to say that I leaned back at last in those arms I had so often dreamed of, and kissed the curls and smooth face, so radiant with beauty, that had dazzled my outward and inward vision since the first interview, November 15, 1850. He had always known I liked him, but not the full extent of the feeling, and owned it had never been indelicately expressed. This relieved me. Heaven itself could not be more blessed than those moments. While life itself shall endure their remembrance will not pass away from a memory charged with much suffering and little bliss.

OCT. 14—the doctor, after talking some little while appeared to return to his former kind feeling for me, caressed me, and tempted me, and finally, after some delay, we adjourned to the next room and spent a quarter of an hour in blissful excitement. I became nearly helpless with the effects of his presence, could hardly let him depart, wept when he bade me try to obviate consequences, and finally bade him a passionate farewell. I was alone. Passion-wasted and sorrowful, sleep was far from me, that night I tossed, and dreamed, and burned till morning, too weary and weak to rise.

Not unexpectedly the defense attorneys representing Mrs. Robinson contend that the diary is an "hallucination." To give their case external ballast, they call a series of witnesses to testify that Dr. Lane, perceived as a devoted husband and dedicated, discreet professional, had neither the opportunity nor the inclination to dally with any of his clients, let alone Mrs. Robinson, who was much older than he and not in particularly good shape. As the argument develops, the entire situation begins to pose extremely knotty problems not solely for the legal and medical profession but for the culture as a whole.

In the first place, the Law of Evidence prevented Dr. Lane from testifying. Next, as Mrs. Robinson's lawyer points out, since "the case against Dr. Lane rested on nothing but Mrs. Robinson's diary which [also] could not be admitted against him . . . it might, therefore, happen that Dr. Lane would be dismissed on the ground that no adultery was proved against him, and Mrs. Robinson would be divorced on the ground that her adultery with Dr. Lane had been proved. He need hardly say what a state of jurisprudence such a state of things would represent. . . ." Then medical witnesses appear to testify that a woman of Mrs. Robinson's years, with her history of ovarian problems, might very well suffer from a "malady" (this kind of "insanity" was then called "erotic monomania") which caused her mind to be "in a state of morbid depression alternating with excitement." Therefore, since the system could not "take her in," as it were, Mrs. Robinson "won" her days in court because a divorce could only be granted with concrete proof of adultery. The judge notes sadly at the conclusion of the trial that Mr. Robinson "remained burdened with a wife who had placed on record the confession of her misconduct or, at all events, even taking the most favourable view, of unfaithful thoughts and unchaste desires." The case of Mrs. Robinson disappears from the pages of Bell Macdonald's clippings at this point and I have not been able to find any record elsewhere of what happened to the unfortunate couple. It is certainly possible to assume that some reasonable out-of-court settlement was reached, but Victorian readers, gluttons for neatly packaged, happy endings, were left hanging without a resolution. It must, I find it difficult not to speculate here, have been at least as frustrating to complacency as William Palmer's cryptic denial of having poisoned Cook with strychnine.

The second *Saturday Review* edition which I had come to Colindale to consult demonstrates quite nicely the sort of reaction—

a peculiar mixture of self-assured outrage and befuddlement—I had by now begun to associate with Victorian orthodoxy, a subject which in itself clearly deserves as much explication as the sensationalism that was antagonizing it. And, in fact, the *Saturday Review* in its extended discussions of Mrs. Robinson manages to touch most of the defense bases of the brigades of respectability.

Mrs. Robinson, the editorialist writes, is prosecuted for adultery on her own confession,

> in the shape of her private journal. A very curious journal it is. It is a feminine edition of the *Lettres à Sophie*—very sentimental, very rhapsodical, and extremely minute and erotic. . . . To be sure, it seems to be pretty clear that the poor lady is a decided monomaniac—her amours are only the creation of a diseased but prurient imagination. . . . It may possibly be that the thing is only a rhetorical exercise—and a clever one too—for it seems hardly possible that any sane woman could write all these glowing annals of her sin with any real purpose. . . . The diary stands self-convicted of insanity. But its consequences are terrible.

It is in the litany of terrible "consequences" that we get a deeper sense of the frightened confusion which Philistine complacency masked. The writer laments the danger of establishing a precedent in which a person such as Lane can be even indicted on the basis of such a questionable document. He deplores the devastation wreaked on the hydrotherapist's life and reputation simply because the issue has been raised at all in public. One of course can question here the overlapping of social ideology in the writer's mind with the purely legal issue, but what is more interesting is that the *Saturday Review* chooses not to merely bemoan the singular problems raised by *Robinson* v. *Robinson*. It appends a second editorial (entitled "The Purity of the Press") which focuses on the news coverage of the case as emblematic of a general deteriorating cultural standard.

We read again of the failure of the Divorce Act (then only six months old) to reduce the number of published accounts of infidelity. "If," the writer declares, "we are to judge from the stream of filth which almost daily flows through the columns of most of our contemporaries," the "new system" is more damaging to England's image than the old (that is, when Crim. Con. proceedings were rampant). As far as the *Saturday Review* is concerned, Mrs. Robinson's jottings, "whether they were true or false, were perhaps about as filthy compositions as ever proceeded from any human pen."

Of course, this latter assertion is an overstatement, and one is inclined to assume that the writer knows it. But, reading on, one wonders if any such assumption is possible. The fact that the "whole of these loathsome productions were reprinted at full length in the *Times* and several other daily papers" seems to have knocked the writer's capacity for clear thinking askew. In any case, what follows is an exercise in incrementally porous—or ideological, if you will—reasoning. He attempts to make distinctions in regard to what should be printed and what not. (There is a definite sense here that the writer does not want to be seen as unreasonable or Philistine about the freedom of the press; he is merely trapped within the limits of what his relatively emancipated but still sorely cramped values can withstand.) He brings up the recent trials of Madeline Smith and of an Italian immigrant laborer named Lanni, who murdered a prostitute in the Haymarket, and finds them, as opposed to *Robinson* v. *Robinson,* printable: "Where lewdness leads to murder, and ends in hanging, the disease and the medicine go together; but the mere details of seduction and adultery are not only not profitable to any human creature, but are the most infallible means of eliciting latent pruriency and stimulating foul curiosity."

The holes in this analysis are obviously numerous. In the first place, the writer has, essentially, contradicted the argument used by the *Saturday Review* two years before in denouncing the coverage of Palmer's case, in which lewdness *did* lead to murder and then to hanging, and the details were printed, and outrage was still evoked. Secondly, Bell Macdonald clipped extensively on Madeline Smith and Lanni and the coverage was—if anything—more rife with sensational details than Mrs. Robinson's case; certainly, they were much more thoroughly, and noisily, exploited. Moreover, Madeline Smith (as I have already indicated) was not hanged at all, nor was she even convicted, and lived a long and interesting life after her trial. So even the temptation to align this particular commentator with the *Newgate Calendar* mentality of "Justice Triumphs" is an oversimplification. The paradoxical diagnosis presented at the Robinson trial returns here: "morbid depression alternating with excitement" leads one to speculate, perhaps prematurely, on what was really so deeply unsettling about the publication of Mrs. Robinson's diaries. The active coexistence of sensuality and bourgeois repression invoked in many a confused morbidity and drove them into chaotic retreat. The spectacle of Mrs. Robinson, whose sexuality was so real and, at the same time, unreal, was positively indigestible. But I am getting ahead of myself here. Let us return to the *Saturday Review*'s curious and sweeping conclusions on the topic, which begin appropriately—as I just left off—with a kind of gastronomic metaphor:

> Clear water may hold in solution the deadliest poison; though it is quite imperceptible either by the smell or by the taste; and we believe that this is emphatically the case with much of the light literature of the day. The principle on which that literature is written is, that it is to contain nothing which a modest man might not read aloud to a modest woman, and accordingly it carefully suppresses all those coarse allusions to the relations between the sexes which we find in Fielding or Defoe; but it indemnifies itself by a sort of luscious sentimentality which appears to us to be infinitely worse. The habit of making the most solemn subjects in the world—death and marriage—mere lay figures for the display of luxurious images, is quite as immoral as undisguised indecency. The exquisitely pathetic deathbeds of beautiful little girls—the fondling love scenes, in linked sweetness long drawn out, and as free from passion as distilled water is free from spirit—the family kissing and coaxing—the slimy apotheosis of the domestic affections—which beautify so many of our popular novels, appear to us to be the first step of a regular process, of which letters from "One more Unfortunate" are the second, and the publication of Mrs. Robinson's journal the third. It may be doubted whether Holywell-street itself carries the series much farther.

This is a most curious—and pell-mell—progression. The "luscious sentimentality" of the various and sundry family intimacies (including the inevitable fondling attendant upon the pathetic death of a little girl) found in popular fiction first leads to prostitution. ("An unfortunate" was a common euphemism for a prostitute, implying of course that the oldest profession was necessarily a joyless and addictive form of slavery. Works such as *My Secret Life* demonstrate that the issue was much more complex.) This in turn leads to nymphomania and adultery in respectable menopausal matrons, and on into the burgeoning underground trade in pornography and perversity centered in Holywell Street just north of the City. What is even more striking is the confusion in the mind of the writer about the nature of fiction as opposed to fact. It is true that popular novels often passed off subversion as sentiment; that London was rife with prostitution; that Mrs. Robinson kept a diary. But the most compelling fact seems to be that these are *published*—whether as literature, letters to the editor, or as police reports—not that they *exist*. In any case the writer has completely blurred the distinction between cause and effect, between perpetrator and victim, even between that which is condemned and that which does the condemning. The exponent of "The Purity of the Press" also is capable of indulging himself in prose not unlike that he finds impure; "linked sweetness long drawn out" has its own undeniably "luscious" qualities.

Again, the Robinson case and the police reports in general provide windows upon nineteenth-century culture, the High as well as the Low. Certainly we can draw from this material inferences about some of the serious thinking of the age on psychology and literature.

First of all, and most apparent to the modern reader, one need not be a radical feminist to appreciate from this discourse what ideological footballs Mrs. Robinson's body and psyche have become. The emphasis in the courtroom remains throughout on how her husband can somehow stretch the law to rid himself of her, and how Dr. Lane is being dragged down—along with various other established systems—by the woman's monomaniacal imagination. Looking at it from her point of view, however, one might emphasize the shortcomings of the system as it fails to provide for *her* welfare instead. It is she, and not her husband or Lane, who is the victim. Not only is she trapped in the suffocating institution of marriage (as it was officially defined for respectable women of the day) but her choice of Lane as literary co-respondent is singularly appropriate. In her excellent 1977 study *Victorian Murderesses,* Mary S. Hartman demonstrates the way in which hydrotherapists at the spas of the mid-nineteenth century often were more sympathetic to their largely feminine clientele than conventional physicians, functioning in a role akin to that of a psychoanalyst. Indeed, in the case of Mrs. Robinson, it would not be too much of a stretch to suggest that her relationship with Lane reflects a form of what Freud was to call "transference." Her acting out merely happens to have been literary rather than physical.

Furthermore, we have been told—by Mrs. Robinson's diary and by the judge—of her interest in phrenology, the trendy "science" by which the shape of skulls were studied in order to analyze character. (Palmer and Lanni and most other major criminals were subjected to it second-hand by the newspapers; and the list of Victorians who took phrenology quite seriously is long and estimable.) Why should this not also be seen as a desperate groping in a world without psychology for someone or something to provide support, something akin to psychotherapy? In my research alone, we have seen Mrs. Robinson as a middle-class example of this need which anticipates Freud's discoveries, and have also observed poor Kitty Littlewood's seeking out of the "wizard" Isaac Rushford to heal her wounds, only to get in return for her trouble sexual exploitation and a dose of seeds of paradise. The "fact" is, if I may revert to that by now much-abused term, that the various attempts through the preceding century to provide some analytic or scientific understanding of the emotions had one thing in common: an insistence on eliminating the emotions, the *feelings* themselves, from consideration. Mesmer's concept of "animal magnetism" assigned psychological states to various bodily fluids, which were then to be regulated or eliminated by the application of glass rods and other external apparatuses. The phrenologist looked for bumps on the head. The wonder is—in exploring these commonplace primary sources of the nineteenth century—that a Freud (and a Marx and a Darwin) did not come along much sooner rather than later. They were sorely needed. And the term "animal magnetism" in conjunction with names synonymous with the id, with industrial dehumanization, and with evolution, recalls for us again the critical position of the beast in the Victorian mind and how the preeminence of that image enabled the Victorian establishment to disregard feelings, focusing on quantitative and materialistic values instead.

In its commentary on the Palmer case, the *Saturday Review* complains about how reading the police reports reflects "one of the lowest appetites of human nature." The relegation of "appetites" or "instincts" to a hierarchical scale was of course one of the distinctive characteristics of Victorian sexual medicine and psychology. And indulgence in an "amative" predisposition suggested nymphomania, which justified locking a woman up, not only for her own good but to protect vulnerable chaste males from a potential "tigress." Poverty was clearly the cause of a lot of the most horrible stories in the papers; but it was also used as an excuse by the establishment for not dealing with them. And these happened to be the very years when evolutionary studies were threatening the stability of the mind-brain dichotomy of conventional psychology which relegated such instinct to the "animal appetites" in men, and, also, women.

This brings us back to literature and the manner in which the various social and scientific ideologies functioned as often in the literary domain as any other. Mrs. Robinson was, even by the *Saturday Review*'s account, indulging herself in a strikingly modernistic literary endeavor. She "fancied herself the heroine of her own amorous reveries." She had "read Dudevant and Balzac till she surrounded herself with the creatures of her own corrupt meditations." If she "had not thought proper to commit her literary amours with a respectable gentleman," her "Ephesian diary . . . would be, like Coleridge's opium poetry, only a psychological phenomenon." This latter phrase, "only a psychological phenomenon," suggests a wide range of readings. The first one important to me here has to do with the debasing of the very term "psychological" into something which is "only" parallel to the externally induced and irrational (setting aside the quality of Coleridge's verse; his reputation during the period is beyond our concerns in this study), recalling again the relentless insistence on separating mind and body and blaming anything distasteful or threatening on the latter. We are confronting, also, the general indifference in certain quarters to making necessary distinctions between literature and life, here attributing to the written word superhuman power to do evil while devaluing it at the same time. Words expressing sensuality or emotion are enemies; to trivialize them is accepted defensive strategy. Indeed, Mary Hartman theorizes that her "lady killers" used their romantically fabricated diaries partly "as escapist fantasy and partly as a means to allow them to integrate socially expected behavior with their own contradictory feelings and urges." At least one of the convicted French murderesses used the phrase "writing my novel" to mean "living my life" in her diary.

This topic will be covered in more detail in my next chapter on the Sensation novel, but what most interests me at this stage is nevertheless related. As I shall argue that the newspapers influenced the Sensation novel and that the criticism of that criminal literary genre even further expands our comprehension of the Victorian state of mind, so I shall also want to demonstrate the key role played by sensational newspapers and Sensation novels in effecting the transition from the nineteenth to the twentieth centuries. More than anything else, the questions raised by the sad case of Mrs. Robinson provide a convenient introduction to such considerations, containing, as it does, a broad range of issues related to the development of modernism.

For example, as I write this, a debate still rages over whether Sigmund Freud (who forty years after Mrs. Robinson managed to establish the *human* value of libidinous drives) had devised his theories of infantile sexuality in an effort to shift, in a *New York Times* paraphrase of Jeffrey Masson, "the emphasis from the real world of sadness, misery, and cruelty, to an internal stage on which actors performed invented dramas for an invisible audience of their own creation." At least equally relevant is the extent to which today we see Dickens, in the words of J. Hillis Miller, as having concluded his career—between *Bleak House* (1852–53) and his death while still writing *The Mystery of Edwin Drood* in 1870—by attempting to come to terms with an England "being slowly destroyed because it cannot find strength to rid itself of the tangible, material presence of the dead forms of the past."

The importance of the relation of the police reports from the 1850s onward to such large issues cannot be minimized. Did the father of psychoanalysis really develop concepts like the Oedipus Complex because he was under social and professional pressure to deny the grim actuality of child abuse, incest, and perversity that fill the pages of *Various Trials Cut from Newspapers?* Can Dickens's great later novels and a significant portion of modernist art be best understood as an act of verbal evasion brought on by the weighty onslaught of unspeakable acts broadcast by the modern media? Did the publication of the Robinson divorce trial contribute to the demise of the happy ending, to the post-modernist tendency to resistance to any "closure" at all?

There is obviously no simple or definitive answer to these questions; but there are two inescapable generalizations to be made. First, without the rapid expansion of the publication of the kind of naturalistic detail we have already encountered in these pages, the questions might never even have had to be asked. Second, one cannot rummage around among the artifacts of nineteenth-century popular culture without stumbling on the controversy over the dissemination of carnal knowledge in police reports and what came to be known as "newspaper novels." It is everywhere.

One final set of brief anecdotes about Dr. Lane and his hydrotherapy practice at the estate called Moor Park in Surrey: back in 1980, I read a brief descriptive paper on Bell Macdonald's collection of cuttings at a Victorian Studies conference. This was duly noted in the newsletter of the association which sponsored the gathering. Soon thereafter, I was contacted by a Park Avenue psychiatrist asking if I had ever encountered the strange story of the Robinsons in my research. I allowed that I had. He was interested, he said, in what had happened to either Lane or Mrs. Robinson after the divorce appeal was refused. His story stopped where mine did (or, rather, where Bell Macdonald's did) with the last allusion to the case—when the judgment was declared—in *The Times* in June 1858. The psychiatrist and I commiserated with one another briefly over the frustration of not being able to follow up such an intriguing story. Then I asked him why he was interested. He said his scholarly research was centered on Charles Darwin— particularly Darwin's health. Apparently there is some question as to whether the author of *Origin of Species* was a hypochondriac. And what, I asked, had this to do with Mrs. Robinson? Well, my new-found colleague replied, Darwin was a regular recipient of the attentions of Dr. Lane at Moor Park and had been quite upset that the hydrotherapist's practice might be damaged by the negative publicity generated in the newspapers.

Some years later, in my casual reading, I came upon an allusion to Jonathan Swift. Swift, I learned, had spent a number of years working as secretary to Sir William Temple. During this period the author of *Gulliver's Travels* had resided with Temple at his country estate: Moor Park, Surrey.

What two more appropriate ghosts to roam these halls—if, indeed, those halls have withstood the wrecking crane of the suburban developer. Swift and Darwin—historical bookends, representing on one end the apotheosis of the age of "coarse allusion" which the *Saturday Review* had decried, and on the other the gentleman-scientist whose discoveries in effect brought down the universe that the intervening "enlightenment" had woven out of progress and prosperity between the beginning of the eighteenth and middle of the nineteenth centuries. In the years I had been studying this period I was myself becoming increasingly skeptical of meaning; so often I felt torn between fantasy-as-fact and fact-as-fantasy. So I countered with a scene of my own. I fabricated in the halls of my imagination three figures, not two: Swift, the unflinching satirist who made monkeys out of men, carries on his shoulders Darwin, the humble fossil collector whose life's work implied that men had been made out of monkeys. Following them, barely lighting the way with flickering candle, is the still incomplete shade of Mrs. Robinson, whose story was too true to be good.

Not many weeks later, another figure intruded, breaking up the symmetry of this imagined trio. I was rereading Altick's *Victorian Studies in Scarlet,* which I had first read in the days before I had become well acquainted with *Various Trials.* There my eye caught the name of Thomas Smethurst. There I read Altick's summary of the accused murderer and bigamist's trials and tribulations with the British legal system. There I discovered that Smethurst had preceded—from 1847 to 1852—Dr. Lane as proprietor of the hydropathic institution at Moor Park, Surrey. In those days a different sort of literary production from Mrs. Robinson's—or Swift's—was taking place. Dr. Smethurst had devoted *his* spare time to editing a periodical called *The Water-Cure Journal.*

12

❖

Critical Passions

I. CONNECTIONS

There are nine million words of newspaper journalism in Bell Macdonald's clippings of courtroom proceedings. And, of course, I have surveyed many more like them in the various sources described in the preceding chapters. Now, as we turn to Sensation fiction, we find that here too we are dealing with a lot of material. Hundreds of novels considered to be of the "Sensation type" were published in the 1860s; moreover, the body of critical commentary about crime writing which appeared during these years is itself enormous.

It is necessary then, before even attempting to draw meaningful conclusions from these stories and reviews, to establish some guidelines. First of all, we need at least a working definition of what a Sensation novel is (and was). Second, by considering the backgrounds of the most prominent authors and books that fall within this definition, we can acquire a sense of the sort of literary and social climate they inhabited—one, it should be noted, strikingly different from the sort of decorous environment prescribed by detractors of the police reports. Finally, by establishing the remarkable number of similarities and parallels extrinsic to the texts themselves, we can then move on to the critics who exemplify the intellectual controversy which the Sensation novel helped inspire. I will analyze the work of these critics in advance of that of the novelists for a relatively basic reason: as the "real" outside relationships of the novelists help us better understand their milieu (and, ultimately, the significance of their writings), so an overview of the idealized social and metaphysical unities which the critics demanded (and which the thriller writers failed to provide) establishes a firm platform from which to comprehend the essence of the Victorian official consciousness of displacement and denial.

The largest collection of British Sensation fiction that I know of is housed in the Sadleir Collection at the University of California, Los Angeles. The Sadleir indexers provide an official definition of the genre. Sensation novels are "those works dependent on a fair smattering of rapes, near rapes, suicides, murders, and other mysterious happenings, often in a setting of winding corridors, dark stairways, trapdoors, abandoned estates. [They] differ from the Gothic novel [of the late eighteenth and early nineteenth centuries] in that no supernatural elements are allowed." This description is certainly accurate enough, but is not as satisfactory—at least for my purposes—as that articulated by Thomas Hardy in a prefatory note to a reissue of his own, largely forgotten, Sensation novel, *Desperate Remedies,* in 1889: "The following story, the first published by the author [in 1871], was written . . . at a time when he was feeling his way to a method. The principles involved in its composition are, no doubt, too exclusively those in which mystery, entanglement, surprise, and moral obliquity are depended on for exciting interest. . . ."

Here, Hardy—like the Sadleir people—acknowledges that these works are thrillers with elements of sex and violence, but he also takes note of the "moral obliquity" which was the scourge of many of his contemporaries. Now, it must be considered that Hardy when he offered this description was in the process of becoming *the* great novelist who most overtly challenged the strictures of Victorian censorship. In his 1890 manifesto *Candour in English Fiction,* he was to plead that novelists be allowed to openly discuss sex, problems of religious belief, and the position of man in the universe; *Tess of the d'Urbervilles* had to be bowdlerized for the sake of propriety in 1891; and the scandal caused by *Jude the Obscure* in 1895 discouraged Hardy from ever writing fiction again. Therefore, his striking this apologetic note suggests how derogatory the term "Sensation" had become among readers; at the same time, however, there is an implicit sense of how seductive sensationalism must have felt to an artistic young man coming of age in the sixties. Hardy's brief recollection captures the meaningful cultural ambivalence of Sensation much more effectively than does the Sadleir Collection's emphasis on grotesque or ridiculous plot elements.

A representative sampling of "Sensation" fiction might include, in roughly chronological order: Wilkie Collins's *The Woman in White* (1860); Mrs. Henry Wood's *East Lynne* and Dickens's *Great Expectations,* (both 1861); Bulwer-Lytton's *A Strange Story* and Mary Elizabeth Braddon's *Lady Audley's Secret* (both 1862); Charles Reade's *Hard Cash* and J. S. LeFanu's *The House by the Churchyard* (1863); LeFanu's *Uncle Silas* (1864); Dickens's *Our Mutual Friend* (1865); Collins's *Armadale* (1866) and *The Moonstone* (1868); and any of LeFanu's stories, particularly "Green Tea" (1869).

Although some of these works are now considered "classics" and others totally forgotten (not without good reason, in some cases) by posterity, when they came out they were more-or-less equally notorious and popular—topping the best-seller lists of the decade. Moreover, they shared a number of interesting external connections, largely radiating out from the person of Dickens who—then as well as now—was the most famous and influential. Miss Braddon, for example, set out quite deliberately in her first novel to imitate Dickens. Wilkie Collins was a protégé, one of his best friends, a frequent contributor to his magazines, and a collaborator with equal billing on such works as *The Frozen Deep* and *The Lazy Tour of the Two Idle Apprentices.* Bulwer-Lytton had been a friend and collaborator since early in the younger writer's career. It was his suggestion Dickens followed in changing the ending of *Great Expectations.* Walter Phillips (in 1918) has pointed out the "mutually affectionate admiration" of Charles Reade and Dickens. Reade openly admired Dickens as he admired no other writer, and Dickens testified, although lukewarmly, on Reade's behalf at the trial in which *Griffith Gaunt* was charged with indecency in 1866. LeFanu, who lived in Dublin, favorably reviewed Dickens's work in his own *Dublin University Magazine;* he also maintained a correspondence with Dickens since he was himself a contributor to Dickens's weekly, *All the Year Round.* Braddon might also have been a contributor there had she not first been tied to a contract with another publisher.

Many of the major Sensation works besides Dickens's own—*The Woman in White, A Strange Story, Hard Cash,* and "Green Tea"—first appeared in *All the Year Round.* And numerous instances show that Dickens was inspired by works he edited for this as well as his other, earlier journals. The mutual influences between Dickens and Collins have frequently been discussed in the last three quarters of a century. The increased tightness of structure of *Great Expectations,* for example, is attributed to the intricate plotting of *The Woman in White,* while *Edwin Drood,* which Dickens left unfinished at his death in 1870, probably owes its Oriental overtones to *The Moonstone.* In very specific ways, *Our Mutual Friend* is indebted to Reade's *Hard Cash,* which preceded it by two years: in the later work both the symbolic dust heaps and Betty Higden, the proud old woman who refuses to go to the workhouse, are amplifications of details in Reade's novel. A relationship can also be inferred to exist between LeFanu's "Green Tea," which appeared in *All the Year Round* on October 23 and November 13, 1869, and *Edwin Drood,* the first chapters of which were being composed in the same months. John Forster's report of Dickens's plans for the plot of *Edwin Drood* postulates that the book, if completed, would have been a dramatization of the self-destructive conflict of surface and depth within a single personality. And indeed, the central figure of *Drood*—John Jasper, a church deacon driven to drug- and sex-related villainy—bears some resemblance to the protagonist of "Green Tea," an Anglican clergyman who is driven by hallucinations induced by drinking green tea to turn away from religion and respectability.

Dickens was not the only link between and among these writers. Collins and Reade were close personal friends, and Reade and Bulwer-Lytton were the only prominent writers who stood openly by Miss Braddon between 1860 and 1880. Nor was it entirely because Braddon was being "vilified" for her sensationalism that such literary and personal comradeship was necessary. Miss Braddon suffered social as well as literary ostracism. She lived illicitly with her publisher, John Maxwell, throughout the sixties, bearing him five children out of wedlock. Only after his wife died in a lunatic asylum in 1874 were they able to have their relationship regularized. Braddon's case typifies the conditions, often psychosexual in nature, which alienated these writers from respectable society and almost certainly intensified their antagonism—however covertly expressed—to that society.

For example, it is well known today that Dickens, after separating from his wife in 1858, conducted a flirtation, or "affair" (according to one's interpretation of the flimsy evidence), with a young actress named Ellen Ternan, until, in the early sixties, he secretly set her up in a house south of the Thames as his mistress. Ellen Ternan is seen by many to have been a model for Estella, Bella Wilfer, and Helen Landless, the heroines of his last three novels; further, the psychological intensity and sense of alienation which pervades these books must, in some degree, have been generated by the author's consciousness of how, at the peak of his financial and artistic success, he was being forced to live a "secret life," exiled from the easy domesticity of English society of which his own life had been considered a symbol. Besides, the personal paradox in which he was caught—having publicly defended the sanctity of that domestic model for so many years and now finding himself in violation of it—intensified the moral confusion which informs his fuller, more developed characters during this period. As a consequence, his own works are charged with ambivalence and bitterness; and it is not, therefore, surprising that he published, in *All the Year Round,* works of similar spirit.

If Dickens and Braddon were the only Sensation novelists to have experienced this kind of alienation, the relationship of such biographical detail to the Sensation novel would be tenuous. However, this is not the case. Collins also had an "irregular" sex life. Details are vague but, between 1859 and the seventies, Collins lived, unmarried and at different times, with two women, Caroline Graves and Martha Rudd, the latter bearing him three children. Graves, as a matter of fact, is reputed to have been the inspiration for *The Woman in White,* since Collins met her on a deserted road in North London as she fled a private lunatic asylum. Collins's life forced him, too, into an ambiguous position in London society. S. M. Ellis states in *Wilkie Collins, LeFanu and Others* (1931) that "the romantic origin of the 'intimacy' might well have cozened the virtuous British Matrons of the time to overlook the irregularity. . . . But they were not to be persuaded . . . and but few 'respectable' females passed the threshold of the houses in Harley Street and elsewhere that he [Collins], later, resided in, though the famous author himself alone, was gladly welcomed to the dinner-tables of his illustrious friends." It is difficult not to assume some relationship between this situation and the work of the man who consistently attacked sexual hypocrisy and the venal elements of the institution of marriage, not to mention his perceptions of private asylums in *The Woman in White* and *Armadale.*

The other novelists' domestic arrangements during the 1860s were no more conventional. Bulwer's marriage, in the words of Robert Lee Wolff, in *Strange Stories* (1971), "collapsed in 1836 in spectacular fashion, and his obsessed and demented wife for decades thereafter made scandalously embarrassing public scenes, and filled the air and pages of her own novels with the most libelous portraits of him and unbridled attacks on his alleged behavior."

Reade lived on an intimate basis with his "housekeeper" (details of their relationship are obscure), never marrying because he was bound to celibacy by an Oxford fellowship, a typically ambiguous Victorian award. Yet his work is characterized by an insistence on frankness and liberty in sexual matters as well as by sado-masochistic undercurrents.

LeFanu, after the untimely death of his wife in 1858, became a virtual hermit in his Merrion Square mansion, and turned from a career devoted largely to Irish historical romances and journalism to the writing of Sensation fiction of crime and the supernatural.

The inference is clear. As the works of these six writers differ from the conventionality of earlier crime fiction, so did their personal experiences differ dramatically from the official Victorian version of domestic bliss. The sensational tales of madness, institutional repression, suppressed sexuality, and disenchantment with orthodox beliefs that they wrote are consistent with what we know of the novelists' lives.

Having said all this as a prelude to demonstrating just how offensive and depraved this fare was considered by conventional readers and reviewers, it must also be admitted that a late-twentieth-century reader—particularly a late-twentieth-century reader who is familiar with mid-nineteenth-century newspapers—will probably find little that is sensational in these books and wonder what the fuss was all about. There may well have been a

kind of subculture of sensationalists which has not—to my knowledge—been discussed in quite these terms; but it is still necessary
to further explore the social and intellectual context in which these
works appeared so as to answer our hypothetical modern reader's
question: what was the fuss all about?

First I suppose one needs to be reassured that there *was* a legitimate controversy and that the novels in question were lumped
together in the controversy. Even a glance at the more prominent
bibliographies of Victorian organs of criticism—Poole's *Reader's
Guide* or the *Wellesley Index to Victorian Periodicals*—makes a strong
case for taking sensationalism seriously. Throughout the 1860s
virtually every leading magazine and newspaper, and many minor
ones, addressed the issue in the form of leading articles or book
reviews. Peeking into the journals themselves illustrates the so-
lemnity with which Sensation literature was treated. In 1865,
W. Fraser Rae of the *North British Review* decried the influence
of Braddon's *Lady Audley's Secret:* "The artistic faults of this novel
are as grave as the ethical ones. Combined they render it one of
the most noxious books of modern times." The *Contemporary Review*, in 1867, accused the Sensation novelists of "studiously, and
of set purpose, seek[ing] to awaken our sympathies for certain
types of characters by involving us in such circumstances as tend
to set us in active opposition to some conventional moral regards."
A critic in the *National Review* in 1863, in another of those strikingly contradictory assertions—since the piece would not have
been written had the books not been best sellers—denied even
their popularity: "There is an aroma of indelicacy, a half-admiration
of profligacy, a familiarity with crime, which an English audience
finds it impossible to forgive. . . . There are no doubt, sets of
people whose proceedings and sentiments they correctly represent; but the great mass of readers regard them with aversion
. . . accord them no welcome in their memories, and reject the
whole picture as a libel upon modern society."

With all this defensive outrage, one might assume that the critics
had stumbled across something not only odious but barely recognizable—strange, different. Therefore, it is no surprise that reviewers, both hostile and friendly, assured their readers that the
Sensation novel *was* a new phenomenon. Margaret Oliphant, from

her lofty and disapproving perch at *Blackwood's,* acknowledged *The Woman in White* in 1862 as the prototypical Sensation novel, which had established "an entirely new position" and thus inspired "a new beginning in fiction." The young Henry James—in *The Nation* in 1865—gave Collins "the credit of having introduced into fiction those most mysterious of mysteries, the mysteries which are at our own doors."

This latter commentary requires some background explanation of the history of mystery thrillers. Some scholars prefer to find the original tales of detection and crime in the distant past—in the Bible, for example, or in classical drama like the Oedipus cycle. And of course—as one writer for *All the Year Round* was to protest serio-comically in an essay called "The Sensational Williams" in 1864—the ground of Shakespeare's plays is littered with corpses. But in terms of popular prose fiction as we know it today, one first finds crime and bestiality—lots of it—in Defoe and his picaresque predecessors of the late 1600s and early 1700s, and in the raunchy backdrops of the earliest English novelists like Fielding and Smollett in the middle of the eighteenth century. But there is not really a concentrated configuration in these years. In fact, a fiction genre whose central thrust is the threat of criminal and sexual malfeasance cannot be found until the last decade of the eighteenth century with the Gothic romance. One of the better known examples of this type is Matthew Gregory Lewis's *The Monk* (1797), which one literary historian has described as "a nightmare of fiendish wickedness, ghastly supernaturalism and sadistic sensuality." Another is Mrs. Radcliffe's *The Mysteries of Udolfo* (1794), in which the innocent English heroine is terrorized in an Italian castle by a degenerate nobleman. These works are not particularly well written and are notable for their very English anti-foreign and anti-Catholic prejudice, not to mention their tendency to set their horrors in long-ago and far-away settings thus neatly distancing them from anyone in the reading public who might feel tainted by association with villainy. Indeed, their most lasting literary contribution is their suggestive influence on Jane Austen's parody of them, *Northanger Abbey* (written in 1805; published posthumously in 1818), and in Mary Shelley's grafting of some of the Gothic techniques onto her philosophical argument about the dehumanizing qualities of modern civilization in *Frankenstein* (1818).

The next criminal genre was the Newgate novel of the 1830s. Here the setting is moved to England but, as a kind of fictional adaptation of *The Newgate Calendar,* the focus of the crime is on real criminals of the past and—although some people were upset about the potential for romanticization of evildoing—any Newgate fiction I have encountered has been clumsy and conventional and safely buried in another age, along with the hanged protagonist. Even *Oliver Twist,* which was reviewed by some as of the Newgate type, cannot compete with Dickens's later work for sensationalism or serious social analysis. It is mere melodrama by comparison. Moreover, neither Gothic nor Newgate stories have detective figures for readers to identify with in their rattling of the skeletons in the closets of respectability, in part because there was no official detective force in London until the 1840s.

Actually, the closest thing to antecedents to the Sensation novel (and therefore to the modern mystery or thriller) are William Godwin's *Caleb Williams* (1794) and Poe's "ratiocinative" detective tales and psychological thrillers of the 1840s. But both Godwin and Poe stood alone in their times (Poe studied Godwin closely), and Godwin, while using contemporary English society as a source of evil, is more concerned with his own theories of political science than with writing a well-crafted thriller. Poe's work is—though fascinating—almost antiseptically "scientific" and, of course, safely set in Paris or Spain or the no-man's-land of the House of Usher.

At any rate, Henry James's commentary on the novelty of *The Woman in White* gives a clear picture of what the historical perspective of the informed reader of the 1860s might be in regard to crime fiction. The "innovation" of Sensation novels, he goes on,

> gave a new impetus to the literature of horrors. It was fatal to the authority of Mrs. Radcliffe and her everlasting castle in the Apennines. What are the Apennines to us, or we to the Apennines? Instead of the terrors of "Udolpho," we were treated to the terrors of the cheerful country house and the busy London lodgings. And there is no doubt that these were infinitely the more terrible. Mrs. Radcliffe's mysteries were Romances sure and simple; while those of Mr. Wilkie Collins were stern reality.

It may be difficult for any reasonably well-read person in the 1980s who is familiar with the Sensation novels to accept that their melange of melodrama and coincidence is exactly "stern reality," but we must try to understand, to put ourselves in the place of Henry James or anyone else living in the middle of the nineteenth century, and attempt to contrast that popular culture with our own. We live in an age with "L.A. Law" and "Miami Vice" on network TV for all to see and movies like *Fort Apache* and *Dirty Harry* on the shelves of our video store. *Fatal Attraction* (not all that unlike *Lady Audley's Secret*) was the hit new film of 1987; and Scott Turow's *Presumed Innocent* still sat atop the best-seller lists in 1988. In each of these exemplars of our popular culture—whatever their wildly differing qualitative values as art—we see a crime-ridden city (a real, recognizable city of our own time and experience) with a legal, political, or social establishment that is tainted or infested with madness and corruption. The villains are often, at first look anyway, unvillainous. Even the "heroes" are likely to be flawed—liars or killers who have managed by chance or technicality to have fallen into the camp of the good guys rather than the bad. It is not my place or intention here to provide an analytical survey of the culture I inhabit, but I can say that in 1860—until the Sensation novel—the Victorians had no really comparable tradition of their own. They were barely digesting the news revolution which I have described in earlier chapters—and the news, at least, usually had something of an inadvertent quality. With the advent of novels with such content, there was now a body of work that seemed willful in its provocative descriptions of monomaniacal noblewomen and murderous pillars of respectability. Certainly, the grip of authority appeared to be slipping rapidly. So the relationship of news and fiction became another, coexistent problem to confront, along with the brazen existence of the novels themselves.

For example, H. L. Mansel, Dean of St. Paul's and an eminent philosopher, took on the Sensation novel for the *Quarterly Review* in 1863. In this essay, he defined the books as "the criminal variety of the Newspaper Novel, a class of fiction having about the same relation to the genuine historical novel that the police reports of the 'Times' have to the pages of Thucydides or Clarendon." These remarks not only underline the connection between journalism and fiction made by eminent Victorians like Mansel, but they also demonstrate the suspicious disapproval with which even *The Times* was viewed. Comparing Thucydides (460–400 B.C.) and the first Earl of Clarendon (1609–1674), the preeminent historians, respectively, of ancient Greece and the seventeenth-century English Civil War, with trial transcripts in a daily paper seems hardly playing fair. Moreover, there are at least a couple of ironies here. Modern historians might today very well find police reports vastly more interesting and representative of an age than any selective official history—and I suspect we can glean at least the dawning of that realization in Mansel's hostile remarks: the police report is what the official version of history would like to repress, *should* have repressed, because of its powerful suggestibility.

In any case, the news and the novels were regularly associated. Another typical passage, certainly more sanguine about the implications of the connection, appeared as the lead to a news item clipped by Bell Macdonald in 1861:

> This is decidedly the age of romance founded on reality. The old writers of fiction, who used to cudgel their brains so indefatigably to construct an ingenious plot interwoven with exciting incidents, would find their vocation at the present time a matter of comparative ease. . . . The most marvellous and melodramatic events are mingled with the occurrences of every day existence, and each law or police reporter . . . flies over the housetops . . . and unroofs all London, for the curious public to contemplate next morning at breakfast time the infinite dramas and intrigues, the comedies, tragedies, and farces, the wild extravaganzas, the screaming burlesques, the pathetic eclogues, which are enacted at every hour of the day and night in London, to the amazement of a community who discover that they have lived so long in indifference or in ignorance of the wonders taking place around them, and to the triumphant confirmation of the aphorism that truth is strange, and stranger than fiction.

The "aphorism" alluded to here is of course a cliché. The notion of finding Amazing Stories behind one's neighbors' closed doors was hardly new in 1861. The point here is that people *thought* it was new. The allusion to the "indifference and ignorance" of the British in general certainly tends to corroborate Steven Marcus's speculations in *The Other Victorians* about a kind of contagion of "dimmed consciousness" in the face of licentious or passionate behavior. And I would like to add that the novelty lay not in the mere existence of unpalatable reality—or even in the awareness of that unpalatable reality in everyday life—but rather in the sense of dumbfounded outrage that so many people, in so many public venues, would be willfully, even joyfully, ready to "unroof" the city and then actually publish their discoveries.

This sense is corroborated in a *Times* review of LeFanu's *Uncle Silas* in 1865, which asserts on the basis of a reading of the week's police reports that no

> flight of imagination, however wild, [can] create greater or stranger horrors than occur among us every day. What sensation novel goes beyond the story of the Plaistow murder, with all its dreadful details of the decapitated corpse gnawed by river rats and buried in vain? What fancied martyrdom can be more singular than that of the wife of the schoolmaster convicted of beating a young pupil to death, who had systematically punished his own infant children in the most senseless manner, at the most tender age, and from whom in spite of ill-usage, no legal decision availed to separate her? What invented story ever came up to the still unforgotten history of the young nobleman who dragged his wife out of her mother's bed for the express purpose of beating her, then lived with another unhappy young creature under a feigned name at an obscure inn, and when the partner of his errors died in her confinement, shot himself, leaving the innkeeper to discover who his inmates had been, and who the new born infant belonged to? As long as these and a hundred more such stories occur in real life, so long will people welcome their shadows in mock memories of romance.

This review in itself exemplifies the very subject it purports to be discussing: by rehearsing with obvious relish the details of the Plaistow murder, among other domestic atrocities, the distinction between the literary and journalistic, between writing about life and life itself, is consistently blurred.

It should be conceded here, of course, that this sort of overkill about killing carries its significance over the 125 years or so into our own age. I have suggested earlier that perhaps the crime columns had created an indifference on the part of the public in the way that TV viewers during the Vietnam War were turned off emotionally by the profusion of cold electronic images of defoliation and pacification which occupied their living room each evening. It seems to me now that 1988 is an even more appropriate age for comparison to the effects of the publication of acts of crime and illicit sexuality in the Victorian era. In the past year or so we have been confronted by such phenomena as the videotape of the confession of Bernhard Goetz (the "Subway Vigilante") being available for rent in video stores; audiotapes of psychiatric sessions with John Lennon's assassin played in a documentary film; a prominent evangelist predicting on TV that future generations will be able to view the Second Coming by a TV satellite hookup; and the general coverage of arrest and conviction of Robert Chambers. Chambers, a young, apparently well-bred, handsome college dropout was accused of murdering Jennifer Dawn Levin, an eighteen year old, about to enter college, from a well-to-do family, during a sexual assignation behind the Metropolitan Museum in Central Park, New York City.

The Chambers case gripped America for over a year—not just because the "Preppie Murder Case" featured a reasonable facsimile of what passes for young, fast, and beautiful in Manhattan, but because the news media exceeded previously accepted bounds of "taste" in reporting the case. Both tabloids and the most solemn journals published accounts of rough sex: hands tied with panties; testicles squeezed; a sexually aggressive young female who had earlier discussed her lover/murderer as a sexual object rather than a human being. In the courtroom, sets of women's underwear were demonstrated at length as exhibits, and the court stenographer (recalling the Palmer case of 1856) claimed that in spite of years of service in criminal courts, the medical testimony was so gruesome and esoteric it was almost beyond his ability to get it all down. Finally, there was the release of the videotape of Chambers's "confession."

To the TV viewer, the tape evokes a subtext of meaning at least as interesting as Chambers's version of the events in the park. This underlying significance is in many ways parallel to the cultural displacement the Victorians must have felt when faced with extended reports and commentary, with illustrations, in the newly cheap newspapers. In the Levin murder, not only was the general public given visual and aural access to a confession while the trial was still going on, but video technology also allowed—and continues to allow—us to record the image and play and replay it at our leisure. We can analyze the demeanour of the accused as we would a touchdown run at the Super Bowl. What before we had to read about in severely edited form, we can now contemplate in perpetuity (not to mention stop-action). So our relationship to criminal and legal proceedings has been radically, and irrevocably, changed. Chambers in close-up on tape is certainly handsome; he also appears sincere, and amazingly calm, as he describes what he alleges was the unintentional snuffing out of Jennifer Levin's life. The quality of tape and sound are high and only the occasional four-letter obscenity—which everyone can infer anyway—is bleeped out. So everyone has an intimacy with the subject heretofore reserved for members of the court and the police.

The point of all this is that new technology is forever becoming cheaper, and more universally available. In this way, there is an ever-expanding sense of the limits of what we know—and of what we think about what we know. And the news, of course, is usually bad. Sometimes the drift of this bad news is to a revisionary understanding of past and present—to the recognition that progress and comfort and all the social services possible cannot change the inherent evil in mankind. In this sense the mass media coverage of the beating to death in 1987 of the child called Lisa Steinberg by her professional-class adoptive parents, at a good address in Greenwich Village, has undermined the possibility of an optimistic outlook on the progress of mankind and, further, reveals doctors, lawyers, adoption agencies, social welfare agencies, the police, and the top-flight public school which the girl attended to be either malevolent or inept. Or both. And the intense scrutiny in December 1988 of the parents—Hedda Nussbaum and Joel Steinberg—in the live TV coverage of Steinberg's trial (including videotapes shown of Nussbaum's horribly beaten body at the time of her arrest), serves to underline my conjectures about the technological significance of the Chambers case.

Child battering, as we have seen most graphically in this text, is nothing new, but it continues to be selectively forgotten until something excessively dramatic breaks into the headlines. In fact only a couple of months after the first news of the Steinberg case, *The New York Times Book Review* was to give first-page status to a study of suppression of information on child abuse in today's society. Even Freud, as I mentioned above, has been accused of complicity in this age-old conspiracy of silence. The Victorians, then, like ourselves could forget, or deny, or actively reject whatever confronted them which they felt was perverse or out of their control.

The reason I've introduced this contemporary subject is that no one knows where the audio-visual technology is taking us. Is the continuing refinement of our techniques for unroofing the city also a constant reinforcement of our drift to nihilism? Is the inner being—up close and more and more personal—too scary to contend with? Do we therefore learn to cope by denying what we can too plainly see? Does it not now seem that the mid-Victorian controversy over Sensation is a sign of a major transitionary stage in society's wholesale drift into denial? Is the tunnel vision of the "Me" generation and the Yuppies but a latter-day version of Victorian Philistinism, generated out of the same resistance to the crushing nullity of the news from Palestine or Ethiopia or Howard Beach?

This brings us back to the 1865 *Times* review of *Uncle Silas*, to the evocation of the Plaistow murder with the corpse eaten by river rats and the schoolmaster beating students to death. This review appeared at the same time as the serial run of Dickens's *Our Mutual Friend* was drawing to a close. In *Our Mutual Friend*, many corpses are pulled out of the Thames and a major role is played by a deranged and brutal schoolmaster. There are mysteries attached to some of the river corpses; these mysteries are published in the papers and discussed at fashionable dinners. The solution to the identity of one corpse becomes the enigma which holds together the rather sprawling plot of the book. The search for an answer to this puzzle leads to the River Thames taking on symbolic value as the flow of information through the city; and the message implicit in this "information," as it spreads through the book and the city of the book, is that London—an agglomeration of dungheaps and old bone shops and unburied dead—is the detritus of a rotten civilization. Paradoxically, the river which delivers this bad news also continues to hold the city together, its denizens united only in the shared knowledge of the bad news, a kind of connection by disconnection. J. Hillis Miller has commented that Dickens in *Our Mutual Friend* abandoned the need for cohesion in his elements, fragmenting them, breaking them apart, with no pretense to be mimetic of reality. His characters "transform their real situations into fictive situations which free them from the steady pressure of reality." As a consequence, the fragmented, confusing, many-voiced nihilism of *Our Mutual Friend* puts the work, in Miller's terms, "on the threshold of the twentieth century."

We have not the data yet to determine where our new knowledge, wrought out of our new technology, is taking us—either artistically or socially. But we *can* suggest where the Victorians were and, with the aid of hindsight, where they were going. We can now postulate that Sensation had plugged itself into the deeper currents of the mainstream of the Victorian mind—in epistemology and religion, for example—and had then blown the circuits.

13

❖

Critical Passions

II. MISSED CONNECTIONS

Henry James had put his finger on what anti-Sensation critics did not want to encounter in their reading: "modern England, the England of today's newspaper." Why? For one thing there was a problem of authenticity. The *North British Review,* for example, found Lady Audley herself to be "at once the heroine and the monstrosity" of Braddon's novel: "Whenever she is meditating the commission of something inexpressibly horrible, she is described as being unusually charming. Her manner and appearance are always in contrast with her conduct. All this is exciting but it is also very unnatural."

What was natural, then? Can one even assume that the reviewer is equating "unnatural" with "inauthentic"? It is after all hard to imagine that many readers of newspapers and active spectators at the stage of city life (among whom I include literary journalists) were disingenuous enough to really agree with the *National Review* that life in Britain was "concentrated upon well-to-do, decorous, and deservedly prosperous people." To answer my question about nature, I believe, we must focus on the end of the *National Review*'s egregious prescription: that Victorian respectability should direct itself to solving not only the problems of "this world but the *next*" (italics mine).

In short, what may appear to us in Victorian book reviews to be a controversy about social realism is actually part of the larger

metaphysical debate about the ultimate destination of man's soul
. . . and how it goes about getting to its terminus. Moreover,
in a kind of reverse paradox, each time we detect this telltale
hint of spiritual agitation in a piece of writing which contrarily
professes to be about the makeup of the material world, we
are consistently pulled back from any contemplation of heavenly
spheres which our nose for subtext evokes. The pieces—overtly
objective treatises on civilization; covertly ideological propaganda
about Christian orthodoxy—take on in their final effect a personally confessional tone of the most worldly character. I suppose
this endlessly contradictory movement is no more than a manifestation of the degree to which what we call religion is really an
expression of our earthbound fears and fantasies. Nevertheless it
is important that we visualize clearly just what form this sort of
wish-fulfillment took in the middle of the nineteenth century.
Everywhere in the period one finds a kind of double vision: on
the one hand, a confident assertion of a perfectly seamless system
in which everything is in its place; on the other, an absolute
terror at the prospect of discovering rents in the fabric of the
system's internal logic. The contradictions in Lady Audley's appearance and behavior are significant not so much because they
may illustrate a money-grubbing sensationalist's capacity for cre-
ating shockingly twisty effects as because they are expressions of
an artist's willful undermining of the neatly symmetrical structure
which had been erected—however foolishly—on a scaffolding of
missed connections.

This devotion to missing the point is nowhere more obvious
than in a solemn dissection of crime-writing (called "The Philosophy of Sensation") that appeared in *St. James Magazine* in 1862.
There the writer complains of the sensation writers' "hybrid combinations of the mean and the noble, the modest and the impure,
the hero and the scoundrel, the angel and the tigress. As the
writer's resistance to psychological complexity is emotional, the
words "hybrid" and "impure" connote a fear of infection that is
quite personal. Moreover, the image of "the angel or the tigress"
has an intensity beyond a mere consideration of popular literature.
At once it recalls William Acton's reassurances in his medical texts
that young men need not fear excessive sexual demands from
women (thus by implication admitting that they *do* need to keep

a sharp eye out for monomaniacal females) and brings to mind another comment by Marcus on the great pornography-collector Ashbee's "displacements": "Such sentences are really about something else and have their referents elsewhere."

One may infer that the "referent" of the author of "Philosophy of Sensation" is his personal terror of a female sexuality that is both voracious and bestial. Such a speculation is at least partially confirmed by a touchingly comical passage which follows:

The novel has really become a domestic institution. In truth so general is its influence, that its presence is felt in almost every link of the great social chain, sometimes, by the way, acting rather as a fetter upon sociality than as a means of communication, as many a traveller must have felt, whose hard fate it has been to sit between two evidently very charming young ladies on a bench placed on a fashionable "Parade" overlooking the sea, whose attention has been engrossed by the interest of the stories they were perusing. In vain he turns his gaze from one intelligent face to the other, in hope of finding an opportunity for saying something that should enable him to accomplish that great difficulty—the first step to a desirable acquaintance. Both pair of bright eyes continue obstinately fixed upon each absorbing page, and he is finally obliged to give up the attempt. . . .

The man who wrote these lines is a disappointed would-be suitor, but he is also a representative of the contradictory Victorian official tendency to blame loss on change. In the sense that he then tries to impose his own sense of "tradition"—whether real or imagined—in order to recoup his losses, he is equally emblematic of his time. The "great social chain" is the idealized—but largely inoperative—orthodoxy which just happens to keep the woman captive in her role as "angel." In this captive state she becomes not only non-threatening but readily accessible. She is in her place as everyone else should be. Of course this sort of observation is commonplace in feminist criticism; what particularly strikes me is the role of the book in the writer's vision. The women are seduced by stories into inattention to the would-be dominant male, or they are metamorphosed into man-eaters. In either case,

Literature—not Sisterhood—is perceived as powerful. Books, we infer, have a prescribed role: they should hold the system together. Instead—as in the Sensation novels—they can and do disrupt the smooth functioning of that machine, allowing it to run amok. And the pre-ordainedly innocent and impressionable girls at the seashore can't keep their eyes off the action.

I do not mean to suggest that the critic's way of conjuring up the universe, or of defending his personal vision, is anything new. The "Great Chain of Being"—a conceptual hierarchical pyramid with God at the apex, wee beasties groveling at the base, and respectable men conveniently placed slightly above women and just beneath the heavenly legions—goes back to at least the Old Testament and pervades English literature from the Renaissance through eighteenth-century neoclassicism. Nor has the belief in such a chain disappeared in the liberated twentieth century—as have Criminal Conversation prosecutions, child labor, and the choking London fog of pre-environmental–control industrialism. Stephen Jay Gould, one of our most respected and popular historians of science, has pointed out as recently as 1987 that today we still share with the Victorians "our almost desperate desire to make humans special and superior among the animals of the earth." The problem with such thinking—today and throughout history— is that it represents, in Gould's terms, "an indefensible conceit," a form of "reductionism," especially as applied to mankind.

What actually makes the Victorians notable, if not unique, is the crazy quilt application of the conceit in which they indulged themselves. I do not use "crazy quilt" lightly because, quite frequently—as in the case of the author of "The Philosophy of Sensation"—there is a sense that the threat of the deterioration of the links in the chain has driven the writer himself slightly loopy. In the critical commentary on a literature riddled with madhouse scenes and allusions to insanity it often seems that we encounter a world in which something has snapped indeed, and in which the inmates have taken over the asylum. Certainly there is a touch of lunacy in the vigor with which guardians of Victorian orthodoxy— when confronted by sensationalism—scrambled to disconnect themselves from their own history at the same time that they so resolutely insisted on the commonality of their own decorous existences, as opposed, of course, to those peculiar beings of inferior races and species with which the British well-to-do unfortunately had to share the habitation of the earth.

Daniel Bell summarizes this Victorian tendency in *The Cultural Contradictions of Capitalism* (1976):

> Central to the imagination of the nineteenth century was a view of society as a web (and in the literary hallucinations as a spider web). Or in the more abstract vein, as elaborated by Hegel, each culture, each "period" of history, and correspondingly each society, was a structurally interrelated whole, unified by some inner principle. For Hegel, it was the *Geist,* or inner spirit. For Marx, it was the mode of production, which determined all other social relations. Thus historical or social change was defined as a succession of fundamentally different unified cultures—the Greek world, the Roman world, the Christian world—each with its qualitatively different mode of production—slavery, feudalism, and capitalism—and each resting on different kinds of social relations and forces of production.

I quote Bell here not because I want to explicate the theories of such original thinkers as Hegel and Marx, but because I want to show how freely their elusive concepts could be reduced to simple-minded prescriptions by Victorian reviewers. One article from the *Contemporary Review* of 1867, titled "The Morality of Literary Art," eloquently illustrates the lengths to which one might go to displace and deny the spider-web hallucinations of crime writing. The author, H. A. Page (writing under the *nòm de plume* of A. H. Japp), announces that he intends to reconcile Morality and Art through a survey of history. He initiates this modest task by introducing his Hegelian "law of Truth": "All art is so far history; but art becomes history not by recording facts but by spiritualizing them, by making them the body of higher truths than history can legitimately deal with, because in the unity of conception, which is the characteristic element of art, there lurks the totality of life of a period."

Art which deals with the past, then, "has a tendency to become false and immoral by (1) setting itself outside the real atmosphere of the time; and (2) by the despising of those elements of progress which must have brought new and quickening light to the moral consciousness of men." The key phrase here is "moral consciousness." Mr. Page has decided that the spirit of his age—of 1867—is one of "moral progress."

> Essential morality never changes but the relation in which each new generation stands to it is modified by the restrictions which must accompany more complex conditions and experiences. Civilization, indeed, takes hostages of art, and requires that her laws be not violated in idea any more than in fact. The wild and unconscious freedom of the artist is thus limited on a hundred sides, simply because as a true child of his time he must respect the laws which a genuine morality has suggested as being necessary for the preservation of social purity.

The reasoning which leads from what could have seemed at first to be a plea for freely expressed realism to the demand for repression in the name of "the preservation of social purity" is startling. No less so is the yoking of technology and morality in the service of censorship. In fact, as we have seen in the newspapers, technology was in the process of doing exactly the opposite of what Page claims for it. By publishing "wild and unconscious" carryings-on of so many Victorians, the papers had created "more complex conditions and experiences" indeed, but their tendency had not been particularly edifying. Page is speaking more of *restoring,* not preserving, purity—if indeed such pervasive cleanliness had ever existed in the real world. Page persists, however, extending his assessment of contemporary culture to a weirdly condescending put-down of the past. There, he claims,

> we find a sharp point of contrast between the two great worlds of art—not, however, the two usually marked off from each other by lines more or less arbitrary—heathen and Christian, classical and romantic. The distinction lies rather between the art which is the outcome of a primitive and simple life, and that which is the result of a highly civilized and artificial one. Homer here contrasts with Horace; the Nibelungenlied with Goethe, and Ossian with Robert Burns. Primitive art was not

immoral, because unconsciousness was its pervading spirit; modern art cannot treat nature as it was then treated, because self-consciousness is its distinctive feature. To be unconscious of evil is in one sense to be free from its taint; and so far as the moderns have entered on the forbidden fields of nature without outraging modern requirements, it has been because of some of the health of early life surviving through all the complications of civilization.

In earlier times spirit and form are found in perfect harmony; this, however, is only because the higher possibilities of man in effort have not yet been realized. The first merit of early art is that it was natural; but of later art that it was victorious over nature—the one was free and spontaneous, the other is everywhere triumphant over obstacle and difficulty. In the one there is a constant tendency to fall into a forbidden sphere, and by consequence self-pleasurings alternate with the self-torturings that always supervene on secret indulgences; in the other no sphere is felt to be forbidden, and no pleasure is prohibited if it has been won in honour.

On the basis of these assertions, Page proceeds to apply himself to all of literary history. Ovid, Virgil, Boccaccio, Petrarch, Dante, Chaucer, and Shakespeare are judged by this standard. Significantly, art which reflects nature and "unconsciousness" is acceptable in inverse proportion to its historical proximity to 1867. Nearness in time converts the abstract to the concretely seditious. Although his elevation of the primitive seems to suggest a sympathy with the great Romantics, he is particularly disturbed by Byron and Shelley. They were poets only "in spite of their conscious revolt against 'what was best and highest' in society; and not because of it, for certainly such revolt lowers them in rank as artists, however large the crowds they may have set agog as agitating quacks do."

Of his contemporaries, Page is particularly unhappy with Swinburne for violating the law of historical truth by patterning himself after Byron's immorality. There is in Swinburne, besides, "a narrowness of sympathy" which "cannot be impartial." His tendency is to "morbid moods and experiences," and "the work of such a one, so far as it is *real,* belongs to the same class as a police report;

so far as it is *ideal,* he has only produced what Hegel takes such care to condemn—a false ideal which is indulged by the isolated imagination, and belongs in no sense to humanity."

Thus we are brought back to the social web. We see the official consciousness as *Geist* placed in contraposition to the police reports, and the two conflicting quantities identified with the *ideal* and the *real*. The immediate bias, at any rate, is clear enough: Swinburne's greatest sin is "the bold and undeclared attack upon ideas or forms which the common sense of the mass holds to be hallowed."

And, as one might anticipate, any discussion which brings in the police reports and seditious ideas is not far from the Sensation novelists. Of Charles Reade, Page maintains, "scarcely a prose-writer of our time has more glaringly violated" the law of historical truth. Reade and Braddon together he classifies among "the falsest writers of our time" because they have "tried to recover the awful brooding unity and fascination of tragedy by setting the emotions in opposition to the intellect in relation to certain points of morality."

One of the major subversive implications of the Sensation novels is manifest here. To develop Page's Hegelian terminology a step further: if "moral consciousness" and "intellect" is the thesis of the age, then the Sensation novels and "emotions" in many ways embody the antithesis. As such, it seems not unjust to suggest that the synthesis of this dialectic—the impulses of modern art toward the naturalistic, the subconscious, and the "morbid"—owes a considerable debt to Sensation fiction.

Lingering over this review-article, some insights emerge about the place of newspapers as opposed to "literature" in the culture. Page seems obsessed—like so many others—with repressing what is instinctive. They are fighting the good fight to be "victorious over nature." It is as if Page and his fellow detractors of sensationalism have willfully missed the quite natural connection between humanity and instinct. They have in fact repressed the very Shakespeare they are so fond of quoting, without having to deal with anything so open or direct as Bowdlerization. (Thomas Bowdler had produced his *Family Shakespeare*—all unnatural passion removed—in 1818.) Instead, the official Victorians want to "spiritualize" fact and fiction alike—at least for their own age. The unspiritualized fact of the texts of recorded history become palatable because the critic assumes they are unconnected to the present. One of the central paradoxes of the nineteenth century is that newspaper police reports and crime novels were denounced for breaking up the "social chain" when in fact they were ensuring that the link to the past—civilized and primitive—remained secure. To pursue this paradox further, one must enter the shadowy realm where religion overlaps with psychology, but first we must examine more closely the Sensation stories themselves as agents of both continuity with the gritty past and discontinuity with the idealized present.

14

❖

The Fishy Extremities
of *Lady Audley's Secret*

Aside from dealing with distressingly criminal or immoral aspects of the human condition, with realistic contemporary English settings, the Sensation novelists are really not all that similar, at least in their surface effects. Dickens of course exemplifies many things: social reformer, humorist, chronicler of urban decay, subtle ironist, prober of the darkest corners of the human psyche. Collins is both master of mystery plotting and sardonic gadfly. Reade weaves convoluted melodramas, most notable for their sense of outrage with institutional oppression. Mrs., Henry Wood is essentially a writer of sentimental romances who seems to wander inadvertently within range of critical opprobrium (by daring in *East Lynne* to suggest that noble women can commit adultery and, through penitential suffering and death, gain a chance at salvation). LeFanu is best known as a "ghost writer" and from one story to the next one is never sure whether to expect to enter the realm of the purely supernatural or that of the psychological thriller. Bulwer-Lytton is now notorious as a long-standing perpetrator (from 1828 when he was twenty-five until his death in 1873) of hack fiction largely notable for its mangled syntax. Still, he was one of the initiators of the Newgate School (with *Paul Clifford* in 1830 and *Eugene Aram* in 1832) and *A Strange Story* is a fascinating—if tedious—sort of anti-Sensation novel, which exploits crime, sex, the war of science and religion, and madness in a frantic effort to counter the general drift of his contemporary crime writers. Miss

Braddon in her dozens of irresistible page-turners is absolute mistress of stringing satire: "jaunty, cynical, and tough," to borrow Winifred Hughes's phrase of 1980.

Nor is there any really extended pattern of imitation of real-life crime from the newspapers. So these are not "non-fiction novels" or "true fiction" of the sort we have been encountering on our own best-seller lists since 1964 when Truman Capote's *In Cold Blood* caused a stir comparable to that of *The Woman in White* a century before. Still, the Sensation novels *are* riddled with details which recall widely reported criminal occurrences of the time. Collins used the infamous "Road" murder case (in which Constance Kent, the twelve-year-old confessed murderess, according to Mary Hartman in *Victorian Murderesses,* may have been "a sacrifice . . . to [male] adult obsessions") as the basis for the mystery plot of *The Moonstone.* He also reproduced, in *Armadale,* the treatment of Dr. Smethurst by the courts. LeFanu and Reade both borrowed specifics—for murder scenes in *Uncle Silas* and *Hard Cash,* respectively—from the carryings-on in John Parson Cook's room at the Talbot Arms in Rugeley, across the street from the Palmer manse.

In fact, almost all the writers used the newspapers as sources of information in one way or another. Indeed, Charles Reade was famous for the voluminous clippings he collected from the papers (*à la* Bell Macdonald), though his focus was more on injustice than criminality, not that the two did not often overlap. On one occasion he wrote to *The Daily Telegraph* after many readers had questioned—in and out of print—the authenticity of his research on the inhumane madhouse bureaucracy in *Hard Cash.* The irascible author publicly challenged any unbelievers to come around to his house (address provided) where he would show them the clippings on which the details were based.

Collins takes the issue a step further in terms of literary technique. In the "Preamble" to *The Woman in White* he lays claim to an innovative narrative strategy. The reader will encounter the story as "a Judge might once have heard it" (if, of course, the wicked premise goes, a corrupt legal system had ever allowed it to get to court in the first place). The multiple points of view will resemble the way "the story of an offense against the laws is told in Court by more than one witness."

The list of such contiguous points between newspapers and novels is potentially endless. But this is hardly as interesting as exploring the texts of the novels themselves in terms of how they undermined the sense of the way things *should* be. This project could be accomplished by looking at any of the stories I have mentioned, but three will do: *Lady Audley's Secret, Armadale,* and "Green Tea."

W. Fraser Rae may have denounced *Lady Audley's Secret* as "noxious" in his 1865 *North British Review* essay but at the same time he had to acknowledge Mary Elizabeth Braddon's talent and influence. "If," he wrote, "the test of genius were success, we should rank Miss Braddon very high in the list of our great novelists. The fertility of her invention is as unprecedented as the extent of her popularity. . . . Three years ago her name was unknown to the reading public. Now it is nearly as familiar as that of Bulwer Lytton or Charles Dickens."

Braddon had indeed come a long way. In 1856 the aspiring actress had written a novel (called *Three Times Dead;* it was finally issued as *The Trail of the Serpent* a decade later) which in many respects imitates *Bleak House.* When it was not published, she turned out anonymous hack fiction for magazines in order to earn her keep. *Lady Audley's Secret* was the first novel to appear under her own name, but in the next three years she produced thirteen titles (by my count) while continuing to write the unsigned "penny dreadfuls." In spite of these impressive numbers, however, *Lady Audley's Secret* remains the essential Braddon and the essential Sensation novel.

The Lady Audley of Braddon's novel (there was a notorious seventeenth-century Lady Audley, of whom Braddon's contemporaries were quite aware, whose husband was executed for forcing her to engage in sexual intercourse with his servant while he watched) is a beautiful young woman who, by marrying Sir Michael Audley, "one of the most influential men in the country," has recently elevated herself from penniless governess to mistress of a great fortune. The Audleys live opulently at a great estate in Essex, Audley Court. Also in residence at the Court is Sir Michael's daughter, Alicia, by his deceased first wife. Alicia and her stepmother are almost the same age.

Sir Michael's nephew, Robert, lives in London. Though devoted primarily to a life of idleness, smoking German pipes and reading French novels, Robert maintains the pretense of purpose by living in rooms at the Temple and fulfilling the residency requirement to become a barrister. One day, Robert encounters an old school chum, George Tallboys, who has just returned from Australia where he struck it rich. He is on his way to rejoin his wife and son, whom he left more than three years earlier to seek his fortune. His wealthy father had disowned George when he married Helen Maldon, the daughter of a drunken retired naval officer. While having coffee with his friend, George reads on the first page of *The Times* the obituary notice of the wife to whom he was so joyously returning.

Robert takes the inconsolable George to Essex for a fishing trip. They visit Audley Court with Alicia. Sir Michael and his wife have been called unexpectedly to London. The young Audleys show George around the house. Her ladyship's rooms are locked, but Alicia reveals a secret passage and they find a lavishly appointed apartment dominated by a portrait of the former governess which shows her as a beautiful woman possessed by a strange inner light. George stares at the portrait for a long time. When they depart, he is gloomier than ever.

Next day, George disappears. Not a trace of George Tallboys can be found. Robert, like the reader, soon suspects Lady Audley of some unexplainable complicity in George's disappearance, and he begins to collect evidence to support these suspicions. Although he has been told by George's father-in-law that George had visited him before returning to Australia, it is clear to Robert that the man is lying. George's son, who is living with his mother's father, mentions a "pretty lady" who has visited the house; and the remains of a "telegraphic message" in the fireplace indicate that the story is a fabrication.

Robert then proceeds to investigate the circumstances of Lady Audley's former life as Lucy Graham and finds that it commenced the day after the former Helen Maldon disappeared from Yorkshire. The body buried at Ventnor under that name is clearly a part of a conspiracy of deception. He presents his case to Lady Audley, who accuses him of madness. She then attempts to murder him by burning down the nearby inn where he is staying. Robert escapes. His step-aunt breaks down and confesses. She is Helen Maldon Tallboys; she pushed George down a disused well on the property, leaving him for dead. And she possesses an even more fearsome secret: she is "mad," having inherited her insanity from her mother who died in an asylum. Robert must now take her to a private asylum in Belgium where she languishes and soon dies.

It is discovered that George Tallboys is not dead but had escaped from the foul well with broken bones and a broken heart to America. Now he returns. Moreover Robert and George's sister, Clara, have fallen in love and married.

At the conclusion, Robert has begun to practice law. He, Clara, and George are living together in a "fairy cottage" on the Thames, near Hampton. Robert and Clara have a baby who plays with George's son on his visits from Eton. Often in attendance are Sir Michael and Alicia, who is engaged to a rich suitor. Audley Court is shut up, and Sir Michael plans to live in a house on the border of the Hertfordshire estate of Alicia and her intended husband. Robert has finally given away his meerschaum and his French novels. Thus, as Braddon tells us in the last paragraph, "the end of it leaves the good people all happy and at peace."

The ending, of course, recalls the strictures of domestic fiction which the reviewer for the *National Review* prescribed for all "acceptable" British fiction: "The real interest of the story is concentrated upon well-to-do, decorous, and deservedly prosperous people who solve, with a good deal of contentment and self-satisfaction, the difficult problems of making the most of both this world and the next." However, it is also quite evident that *Lady Audley's Secret* does not otherwise fill the prescription. The primary focus of the novel, besides the process of "detection," is the character of Lady Audley. As such, it is a novel of sexual irregularity and madness, and it is convincing in that it boldly asserts its contemporary realism, and it develops a subversive social theme about the reality of life in England in 1861.

This contemporary verisimilitude is established in a number of ways in *Lady Audley's Secret*. Unlike most fiction of the period, contemporaneous dates are emphasized. The book ends in 1861, the year in which it began to appear in installments in the magazine *Robin Goodfellow*. Written communications are dated exactly. Robert takes specific trains at specific times from specific stations. The dates of newspapers are given. It is difficult today to imagine just how brazen these gestures were in the context of the time. We must remember Page's strictures about *Geist* and the inappropriateness of sensational material to the 1860s. Braddon is, in effect, casting the law of historical truth back in the lawmakers' faces.

Circumstances which seem improbable today can also be authenticated by reading contemporary newspapers. For example, Helen Maldon had wiped out her entire past before she applied for her position at Audley Court. It is common, in Bell Macdonald's clippings, to encounter lawsuits involving people with a disguised or suppressed past. One paper even editorialized about the great threat to British domestic security posed by servants, usually foreigners, who might turn out to be secretly married, or worse, Roman Catholic. Just as certainly, the author clearly takes a perverse enjoyment in assigning this intimate acquaintance with courtroom proceedings to her omniscient narrator. When George and Robert arrive at Audley for their visit, George, "in the first taste of rustic life," experiences a "kind of sensuous rapture." Then George's bucolic euphoria is rudely interrupted by the Braddon version of the world of Bell Macdonald's clippings:

> We hear every day of murders committed in the country. Brutal and treacherous murders; slow, protracted agonies from poisons administered by some kindred hand; sudden and violent deaths by cruel blows, inflicted with a stake cut from some spreading oak, whose every shadow promised— peace. In the country of which I write, I have been shown a meadow in which, on a quiet summer Sunday evening, a young farmer murdered the girl who loved and trusted him; and yet, even now, with the stain of that foul deed upon it, the aspect of the spot is—peace. No species of crime has ever been committed in the worst rookeries of the Seven Dials that has not been also done in the face of that rustic calm which still, in spite of all, we look on with a tender, half-mournful yearning, and associate with—peace.

This single paragraph neatly foreshadows George's impending accident, but it can also be read as a direct assault upon the more pastoral conventions of Romanticism, on the English faith in domestic and rural tranquility, and on the pieties of *The Newgate Calendar*. It is also typical Braddon prose—clear and sharp, almost always on the cutting edge of satire. One thinks of a restrained version of Edward Whitty of *The Leader*.

In any case, by the time Robert has begun to penetrate to the core of the mystery, the most banal corners of England have taken on the contours of treachery. As Robert arrives in the Yorkshire seaport of Wildernsea, where George Tallboys and his wife, Helen, had lived together, we are told:

> This northern road was strange and unfamiliar to the young barrister, and the wide expanse of the wintry landscape chilled him by its aspect of bare loneliness. . . .
> "I wonder whether settlers in the backwoods of America feel as solitary and strange as I do tonight?" he thought, as he stared hopelessly about him in the darkness.

As this consistently impending sense of crime and doom makes the English garden a jungle, Braddon does not miss the sense of urban blight either. The many homes of the itinerant family of George's wife are described in unsparing—and rather hilarious—detail. In Southampton,

> Mr. Maldon had established his slovenly household goods in one of those dreary thoroughfares which speculative builders love to raise upon some miserable fragment of waste ground hanging to the skirts of a prosperous town. Brigsome's Terrace was, perhaps, one of the most dismal blocks of building that was ever composed of brick and mortar since the first mason plied his trowel and the first architect drew his plan. The builder who had speculated in the ten dreary eight-roomed prison houses had hung himself behind the parlour door of an adjacent tavern while the carcasses were yet unfinished. The man who had bought the brick and mortar skeletons had gone through the bankruptcy court while the paper-hangers were still busy in Brigsome's Terrace, and had white-washed his ceilings and himself simultaneously.

The charnelhouse imagery not only serves here to enhance the sense of decadence in suburban development, but keynotes a sepulchral undercurrent—and black humor—which runs through the book. It also provides an implicit sympathy for anyone—villain or hero—who has come out of all this alive. Moreover, it is based on reality. In 1854, cholera, spawned in the unsanitary conditions of such housing developments, killed tens of thousands of people. And the plague was broadcast by the newspapers as no other had been before.

Within this larger vision of the treacherous nature of all England, there lies a more insidious statement on social corruption. Audley Court, symbol of the past and the traditional security of the hierarchical social structure, is threatened with decay. Lying "in that sheltered valley, which seemed to shut in the old house from all the clamour and hubbub of the everyday world," its images recur in Robert's subconscious:

> In those troublesome dreams he saw Audley Court, rooted up from amid the green pastures and shady hedgerows of Essex, standing bare and unprotected upon that desolate northern shore, threatened by the rapid rising of a boisterous sea, whose waves seemed gathering upward to descend and crush the house he loved. As the hurrying waves rolled nearer and nearer to the stately mansion, the sleeper saw a pale, starry face looking out of the silvery foam, and knew that it was my lady, transformed into a mermaid, beckoning his uncle to destruction.

In the dream, the waters retreat and the house is left unharmed, foreshadowing—on one level at least—the denouement of the story. But it is clear that Robert is not solely "villain-finder," as he was called in the *Times* review of the novel (the concepts of "amateur sleuth" and "private detective" not having quite taken hold yet) but defender—and a rather ineffectual one—of the faith.

It is Lady Audley, née Helen Maldon, who plays the criminal role, and embodies the menace to that order. *Lady Audley's Secret,* like *Great Expectations,* can be reread as a kind of perverted Horatio Alger tale with its ironic unravelings functioning as a defoliation of complacent respectability. Her new life, with her chest of jewels, her paintings, her china, the Audleys' invaluable collection of "plate," her adoration by the people of the country for both nobility of appearance and good works, becomes the apotheosis of a poor child's fairy-princess fantasy. And she has achieved it by abandoning her child, misrepresenting her identity, and committing bigamy. Then she twice attempts murder to preserve the status she has so perfidiously attained. In short, Lady Audley's career is a summing up of the warnings, implicit and explicit, of the newspapers. As such, the book provided the ideal culprit on which reactionary critics, as we have seen, could heap their retribution.

Nor does the fact that she is caught and punished by incarceration until death used by the author to soothe the ruffled feathers of bourgeois sentiment. In one of the most brilliant touches of the book, the proprietor of the asylum in Belgium where Lady Audley is taken has been told that money is no object, and the rooms into which Lady Audley is ushered, in bitter paradox, are the best money can buy. The best madhouse rooms, that is: they present, in contrast to the voluptuous splendor of Audley Court, a chilling parody of that materialist fantasy. The proprietor

> opened the outer door of a stately suite of apartments, which included a lobby, paved with alternate diamonds of black and white marble, but of a dismal and cellar-like darkness; a saloon furnished with gloomy velvet draperies, not particularly conducive to the elevation of the spirits; and a bed-chamber, containing a bed so wondrously made, as to appear to have no opening whatever in its coverings, unless the counterpane had been split asunder with a pen-knife.
>
> My lady stared dismally round at the range of rooms, which looked dreary enough in the wan light of a single wax-candle. This solitary flame, pale and ghost-like in itself, was multiplied by paler phantoms of its ghostliness, which glimmered everywhere about the rooms; in the shadowy depths of the polished floors and wainscot, or the window-panes, in the looking-glasses, or in those great expanses of glittering something which adorned the rooms, and which my lady mistook for costly mirrors, but which were in reality wretched mockeries of burnished tin.

If the "wretched mockeries of burnished tin" serve as metaphors for the perverted ideals of Helen Maldon's life, they just as certainly cast a fun-house image in the face of domestic sentiment. Since the chapter is titled "Buried Alive" the ironies multiply as well, and Helen Maldon–Lucy Graham–Lady Audley has been retitled again: in deference to the good name of the Audleys, she is registered in the asylum simply as "Madame Taylor." There is sympathy here for this rather pathetic woman, not only by virtue of the narrator's outspoken scorn for the system which ultimately defeats her protagonist, but through a consistent—if implicit—sense that Lady Audley is as much a victim as a perpetrator in the larger scheme of things. This idea is most vividly hinted at in Braddon's treatment of her "abnormal" emotional condition.

As Norman Donaldson has pointed out in his introduction to the Dover reprint (1974) of *Lady Audley's Secret,* her secret is not her bigamy nor her attempt to murder her first husband, as most readers and critics would have it. Her secret is that her mother was insane and that she believes the madness has descended to her. Like many women who turned up in police reports of court proceedings accused of madness and on their way to asylums, Lady Audley's first awareness of her "insanity" came with the "milk-fever" which accompanied her pregnancy. It develops into a kind of *idée fixe*—"monomania" is the term Braddon applies both to Lady Audley and to Robert as his obsession with solving the mystery sends his mind teetering to the brink. The question is, to the brink of what? In Robert's case, his imbalance certainly symbolizes the potential collapse of Audley Court. In the case of his uncle's wife, it is something else, something unspeakable. As she loses control of her proper social posture, "an unnatural lustre gleamed in her great blue eyes. She spoke with an unnatural rapidity. She had altogether the appearance and manner of a person who has yielded to the dominant influence of some overpowering excitement." In one of Robert Audley's dreams, she appears

hanging on his arm, when suddenly they heard a great knocking in the distance, and his uncle's wife wound her slender arms around him, crying out that this was the day of judgment, and that all wicked secrets must now be told. Looking at her as she shrieked this in his ear, he saw that her face had grown ghostly white, and that her beautiful golden ringlets were changing into serpents, and slowly creeping down her neck.

It is hard to deny the implications of these two passages. In the first, her "madness" is seen in terms of physical passion; in the second, her threat to Audley Court, at least in Robert's subconscious, is explicitly sexual. Combined with the fortuitous concurrence of the onslaught of this madness with the fruit of her first sexual experience, these passages and others like them—which contemporary critics called "voluptuous"—insist on the recognition of women's sexuality which the medical and moral establishments were intent on denying. Nor is Robert Audley unaware of these contradictions. Braddon tells us that "a shiver of horror, something akin to fear chilled him to the heart as he remembered the horrible things that have been done by women since that day upon which Eve was created to be Adam's companion and helpmeet in the garden of Eden."

The daily reviewer of *The Times*—when the novel appeared in 1862—most succinctly conjured up Braddon's accomplishment and the problems which it posed to the age: "It is not easy to represent a woman in such a position . . . to combine so much beauty with so much deformity; to depict the lovely woman with the fishy extremities."

The conclusion of the novel, moreover, far from being the conventional return to order it appears on the surface, reveals that the author herself refuses to relinquish her scornful attitude to the "respectable" otherworld (i.e., other from the world of the police reports) she has created. The final chapter is entitled "At Peace"—recalling the earlier mockery of the impossibility of "rustic calm." The legal success which Robert has achieved has come "in the great breach of promise case of Hobbs v. Nobbs," in which he "has amused the court by his deliciously comic rendering of the faithless Nobbs' amatory correspondence." In other words, he has become a featured performer in the kinds of sexual litigation revealed by Bell Macdonald's clippings, like the madcap "Merry Tale from Croydon," or the untangled skein of *Robinson* v. *Robinson*. This is hardly a noble profession. To boot, Alicia Audley has resigned herself to marry the rich fool whom she has spent the novel avoiding; and the Eton which little George attends, in terms of the value structure of the book, can hardly be an admirable place. Audley Court, though officially closed (in a touch prophetic of twentieth-century tourism), is often shown to "inquisitive visitors." The pre-Raphaelite painting of Lady Audley, who has died in Belgium of "maladie de langueur," is covered, for the sake of delicacy, with a curtain. Robert has had to give away his only pleasures, the pipe and the French novels, in exchange for domestic bliss—with a depressed brother-in-law in residence—in his "fairy cottage." In this light, the closing paragraph of the book is bitingly sardonic: "I hope no one will take objection to my story because the end of it leaves the good people all happy and at peace. If my experience of life has not been very long, it has at least been manifold; and I can safely subscribe to that which a mighty king and a great philosopher declared, when he said, that neither the experience of his youth nor of his age had ever shown him 'the righteous forsaken, nor his seed begging their bread.' "

My interpretation is confirmed by the way in which these lines echo a famous passage in Thackeray's *The Newcomes* (1853–55; this similarity was pointed out to me, by the way, by Gordon Ray). The Biblical reference is to Psalm 37:25, which reads: "I have been young and now am old, yet I have not seen the righteous forsaken, nor his seed begging for bread." In Thackeray's novel, the psalm is intoned, insensitively, before a group of pensioners in the alms house of Grey Friars Hospital. Pendennis is moved to ask: "But in the presence of eighty old gentlemen, who have all come to decay, and have all had to beg their bread in a manner, don't you think the clergyman might choose some other Psalm?" Certainly in *Lady Audley's Secret,* the irony is no less stinging.

In this line it should be noted as well that *Lady Audley's Secret* has strikingly modern qualities, providing a rich vein of inter-textual readings. It is chockful of references to the popular culture in which it is firmly rooted and at the same time—by virtue of its naughty playfulness of allusion—from which it is breaking away. Not only are Thackeray and recent news headlines evoked—re-played, if you will, in an altered context—but elementary resemblances, as I have already hinted, to *Great Expectations* and *The Woman in White,* for example, are obvious. Dickens's novel is recalled in the gentleman-hero who lives comfortably in the Temple on an "independent" income pretending to read Law but really playing around; in the return of a protagonist from a lost sojourn in Australia—materially successful but lost and unhappy; in the sense of "civilized" England as wasteland. *The Woman in White* explicitly shares this wasteland imagery, and also includes much which is recycled in *Lady Audley:* the unassertive amateur detective terrified by a woman's beastly sexuality; the mistaken identities, complete with the fake tombstone; and details here and there that turn up frequently.

In any case, the artistic and moral subtext of Braddon's sensationalism is happily packaged along with her breezy, thumb-your-nose attitude toward the official consciousness. In this she joins a heretofore unheralded class of journalists, critics, and fiction writers. Some of these were well known, some—like Whitty—virtually anonymous. But they emerge in full form today only to the student of primary sources in mid-Victorian periodicals.

Eventually, like Dickens and Thackeray among others, Braddon came to control her own magazine. It was, like *Temple Bar* and *Cornhill,* named for a section of London: *Belgravia.* In this journal, in 1868, she was able to print a piece by George Sala, Dickens's longtime crony and colleague, which perhaps best exemplifies the more openly flippant side of this counterculture. The piece is called "On the 'Sensational' in Literature and Art." I take the title alone to be a gesture of mock-solemnity, poking fun at such ponderous pieces as "The Philosophy of Sensation." At the same time it reinforces our sense of how pervasive the controversy had become over the dozen years since the Palmer trial.

According to Sala, "In the opinion of dolts and dullards and envious back-biters, everything is 'sensational' that is vivid, and nervous, and forcible, and graphic, and true." Millais and Holman Hunt in painting, Ruskin in art criticism, and Darwin as a "philosopher" are "sensational." In matters of magazines, novels, and newspapers, "*Belgravia* is a sensational magazine," and, along with Dickens, "Miss Braddon is a dreadfully sensational novelist." The *Grub-Street Journal* and *Daily Intelligencer* do not qualify for the epithet, while three of Bell Macdonald's favorite papers, "the *Telegraph,* the *Standard,* and the *Star,* are clearly sensational."

Sala concludes by proposing "no more sensation novels, no more sensation leading-articles, no more sensation pictures, no more sensation sermons, no more sensation speeches." Instead, England can return to the "calmly dull, to the tranquilly inane, to the timorously decorous, to the sweetly stupid." Let the Bishop of London, "in a wig like a bird's nest, preach a sermon in St. Paul's against photography and the Electric Telegraph. Don't let us move, don't let us travel, don't let us hear or see anything; but let us write sonnets to Chloe, and play Madrigals on the spinet, and dance minuets, and pray to Heaven against Sensationalism, the Pope, the Devil, and the Pretender; and then let Dullness reign triumphant, and Universal Darkness cover all."

Once again we hear the echo of the laughing gallery at the Crim. Con. trials. Braddon and her colleagues as spokespersons for that part of the population were quite happy to go to extremities—however fishy, however un-Victorian.

15

❖

Armadale: "A Sensation Novel with a Vengeance"

Wilkie Collins is still a familiar name to many readers. *The Moonstone* is considered by some literary historians to be the first modern mystery novel; and *The Woman in White* remains in print and is often assigned to students in Victorian studies as an example of "popular culture." Each of these works is openly antagonistic to British respectability, although many modern readers miss this. The oversight is probably the effect of the fact that each is immensely readable as a mystery thriller, a quality which Collins's other "sensation" novels of the sixties—*No Name* (1862) and *Armadale* (1866)—do not possess, at least in any significant measure. This is not to say the lesser-known books are without interest. *No Name* has an interesting social cause—to protest the law which determined that illegitimate children had no rights of inheritance from their parents—that is at least worth a footnote in history. *Armadale,* however, is something else entirely. It is probably Collins's most ambitiously subversive work and the spectacular manner in which it fails compels the attention of anyone curious about crime and sexuality in nineteenth-century literature. While it can be said that *The Woman in White* and *Lady Audley's Secret* set the basic patterns for the Sensation novel, *Armadale* can be seen to break out of them and, perhaps, as well out of the confines of the novel form as it was then known—"with a vengeance," as H. F. Chorley put it in his *Athenaeum* review in June 1866. It is a book so bursting at the seams with venom, social protest, and shocking behavior that its primary weakness seems to be that it tries to comprehend too much, in plot, theme, and literary experimentation. In its fulsome brew of coincidence and sardonic irony—apparently designed to undercut any notion of comfort or universal harmony in its readership—*Armadale* can be said to represent a meaningful, if flawed, proto-modernist experiment. And these form-shattering qualities now seem only logical developments, stylistic and substantive, of the newspapers of the late fifties and fiction of the early sixties.

The plot of *Armadale* must first be contended with, however. One critical biography has called it "so complex and tortuous as to defy summary"; another terms it "labyrinthine"; yet another complains that the Prologue to the novel alone "has material enough for a whole sensation novel." And—as it turns out—two of these three published studies of Collins's *oeuvre* manage to get the plot wrong! It seems to me that this is reason enough to make sure that we get an accurate paraphrase of the events narrated in *Armadale* before moving on to any interpretive gesture. So let us begin at the beginning.

The Prologue deals with the arrival of a dying Englishman, accompanied by his mulatto wife and baby son, at a German spa. Too weak to lift a pen himself, he summons a Scottish guest at the hotel to act as amanuensis for a deathbed confession. His tale is bizarre, even by Sensation standards.

Born Allan Wentworth, in Barbados, he became heir to the largest estates in those islands when an English cousin, Allan Armadale, was disowned by his father, who happened to be Wentworth's godfather. The only stipulation to the bequest was that Wentworth change his name to Allan Armadale. Here the plot (as well as the identity confusion which is the central focus of the plot) begins. Because Wentworth/Armadale needs to find a wife with a fortune comparable to his own, his mother arranges for him to meet the daughter of a former suitor of hers named Blanchard, the master of a large Norfolk estate called Thorpe Ambrose. Wentworth/Armadale is happy about the prospect, having become enamored of a miniature portrait of the girl. He makes plans to sail to Madeira (all the way across the Atlantic from the West Indies!) where the Blanchards are on holiday. Just before embarking, he falls ill. It is suspected that he has been drugged, inexplicably, by a young clerk named Ingleby whom he had recently hired and befriended. Ingleby has disappeared. When Wentworth/Armadale recovers, he embarks on the next boat to Madeira and there finds Miss Blanchard already married to Ingleby, who has represented himself as Allan Armadale. In fact, he is the *real* Allan Armadale, taking revenge against his cousin for inheriting his fortune (that is, the fortune which rightfully belongs to Armadale/Ingleby). Miss Blanchard has been brought into the conspiracy as well, aided by a "precocious" servant girl who forged a letter of consent to the marriage under the name of "Mrs. Wentworth."

A duel is arranged between the two young men, but before it can take place Armadale/Ingleby escapes with his bride and the little maid aboard a timber ship bound for Lisbon. Wentworth/Armadale disguises himself as a sailor and ships aboard the enraged Mr. Blanchard's yacht in pursuit of the fleeing trio. The timber ship is discovered foundering in the sea. The crew and the two women are saved, but the fugitive is found in his cabin below, drowned. The door to the cabin is locked from the outside.

The narration now shifts forward to Germany. The dying man confesses that he, Allan Armadale, formerly Wentworth, had murdered his cousin by locking him in the cabin. The reason for his confession is ominous: he has recently discovered that the former Miss Blanchard was pregnant when she was widowed. She lives in England with a son to whom she has given his father's real name. Wentworth/Armadale's son is *also* called Allan Armadale. The old man's last words are addressed to his only child: "Never, to your dying day, let any living soul approach you who is associated, directly or indirectly, with the crime which your father has committed. Avoid the widow of the man I killed, if the widow still lives. Avoid the maid whose wicked hand smoothed the way to the marriage—if the maid is still in her service. And more than all, avoid the man who bears the same name as your own." The novel itself is devoted to the working out of the "fatality" of this warning.

The three main characters are Allan Armadale, son of Mrs. Armadale née Blanchard and, posthumously, Armadale/Ingleby; the man who is the son of Allan Wentworth/Armadale and his mulatto wife, who is legally "Allan Armadale" but who has changed his name to Ozias Midwinter (this is the point at which the critics get confused); and finally the little maid, now grown up. Her name is Lydia Gwilt. The three are brought together by an incredible— even by Sensation standards—series of circumstances. In 1850, when Allan is twenty-two, Midwinter twenty-one, and Gwilt a youthful thirty-five, Midwinter turns up in the Devon coastal town where Allan lives with his mother, that is, with the former Miss Blanchard of Thorpe Ambrose. Allan and Midwinter become fast friends. Midwinter thinks it a coincidence that his new friend's name is identical to his concealed one until he inherits, along with a small but comfortable income, the transcript of his father's confession. He is ambivalent about the relationship: though fore-warned by the confession and suffused with a sense of doom, he also feels protective of Allan who is, after all, a not-so-distant cousin. Midwinter decides to remain silent about the secret.

In the meantime, Allan's mother dies and he soon becomes heir to Thorpe Ambrose through the untimely—and extremely coincidental—deaths of three healthy male relatives who stood ahead of him in line of succession. He is now one of the wealthiest young men in England. He persuades Midwinter to join him at Thorpe Ambrose as companion and steward. The two young men first take a sailing holiday to the Isle of Man. There, they become stranded—after abandoning their own yacht—aboard the wreck of *La Grâce de Dieu* which is the very boat on which Wentworth /Armadale had murdered Armadale/Ingleby. Allan naps for a while on the deck of the death ship and has a dream which foreshadows the entanglements to come. Briefly stated, the dream portends the entry of a beautiful woman into his life, the threat of his destruction by a man resembling Midwinter and, subsequently, his own destruction at the hands of the beautiful woman.

At Thorpe Ambrose, Miss Gwilt, the woman in the dream, enters the story. The death of Allan's mother has cut off the money she had been collecting from her former mistress in exchange for her silence about the events surrounding the marriage on Madeira. Miss Gwilt has designs on Allan and his fortune. Her plan, financed by an unscrupulous woman, Mrs. Oldershaw, is to obtain em-ployment as governess to the teen-aged daughter of Colonel Mil-roy, who lives on the estate, thereby gaining access to Allan, whom she will seduce and marry. Allan's romantic interest in Nellie Milroy and certain domestic complications involving Colonel and Mrs. Milroy foil the conspiracy. Meanwhile, however, Gwilt has attracted the attentions of Midwinter, whom she finds much more interesting than Allan. When Midwinter confesses the secret of his true identity to her, she conceives an alternate scheme. She will marry Midwinter under his "real" name of Allan Armadale, dispose of Allan first and then Midwinter, and return to Thorpe Ambrose in triumphant widowhood, bearing evidence of her legal marriage to one "Allan Armadale." In so doing she will provide herself with an annual income, for life, of £1,200. (There is no simple table of equivalents, but this would translate into at least a quarter of a million 1988 U.S. dollars; a tidy sum in any event.)

Gwilt and Midwinter tie the knot. Midwinter obtains employment as a newspaper correspondent in Italy and takes his bride to Naples. They are visited by Allan; and Gwilt, in a scene which fulfills the climactic prophecy of Allan's shipboard dream, attempts to poison him. Midwinter begins to crumble under the strain of the guilt he feels because of Allan's danger. He does not suspect his wife of being the agent of that danger; he is simply fearful that he is an omen of bad luck for Allan. Therefore, he refuses to go sailing with him (one would think the family would have developed hydrophobia by now). Gwilt seizes the opportunity to conspire with a former lover to drown Allan alone at sea. Confident of the success of her blackguardly accomplice, Gwilt returns to England armed with proof that she is Mrs. Allan Armadale to prepare to claim the estate. Midwinter, ignorant of her plan, remains in Italy.

The wreckage of Allan's ship is found and his presumed death is announced in the newspaper. However, when Gwilt's preparations are complete, Allan turns up unharmed. With the aid of a corrupt physician friend of Mrs. Oldershaw named Dr. Downward (now changed to Le Doux), who has opened a "private sanitarium for nervous invalids" near Hampstead, she lures Allan there for a final attempt at murdering him before he can announce to the world that he is not lost at sea. A bedroom at the sanitarium is rigged up so poison gas can be introduced into it as the victim sleeps. The plan is aborted by coincidence. Midwinter, unaware of all that has happened since his wife's return to England, encounters Allan by chance at the railway station. Suspicious, though unaware of Gwilt's involvement, he insists on accompanying him to the sanitarium. There, he takes a room next to Allan's.

When everyone in the establishment is asleep, Gwilt sneaks into the corridor to begin administering the poison. After the fourth of five doses, she glances into Midwinter's room and finds that he has switched with Allan and that she has been poisoning her husband whom she still actually loves. Frantic, she pulls Midwinter, unconscious but still alive, into the corridor. Realizing that all is lost, she writes a farewell note, puts the final dose into the murder room, and locks herself in, thus taking her own life.

The novel closes with the two friends, Armadale and Midwinter, back at Thorpe Ambrose looking somberly into the future. Allan is to marry the Milroy girl. Midwinter has kept secret the circumstances of his birth from Allan, and he has begun to acquire new faith from his recognition that Allan's dream was not so much fatalistic as it was ominous, a warning sent to protect Allan from conspiracy. A new dawn is breaking, but it is still far off.

Even if this plot summary manages to provide some idea of the wildly agitated state of nature and society which Collins envisions, it can in no way do justice to the extent to which Collins has openly declared war on what Chorley calls "the cant of conventionalism."

First of all, in the view of Chorley, the *Athenaeum* critic (who admitted that the story was "powerful"), the novel is based on the lives of "vermin," most particularly Miss Gwilt, "one of the most hardened female villains whose devices and desires have ever blackened fiction." Worse, this "horror" is displayed "without a suggestion towards its cure."

Collins of course had anticipated this sort of response. In his prefatory note to the book version, he had written:

> Readers in particular will, I have some reason to suppose, be here and there disturbed, perhaps even offended, by finding that "Armadale" oversteps, in more than one direction, the narrow limits within which they are disposed to restrict the development of modern fiction—if they can.
>
> Nothing that I could say to these persons here would help me with them as Time will help me if my work lasts. I am

not afraid of my design being permanently misunderstood, provided the execution has done it any sort of justice. Estimated by the clap-trap morality of the present day, this may be a very daring book. Judged by the Christian morality which is of all time, it is only a book that is daring enough to speak the truth.

Significantly, Collins's targets have broadened since *The Woman in White* (which also included an explanatory Preface). There the "Law" and its susceptibility to corruption was the stated issue. In *Armadale* the attack moves "in more than one direction." The belligerently combative tone of the Preface is matched by the text itself in the breadth and depth of its antagonism to respectability. All levels of society, from hardened criminals to average businessmen, are presented with a jaundiced eye: the mad-doctor of the private sanitarium is a former abortionist; a butcher at Thorpe Ambrose thinks Midwinter is insane because he is soft-hearted enough to feed a stray dog.

Victorian architecture, and its cultural implications, fare no better. The mansion at Thorpe Ambrose "presented the spectacle of a modern manufactory trying to look like an ancient temple." (One today hears the Prince of Wales decrying the London architects of the late twentieth century in comparable terms.) The description of a rising housing development where the sanitarium is located underlines the sense of waste and death, echoing Braddon's descriptions of suburban blight:

Fairweather Vale proved to be a new neighbourhood, situated below the high ground of Hampstead [this would be Camden Town today], on the southern side. The day was overcast, and the place looked very dreary. We approached it by a new road running between trees, which might once have been the park avenue of a country house. At the end we came upon a wilderness of open ground, with half-finished villas dotted about, and a hideous litter of boards, wheelbarrows, and building materials of all sorts scattered in every direction. At one corner of this scene of desolation stood a great overgrown dismal house, plastered with drab-coloured stucco, and surrounded by a naked, unfinished garden, without a shrub or flower in it, frightful to behold.

The text of the novel is full of small, ironically subversive details: the wrong side of the tracks in Thorpe Ambrose, where Gwilt moves after being put out of the Milroy home, is called "Paradise Place"; and she tidies up the final arrangements for her marriage conspiracy from "All Saints Terrace" in London.

A group of women who visit the sanitarium provides Collins with the opportunity for a frontal attack on domesticity: "In the miserable monotony of the lives led by a large section of the middle classes of England, anything is welcome to the women which offers them any sort of harmless refuge from the established tyranny of the principle that all human happiness begins and ends at home."

The central theme here is obvious enough. The most interesting aspect of it is the way in which Collins supports this cynical outlook with newspaper-based "realism," and the manner in which this material is then expanded to add new anthropological dimensions to the novel.

In his "Appendix" to *Armadale,* Collins insists on the verisimilitude of various occurrences in the novel on the basis of specific newspaper accounts. In the novel itself, Allan's lawyer, Mr. Pedgift, holds forth on the criminality of the times and the leniency of the courts in dealing with it. He warns Allan: "Read your newspapers, Mr. Armadale, and you'll find we live in piping times for the black sheep of the community—if they are only black enough." Miss Gwilt gets her inspiration for eliminating Allan from a newspaper court report—the same kind of source which inspired the plan used to do away with a man to whom she was married some years before. When it is revealed that Miss Gwilt had been tried and convicted of murdering that husband and then had been pardoned, it is the role of the newspapers in that case which is emphasized, and this emphasis serves to mock both the Victorian legal establishment and the gullible public.

It also happens that these latter circumstances—as I have indicated earlier—are based on one of the most intensely reported cases in Bell Macdonald's clippings. This is the trial of Dr. Thomas Smethurst for the murder of his wife. Here also a conviction was overturned when the press seized on conflicting medical evidence. One of Bell Macdonald's clippings states the case succinctly:

> Dr. Smethurst, after his trial at the Old Bailey, is being tried a second time by the Press. By that great jury he has been acquitted. It is interesting to mark the progress of this new investigation. When, originally, we repudiated the verdict, it was amid a general confusion of opinion, the public hesitating to protest against the issue of a legal scrutiny so solemn, formal, and deliberate. Within forty-eight hours a great change had taken place. The *Times* became dubious and apologetic; our other daily contemporaries, with a single exception, agreed that the sentence must be reconsidered. . . . But the crowning fact is, that neither by the legal nor by the medical press has the conviction of Dr. Smethurst been regarded as satisfactory.

The resemblance of Miss Gwilt's trial to Dr. Smethurst's is underlined when the reader of *Armadale* is told that, after Gwilt's pardon, a "general impression prevailed directly that she was not quite innocent enough, after all, to be let out of prison then and there!" The solution was to "punish her a little." Gwilt was, therefore, sentenced to two years for burglary, convicted of carrying away some of her deceased husband's family jewels. In Smethurst's case, the reprieved doctor was later convicted and jailed for bigamy.

Collins is also probing in this book for new psychological insights. We see this most clearly in the relationships of the three main characters. Allan and Midwinter represent a metaphorical exploration of the split personality; while Miss Gwilt, in her relationships with the two men and with society in general, represents the furthest development in Sensation fiction of the disturbing admixture of Good and Evil in one woman, the angel-as-tigress.

Allan and Midwinter are blood-related, have the same name, and their fates are inextricably entwined by the prophecy. Beyond this, all resemblance ends. Allan is fair, large, handsome, and uncomplicated. He is also often stupid. Midwinter, on the other hand, is exotic and possesses an intricate intelligence. While Allan comes from the best English stock, we know that Midwinter is the issue of a colonial murderer and a mulatto. Mr. Brock, the rector of Allan's mother's parish, meets Midwinter—admittedly, when the long-suffering Ozias is barely recovered from "brain fever"—and his "healthy Anglo-Saxon flesh crept responsively at every movement of the usher's supple brown fingers, and every passing distortion of the usher's haggard, yellow face."

The dramatic irony is that Midwinter's ultimate role is to protect the Anglo-Saxon Allan. Collins plays with this racial ambivalence in a number of ways. First of all, Midwinter seems to embody both the alienated Romantic hero and the noble savage. When Allan shows him kindness, Midwinter's reaction recalls Frankenstein's monster: "He showed a horrible sincerity of astonishment at having been treated with common Christian kindness in a Christian land." Midwinter says to Brock, "I beg your pardon, Sir . . . I have been used to be hunted, and cheated, and starved. Everything else comes strange to me."

It is easy to acknowledge the debt of these passages to works like *Frankenstein* and the Romantic movement in general. But what is remarkable in *Armadale* is that Midwinter's heroism does not derive from some simple primitive performance of physical and sensual superiority, but comes from a paradoxically more complex and advanced level of awareness. In the last passage cited, Midwinter understands fully the ambiguity of his position, not certain whether he is "vagabond man" or "vagabond animal." When he does save Allan, it is through equal parts of intelligence, coincidence, and his curious sensual prescience. It is, in fact, impossible to resist the implication that Midwinter represents not only progressive reason but the subconscious, sensual side of the dual human metaphor he forms with Allan. Midwinter prevails as a figure in this story because he represents a racial mixture of light and dark, but also an instinctual mixture of rational and irrational.

The assignation to Midwinter of these various "mixtures" is in fact a tipoff that the uneasy alliance of social science and religion in Victorian orthodoxy will once again be shaken up. As Lady Audley's split personality undermined notions of femininity and respectability, so Midwinter plays a peculiarly metaphysical role in the events of *Armadale*. This is seen, for example, when a doctor on the Isle of Man attempts to impose a "rational theory" on Allan's dream of the wreck. His interpretation is representative of the prevailing belief in Associationism. Everything in the dream is a duplication of an image lingering in Allan's memory from the preceding day. As Robert MacLeod, an historian of psychology, put it in 1975, this sort of mechanistic analysis was typical of the empiricist school which wanted not uncertainty but a guide for human conduct and therefore insisted "that mind can be reduced to its elements and thereby explained." Midwinter, however, is operating on a different wavelength; is not convinced; and it is his skepticism which saves the credulous Allan's very English body, if not his soul.

Midwinter's prescient skepticism therefore undermines a basic principle of nineteenth-century Christianity. Dean Mansel, one of the principal antagonists of Sensation, for example, had argued in his best-known work, *The Limits of Religious Thought Examined* (1858), that the essences of God and of "absolute morality" are beyond the reach of human knowledge. As a consequence, the citizenry had better do only as it was told. Midwinter—although hardly rebellious—finds it impossible to lead an unquestioning or complacent life. This quality of character is clarified in a letter Reverend Brock writes to Midwinter when he is about to leave Thorpe Ambrose to marry Miss Gwilt. Brock is convinced that Midwinter has decided to remove himself from Allan to protect his friend from the destiny foreshadowed by the prophecy and the dream: "The one object which I have it at heart to attain is to induce you to free yourself from the paralyzing fatalism of the heathen and the savage, and to look at the mysteries that perplex, and the portents that daunt you, from the Christian's point of view." In short, the dark-skinned stranger should find freedom by giving up freedom—i.e., any responsibility or responsiveness to his feelings or instincts. If Midwinter is not able to see things from this submissive Christian point of view and persists in the "fatalistic" one, Brock warns that such a belief will end "in the darkness in which you are now lost; in the self-contradictions in which you are now bewildered; in the stubborn despair by which a man profanes his own soul, and lowers himself to the level of the brutes that perish." Brock counsels, instead, a faith that "God is all-merciful, God is all-wise: natural or supernatural, it happens through Him."

These spiritual reflections become curiously mixed up with

more fleshly matters, almost from the first plot entanglement. Brock, when he counsels Midwinter, knows nothing of Gwilt; but, to Midwinter (and, of course, the reader), the "darkness" and "self-contradictions" of which Brock speaks cannot but help suggest Gwilt and her rampant sexuality, not to mention the equally seductive orderliness of the "fatality" of prophecy and dream. What is "heathen" is related equally to the "supernatural" and the "animal," or "brute," and all of these seem inextricably tied up with the libidinal aura surrounding Miss Gwilt. Unfortunately, it would be stretching the point to assert that Collins had resolved these elements into some clearly developed theme. Like most of the better Sensation novelists, he was attempting, as he says in his Preface, to transcend traditional restrictions on fiction writing. In so doing, he seems here to have run into deep water. Yet the attempt is remarkable. In his treatment of Midwinter and the dream of the wreck, Collins has managed to satirize the mechanistic thought of the pre-psychoanalytical establishment; he has put into negative light a questionable religious position remarkably similar to that of Dean Mansel; and he has suggested an intricate reversal of conventional notions of race and appearance.

It is in the person of Miss Gwilt that we see Collins most coherently struggling with these motifs. An 1866 review in *The Spectator* states that *Armadale* is successful in "overstepping the limits of decency, and revolting every human sentiment." It is Gwilt who is primarily responsible for this judgment, according to the reviewer. *Armadale* has "for its heroine a woman fouler than the refuse of the streets, who has lived to the ripe age of 35, and through the horrors of forgery, murder, theft, bigamy, gaol and attempted suicide, without any trace being left on her beauty." Gwilt subverts religious faith as well as most of the social and psychological conventions of contemporary literary criticism.

The details of Gwilt's early life demonstrate that she is a victim of an indifferent, corrupt, and often hypocritical social system. Her first memories are of a foster home where she was beaten and starved. Sold by her foster parents to Mrs. Oldershaw, she was used to advertise hair oil in a traveling medicine show. The Blanchards treated her as a "new plaything" until the unpleasant events in Madeira took place. She was then shipped to a school in France, where a middle-aged schoolmaster, who showed an exceptional interest in her (presumably sexual), went mad and attempted to blow his brains out. She came under the spell of a fanatic priest and entered a convent school, where she was discriminated against because of her good looks. Considered by the priest to be possessed by the devil, she was ultimately dismissed. She came under the influence of a baroness, who used her as a lure in a card game. A wealthy Englishman, who caught on to the cheating in the game, offered her the alternative of giving herself to him or being turned over to the police. This is the man she married and whom she was later accused of murdering. It is not a lovely story, and it is considerably less attractive in the thoroughly detailed private investigator's report, which is the form in which her story appears in the novel. As the cynical detective comments at one point: "Everything was right, everything was smooth on the surface. Everything was rotten and everything was wrong under it."

Nor did Gwilt's looks help her with the reviewers of *Armadale*. As with Lady Audley, who was attacked for her blonde ringlets and voluptuous tastes, Gwilt's sensuality is quite explicit in the novel. She has "superbly, luxuriant" red hair, the "unpardonably remarkable shade of colour which the prejudice of the Northern nations never entirely forgives." She possesses a high, sloping forehead, straight nose, lips which are "full, rich, and Sensual"; her skin is "softly white," and is "delicately bright in its rosier tints"; her chin is round, dimpled, and unblemished. Most often referred to is her striking "figure."

It is not only Gwilt's physical characteristics which defy conventional morality. Within the quasi-epistolary structure of the novel we are most directly confronted with Miss Gwilt through her diary, by her own words rather than those of others. As *The Spectator* reviewer put it, Gwilt's story "is frankly told in a diary which, but for its unreality, would be simply loathsome. . . ." One remembers Mrs. Robinson's real-life diary being denounced in almost identical language. In any case, Gwilt steadfastly refuses to conform to either the conventional image of the passive, frail female or that of wild-eyed she-wolf. Miss Gwilt is coolly ironic and sure of herself. Here is a typical entry:

I shall write no more today. If so lady-like a person as I am could feel tigerish tingling all over her to the very tips of her fingers, I should suspect myself of being in that condition at the present moment. But, with *my* manners and accomplishments, the thing is, of course, out of the question. We all know that a lady has no passions.

And this comes from a woman whose passions—besides sex and murder—are for Beethoven and laudanum (the alcohol-and-opium drug to which Collins himself was addicted). Gwilt, as we can see, doesn't exactly fit in.

At the climax of the novel, in the tradition of Lady Audley, Gwilt is in her own unique way both culprit and victim. She is obviously guilty of crime and conspiracy but, as a witty and perceptive human being, her villainy is mitigated. Hemmed in between her own evil and that of society, she destroys herself, and her end is a kind of tragedy although, unlike Lady Audley, she is able to control destiny, however impetuous and masochistic is her final act. There is no question that she is one of those of God's children whom the "clap-trap morality" cannot abide. Her essential humanity is therefore highlighted by contrast to the respectable world and the reader cannot help but feel a sense of lost promise.

Gwilt's end is made all the more unhappy when it is juxtaposed in the conclusion of the novel with the continuing career of Mrs. Oldershaw, recounted by the lawyer, Pedgift. He describes a performance at a theater during a visit to London. It is a kind of prayer meeting billed as "Sunday Evening Discourses on the Pomp and Vanities of the World by a Sinner Who Has Served Them." Giving a "fashionable tip" of half a crown into a well-filled plate, Pedgift discovers Mother Oldershaw on the stage:

You never listened to anything more eloquent in your life. As long as I heard her she was never once at a loss for a word anywhere. I shall think less of oratory as a human accomplishment, for the rest of my days, after that Sunday evening. As for the matter of the sermon, I may describe it as a narrative of Mrs. Oldershaw's experience among dilapidated women, profusely illustrated in the pious and penitential style. You will ask what sort of audience it was. Principally women—

and, as I hope to be saved, all the old harridans of the world of fashion whom Mother Oldershaw had enamelled in her time, sitting boldly in the front places, with their cheeks ruddled with paint, in a state of devout enjoyment wonderful to see!

The image is at once brilliant and depressing. Christianity and cosmetics are confused. Materialism and cant lie at the heart of both religious faith and scientific progress in the mid-nineteenth century. Beneath surface respectability is rotten essence. As Pedgift's son remarks on the continued ascendancy of Dr. Downward, the abortionist, conspirator, and fraudulent "psychiatrist": "We live . . . in an age favourable to the growth of all roguery which is careful enough to keep up appearances. In this enlightened nineteenth century, I look upon the doctor as one of our rising men."

16

❖

"Green Tea": A Forerunner of
Dr. Jekyll and Mr. Hyde

In her Introduction to a 1947 reprint of J. S. LeFanu's 1864 novel, *Uncle Silas,* Elizabeth Bowen refers to that story as "not the last, belated Gothic romance, but the first (or among the first) of the psychological thrillers." And indeed it is convenient for us to follow Bowen's lead here by seeing LeFanu's fiction in the 1860s as exemplifying a progress from the older form of thriller to the newer Sensation genre (in this sense parallel to the evolution of the newspaper reports from *The Newgate Calendar*) and, ultimately, to a striking symbolic anticipation of the modern consciousness. In *The House by the Churchyard* (1863) the traditional historical romance is informed by the contemporary criminal aspect and subversive point of view. *Uncle Silas* (1864) refines and intensifies these qualities. "Green Tea" (1869) manages to create a situation that moves beyond the merely cynical and/or shock-oriented symbolism—which predominates in the split figures of Lady Audley or Lydia Gwilt—and advances into a shadowy domain where spiritual and emotional and instinctual matters constantly eddy about, overlapping each other.

Although "Green Tea" is a longish short story, it is easy enough to summarize. Ostensibly extracted from letters written by Dr. Martin Hesselius, a German physician, to an English physician-disciple who had once acted as his medical secretary, it tells of the breakdown and ultimate suicide of an English clergyman named Jennings. Jennings, wealthy and genteel, is introduced to Hesselius as a normally jolly man whose "health fails him" whenever he goes to his vicarage in Warwickshire. Recognizing Hesselius as the author of a book he has admired (the power of the Word again!), the vicar consults him about the problem.

Jennings had embarked four years before on a study of the "religious metaphysics of the ancients." Because of his habit of writing late into the night, he had to drink large quantities of green tea to keep alert. Returning one night from research among some "odd old books," the apparition of a red-eyed monkey manifested itself to him while he was riding in an omnibus. Since then, the beast has periodically appeared, interfering with Jennings's clerical duties and speaking to him, "urging" him to "crimes." The good reverend fears that, under the beast's influence, he will injure himself or others. Hesselius reassures the frightened cleric and takes a room for the night at a nearby inn to devote himself to finding a "cure" for this alien vision. Unfortunately, he has informed no one of his whereabouts, and when he returns to his lodgings the next day, he finds an urgent message from Jennings's servant. Arriving at the clergyman's house, he finds that the master has already slit his own throat.

As I have suggested, "Green Tea" lends itself to fairly obvious psychoanalytical interpretation. Any informed reader in the second half of the twentieth century will find it difficult to avoid the inference that Jennings, who is tall and thin, middle-aged, and "dresses with a natty old-fashioned, high-church precision," is in appearance an example of a dominant and regulatory superego; or that the monkey which he finds himself in conflict with represents his id, or, more generally, his suppressed passions. That the monkey clashes dramatically with Jennings's "slight, timid, kindly, but reserved" exterior, and that its "satanic captivity" of this otherwise reasonable man leads to his destruction, enhances, of course, the thrilling effects of the story as entertainment.

However, as in Stevenson's *Dr. Jekyll and Mr. Hyde* (which was an immediate success when published in 1886), the singular "cultural" context in which the characters exist, and what I interpret as a doubly ironic conclusion, combine to develop the subversive Sensation themes to their most concentrated form, and to promise most clearly the new areas of experimentation in fiction, not to mention the social sciences, which were to follow. The Dr. Hesselius of the story is concerned with the metaphysical rather than the biological aspects of disease. He calls himself a "medical philosopher" and has written a book called *Essays on Metaphysical Medicine*. His basic philosophical position suggests not only a rejection of established medical practice but a development of the embattled heroine's reflections in the last lines of *Uncle Silas:* "I may remark, that when I here speak of medical science, I do so, as I hope some day to see it more generally understood, in a much more comprehensive sense than its generally material treatment would warrant. I believe the entire natural world is but the ultimate expression of that spiritual world from which, and in which alone, it has its life."

Hesselius's position in the same line corresponds rather closely to the books by Swedenborg which he finds Jennings has been reading. There he discovers that "external vision exists from interior vision," that there are "with man at least two evil spirits" which, "when seen by other eyes than those of their infernal associates," present themselves, by "correspondence," in the shape of the "beast (feral) which represents their particular lust and life, in aspect dire and atrocious." We are reminded of the opposition such a theory presents to the sequence of inadequate medical opinions we have encountered in both newspapers and novels. Jennings tells Hesselius of a Dr. Harley, "one of the very greatest fools" he had ever met, "a *mere* materialist," who seems "one half, blind—I mean one half of all he looks at is dark—preternaturally bright and vivid all the rest; and the worst of it is, it seems *wilful*. . . . I've had some experience of him as a physician, but I look on him as, in that sense, no better than a paralytic mind, an intellect half-dead." Harley's name—that of the street which is the address of the most eminent and fashionable doctors in London—gives away his allegorical function, signifying the reluctance of his moribund profession to cope with the dark reaches of the mind. Jennings's feelings and instincts have been neglected by the medical establishment under the cover of empirical science and in the service of a materialistic ideology determined to exclude human passion. And, of course, we are also reminded here of the ineptitude of the medical establishment in the Palmer case, and, in a deeper sense, of the intellectual incompetence of the doctor in *Armadale* who attempts to imprison Allan's dream in a strait-jacket of literal-mindedness.

In any case, *Lady Audley's Secret, Armadale,* and "Green Tea" function—with varying degrees of covertness—not only as thrillers but as attacks on a cast (I use the metaphor calculatedly) of mind peculiarly powerful in Victorian culture. As I have demonstrated, the most obvious issues addressed in this criminal context were the most elemental human concerns: sex and femininity, religion and science, and so forth. These "problems" were of a sort which also attracted the ire of the most hidebound and traditionally ori-ented critics: those with vested interests in long-established prin-ciples, such as Mansel, the Dean of St. Paul's. It is important at this stage to remember, however, that the cultural conflicts brought to the surface by published accounts of crime are not always so easily explicable as is H. L. Mansel's straightforward assault on irreverent insubordination. I am thinking now of course of the more intellectually ambitious critical reviews we have al-ready encountered; but what comes most dramatically to mind, in the wake of LeFanu's satirical treatment of the Harleys (and Harley Streets) of the world, is an authoritative—and most highly fanci-ful—*History of Civilization in England* by Henry Thomas Buckle, first published in 1857.

One of the first subjects Buckle tackles in his massive work is morality and crime. He asserts that the "actions of men are by an easy and obvious division separated into two classes, the virtuous and the vicious; and as these classes are correlative, and when put together compose the total of our moral conduct, it follows that whatever increases the one, will in relative point of view diminish the other." Buckle's position here not only implies a considerable complacency but also demonstrates a powerful reliance on the reducibility of human behavior to oversimplified mathematical for-mulae. Dealing specifically with murder, these qualities are even more apparent:

> Of all offences, it might well be supposed that the crime of murder is one of the most arbitrary and irregular. For when we consider that this, though generally the crowning act of a long career of vice, is often the immediate result of what

seems a sudden impulse; that when premeditated, its com-
mittal, even with the least chance of impunity, requires a rare
combination of favourable circumstances for which the criminal will frequently wait; that he has thus to bide his time,
and look for opportunities he cannot control; that when the
time has come, his heart may fail him; that the question
whether or not he shall commit the crime may depend on a
balance of conflicting motives, such as fear of the law, a dread
of penalties held out by religion, the prickings of his own
conscience, the apprehension of future remorse, the love of
gain, jealousy, revenge, desperation;—when we put all these
things together, there arises such a complication of causes,
that we might reasonably despair of detecting any order or
method in the result of those subtle and shifting agencies by
which murder is either caused or prevented. But now, how
stands the fact? The fact is, that murder is committed with as
much regularity, and bears as uniform a relation to certain
known circumstances, as do the movements of the tides, and
the rotations of the seasons.

One recalls here the newspaper editorialist in 1824 who defended
the reportage of the Thurtell murder case by asserting that murder
was largely a foreign occupation—"Not British," as Podsnap might
say. But Buckle is at once even more aggressively single-minded
and "scientific." He is happy to skim, rather than plumb, the un-
fathomable depths of suicide as well. This "law of uniform and
periodical repetitions," Buckle goes on to explain, "will appear
strange to those who believe that human actions depend more on
the peculiarities of each individual than on the general state of
society." Suicide, he points out, is "more clearly the product of
his (the self-murderer's) own volition than any other offence could
possibly be." Yet, of this most "capricious and uncontrollable" of
crimes, Buckle concludes that "the individual felon only carries
into effect what is a necessary consequence of preceding circumstances. In a given state of society, a certain number of persons
must put an end to their own lives."

This sort of thinking can be simply dismissed as representative
of utilitarian or Malthusian early-nineteenth-century schools of
thought, of which there are more noteworthy examples than

Buckle. But what we must try to comprehend here is the fact that both Carlyle—in the thirties and forties—and Dickens—particularly in *Hard Times* in 1854—had already quite effectively railed against the inhumane implications of such cramped reasoning. Carlyle and Dickens had quite explicitly advocated the primacy of subjectivity and imagination in the human mind. Still the fact is that Buckle's reduction of history to a set of fixed environmental laws had come in the late fifties to represent mainstream Victorian intellectual progress (*The History of Civilization* was popular and influential). Moreover, Buckle's early emphasis on the double issue of murder and suicide very strongly suggests not only the persistence of the ideology of displacement and denial in the face of unacceptable passionate acts but the preoccupation of the mid-Victorians in general with crime (and the literature of crime) as significant omens of cultural breakdown. In any case, one thing seems certain: Buckle's cast of mind is precisely that to which LeFanu in "Green Tea" opposes the terrors of the unexamined psyche.

Buckle is not unaware of potential opposition, allowing that "the cultivators of physical science" find themselves constantly opposed by the "moralists, the theologians, and the metaphysicians" who find in science "an undue confidence in the resources of human understanding." His proposal, then, to "mediate between these two parties and reconcile their hostile pretensions," is clearly biased. LeFanu's story, however, while no less ambitious in scope, does present a viable alternative to the two irreconcilable positions. Conventional "moralists, theologians, and metaphysicians" offer no more sense of salvation to the tormented Jennings than does the mechanistic universe for which Buckle argues. The visionary "malignant" monkey of "Green Tea" is at once fearsome and offers a metaphor for nineteenth-century man. Jennings complains: "The thing exhibited an atrocious determination to thwart me. It was with me in church—in the reading desk—in the pulpit—within the communion rails. At last, it reached the extremity, that while I was reading to the congregation, it would spring upon the book and squat there, so that I was unable to see the page. This happened more than once." Religious dogma is thus thwarted, while the laws of science are inadequate. Through the image of the leering monkey, LeFanu suggests that there is another element, the animalistic subconscious, which conventional thinkers of the age have managed to overlook or simply deny.

That Jennings dies, and that Hesselius complacently asserts that he has not lost the patient but has merely run out of time in searching for some materialistic prescription of his own, is but a more bitterly ironic commentary on the refusal of man to acknowledge his subconscious and his indeterminate state in a chaotic universe. Perhaps Hesselius's final attribution of Jennings's "case" to a "complication" of "hereditary suicidal mania" is an even more subtle commentary on the libidinal inheritance of man. Ultimately, the aftertaste of "Green Tea" is bitter, and one gets the sense that the author might have expected better than he got in his lonely waning years from nineteenth-century scientific progress.

In any case, Buckle's predisposition to intellectual rigidity, his relying on strict, unchanging laws to prescribe human behavior, recalls a much better known Victorian prose work which also, so far as I am aware, has not been heretofore related to the nineteenth-century controversy over sensational writing. This is Matthew Arnold's essay of 1864, *The Function of Criticism at the Present Time*. In this work, Arnold directly confronts the Philistine tendency of the English to distrust ideas and resort to "immediate political and practical applications" of any ideas they cannot manage to avoid. This tendency of course leads to an overreliance on simplistic or legalistic solutions, like Buckle's, a weakness which Arnold feels can only be overcome by "disinterestedness" or "the free play of the mind." Arnold finds among the chief offenders against open-mindedness some of the journals we have encountered in our survey of criticism of the Sensation novel. The *Edinburgh Review* is Whig; the *Quarterly Review* is Tory; *The Times* is for the "common, satisfied, well-to-do Englishman." *Blackwood's* is the organ of the Scots Tories, noted for "narrow . . . conservatism" and "uncompromising Tory righteousness and . . . old-fashioned dress"; the *North British Review* aimed to be "both Liberal in politics and Christian in tone" but opted for the latter in 1857 when an editor who questioned the "verbal infallibility of Scripture" was forced to resign. Each of these organs, according to Arnold, is limited to only as much free play of the mind as the definition of its constituency allows.

Arnold's key phrases here—"Philistine," "disinterestedness," and "free play of the mind"—still resonate in Victorian Studies lectures; what seems to have been forgotten is the significance of the source which Arnold used for what I take to be the most striking passage in the essay. In this section, Arnold comments on recent remarks of two Philistine public figures, John Roebuck and Sir Charles Adderley. Roebuck (1801–1879) was a radical reformer, and Adderley (1814–1905) a conservative politician. In speeches made to groups of industrial and agricultural workers, these men of conflicting political viewpoints had each displayed what Arnold calls an "exuberant self-satisfaction" about the "state of England." Adderley had described the Anglo-Saxon race as "superior to all the world," while Roebuck extolled the "unrivalled happiness" and "perfect security" of England. In opposition to those complacent statements, Arnold reproduces a newspaper item which he feels will effectively undermine them: "A shocking child murder has just been committed at Nottingham. A girl named Wragg left the workhouse there on Saturday morning with her illegitimate child. The child was soon afterwards found dead on Mapperley Hills, having been strangled. Wragg is in custody." Arnold then masterfully summons up the meaningful reverberations of this police report in the 1860s:

Nothing but that, but, in juxtaposition with the absolute eulogies of Sir Charles Adderley and Mr. Roebuck, how eloquent, how suggestive are those few lines! . . . And "our unrivalled happiness";—what an element of grimness, bareness, and hideousness mixes with it and blurs it; the workhouse, the dismal Mapperley Hills,—how dismal those who have seen them will remember;—the gloom, the smoke, the cold, the strangled illegitimate child! . . . And the final touch,—short, bleak, and unhuman: *Wragg is in custody.* The sex lost in the confusion of our unrivalled happiness; or (shall I say?) the superfluous Christian name lopped off by the straightforward vigour of our old Anglo-Saxon breed! There is profit for the spirit in such contrasts as this. . . . Mr. Roebuck will have a poor opinion of an adversary who replies to his defiant songs of triumph only by murmuring under his breath, *Wragg is in custody*; but in no other way will these songs of triumph be induced gradually to moderate themselves, to get rid of what in them is excessive and offensive, and to fall into a safer and truer key.

The point here is that Wragg's story, as Arnold realized (and as we do now, having surveyed Bell Macdonald's clippings), was hardly exceptional; only the grim appropriateness of her surname lends the paragraph singularity. It is a murder story, a nasty police report; and, while posterity has managed to remember *The Function of Criticism* as a seminal essay opposing the complacency of the Philistines in Victorian England, we seem to have missed the relevance of the newspaper police reports from which Arnold derived much of his critical energy. News reportage of crime— we see again—managed to provoke inspired litanies of protest from other columnists, prominent novelists, and critics alike. These protests in turn invoked counterprotests from orthodoxy, which brought even wider attention to the issue.

And the discussion of the dynamic interaction of protest and counterprotest raises a crucial question in social history. Does the mass invasion of crime into the Victorian consciousness represent the "trickle-down" or "trickle-up" effect? That is, were these concerns initiated from above, from the High Culture, to then somehow proliferate in the Low Culture of mystery stories and popular newspapers? Or did Fleet Street and Grub Street infest the lofty minds of their betters with tales of sex and gore? I suspect it was a bit of both. There is no clear line which can be drawn. What we do know is that the greater availability (in terms of cost and distribution) of the papers was new after the 1840s, and also that there was no definable genre of best-selling realistic crime fiction before 1860. At the same time we must recognize that not only newsmen and thriller writers were able to display in their works a fascination with criminal life and the bestial implications of sexuality. It is easy to make up a virtual All-Star team of eminent nineteenth-century literary names who wrote about crime and crimes of passion: De Quincy, Hazlitt, Browning, Ruskin, and Hardy—to name but a few. So we have to assume there was a back-and-forth process taking place, not a simple ascent or descent. But the technological and social conditions which changed the newspapers did profoundly intensify and illuminate the interaction of Sensation and respectability.

But *then* what happened? Why do we remember the Victorian age in simplistic, black-and-white terms? Why was it passed down to us this way? Perhaps these questions can never be fully answered, but one thing does seem certain: the "shock of the new" which the newspapers and novels represented in the fifties and sixties was somehow dulled and fragmented—how I do not know—but it did not vanish. Instead, we find the various subversive components of early police reports and mystery fiction miraculously reappearing as integral parts of the works we most closely identify with the transition to modernism: not only in *Our Mutual Friend* and *Dr. Jekyll and Mr. Hyde,* but in *The Picture of Dorian Gray, Heart of Darkness,* and—of course—various studies by Sigmund Freud. Moreover, it should be noted here, the raw formlessness of the printed trial testimony—like today's rough and shocking videotapes of confessions and trials—had to contribute to an undermining of faith in a complacent social vision, and also to a breaking away from prescribed artistic form. In any case, the nineteenth-century culture was riddled with what was then called "Sensation." One only has to look for it. It seems to have been on everyone's mind.

17

❖

A "Mysterious Something Between Sensation and Thought"

In my analysis and interpretation of literary artifacts of the mid-nineteenth century I have somewhat lost touch with the narrative of my own late-twentieth-century essays in scholarly detection. Therefore I would like to recapitulate a bit before moving forward. I began this project looking to substantiate a very preliminary hypothesis that the best-selling but critically savaged Sensation novels of the 1860s constituted a significant attack on the Victorian official consciousness. While I found the prudish complacency of orthodox respectability general—as epitomized in such writings as the Preface to an 1860 edition of Addison and Steele's *The Spectator,* where the anonymous editor deplores the "raging profligacy" of the Restoration while asserting, of his own age, that "English Literature is now pure"—I also encountered an at least equally powerful spirit of dissent and discontent. These latter sentiments were manifested in crime novels but even more blatantly in newspaper crime reportage, a medium which had grown enormously in quality and quantity after the early 1850s. The Sensation novels which followed these changes in journalism then seemed to have incorporated the domestic realism, immediacy, and iconoclastic drift of the papers in such a manner as to persuade contemporaries that, first, the authors had set off in a new (for the nineteenth century) artistic direction and, second, that the path they were following was mined with the potential for tainting a supposedly "progressive" society with immorality and instability.

When I went on to probe beneath these surface manifestations of significant social subversion, I found deeper, more complex intellectual currents exposed. By reviewing police reports and crime novels I found that I was able to illuminate political, social, and metaphysical components of the Victorian *Zeitgeist* from an angle of vision which had not before been undertaken in any coherent or comprehensive way.

In the course of this endeavor, I read mid-nineteenth-century novels, criticism, and newspapers. I was lucky enough to benefit from the largesse and vision of a senior adviser, Gordon N. Ray, particularly in his discovery of a lost archive of newspaper court reports. I was able to visit the British Museum Library and the Museum's newspaper branch in Colindale and begin to acquire a larger vision of the significant cohesions of all this criminal material. I was fortunate to meet another older and wiser man, Alan Macdonald—great-grandson of the collector who had put together the lost archive between 1839 and 1862 in the first place—who at his houses in Scotland and in France likewise provided me with counsel and access to materials I would not otherwise have come upon.

So far, the story tracks quite neatly. What I have not yet sufficiently accounted for here are the kinds of piecemeal evidence which accumulate more or less randomly to anyone who has invested himself in a long-term research project and remains—even when relatively inactive or uninspired—on the job, vigilant.

For example, a relatively conventional "academic" exercise ultimately led me down one of the more curious, and rewarding, avenues of my bookish travels, providing me with a kind of anchor, a central meaning to which all (or most) speculative readings might be attached. This came in the course of pursuing the etymology of the word "sensation" in the sense in which it was applied to the criminal materials at hand.

The *Oxford English Dictionary* attributes to W. M. Thackeray the first use of the term "sensation" in reference to "a particular literary or dramatic phenomenon." Following this lead I found that the term had appeared in the author's own *Cornhill Magazine,* in September 1861. There Thackeray describes fishing for a subject for one of his "Roundabout" essays with "that ocean *The Times* newspaper" spread before him. The first topic which comes to his attention is the infamous "Northumberland street encounter which all the papers have narrated." In this incident, a Londoner went to a moneylender in the heart of the West End at midday. To his surprise, the "agent" emerged from the back room with two ivory-handled pistols and blew part of his head off. The theaters have a new name for such scenes, says Thackeray: "Sensation Dramas." After such an occurrence, quite near the Adelphi, he asks, "what is the use of being squeamish about probabilities and possibilities in the writing of fiction?" Indeed, even a street preacher would find a sermon on Northumberland Street's implications to be "too dark" to use.

Reading such lines from Thackeray himself was worth the visit to the library, enlarging, as it did, my sense of the pervasiveness of the controversy over newspaper crime and Thackeray's profound understanding of the message such stories sent to the Evangelical crowd. But I was more interested by this time in etymology and I knew that Thackeray could not have exactly coined the term since he was treating it here as if it were already in general use. Looking further in my reading, I consulted Kathleen Tillotson's Introduction to a 1969 edition of *The Woman in White,* "The Lighter Reading of the Eighteen-Sixties." There Tillotson claims that the first specific allusion to Sensation novels can be found in *The Sixpenny Magazine,* in the same month as Thackeray's "Roundabout Paper," in an article on Braddon, Collins, and Dickens. However, Tillotson allows, the term "in its popular sense . . . first appeared in news reports and headlines." This had already been amply illustrated to me in Bell Macdonald's clippings. One memorable case (which I have not yet cited in this study) came to mind. It seemed then—and still does—particularly relevant. This was an 1861 case of "the cruel treatment of a child by a schoolmistress," in which the child's testimony that the teacher had forced her to eat human excrement "caused considerable sensation in the court." This memory led me back, in any case, to the *OED,* to look up a variant meaning of the word—"a strong impression (e.g. of horror, admiration, surprise) produced in an audience or body of spectators, and manifested by their demeanour." I found examples of the usage cited as far back as 1779. They included Dickens in *Pickwick Papers* in 1837 ("a slight sensation was perceptible in the body of the court"). Then I recalled that Macdonald had also clipped an editorial which commented on the significance of the 1861 excrement-eating case. There (I had a copy in my notebook) the word is used in another, even older form: to communicate simply "perception by means of the senses." The schoolmistress struck the student, we are told, "with a stick over the head and shoulders; she whipped her until her limbs were blackened; she cut her with a cane to the very blood; she half-scalped her with a sharp stick; then weary of the rod she employed a poker or a shovel, and then, to enjoy a new sensation, she submitted the young girl to indescribably bestial insults."

I realized after mulling these definitions over that what I was dealing with here was a word being used to evoke two somewhat contrary senses: of "cognition" and "emotion" at the same time. The dichotomy of meanings, I could see, underlined the horror and invoked a particularly monstrous image of the schoolteacher specifically because she was not, after all, a simple beast. The punitive woman is at once a coolly detached authority figure out of control and an example of pure feelings gone haywire. The physical urge and mental intent overlap, leaving open the possibility that there is no convenient way of separating the body and mind.

At this point, I had to drop my semantical pursuits for the time being. Just the same, these new insights continued to percolate for quite a while. After all, I was vaguely aware that a mind-body (or subject-object) dichotomy had been the subject of psychological debate at least since the seventeenth century when René Descartes had postulated a mechanistic physical world entirely divorced from the mind, the only connection between the two being by intervention of God.

In any case, in the days and weeks that followed I continued my reading of and about nineteenth-century Sensation writers, keeping an eye out for further clues to a better understanding of the word "sensation" in its literary applications. I became familiar with the *Wellesley Index to Victorian Periodicals,* where one can look under the titles of major journals of the time and find the contents of each volume as well as identification of the authors of many of the unsigned articles. There I encountered a listing for a review of new fiction in *Blackwood's* in May 1855 by Mrs. Oliphant which included a discussion of Wilkie Collins's first three novels:

Antonina (1850), *Basil* (1852), and *Hide and Seek* (1854). Here
Oliphant declaims: "Something new! Happy people of Athens,
who had it in their power to say or to hear every day some new
thing! In our times we know no such felicity, and far and wide
are our researches for the prized and precious novelty which it is
so hard to lay hand upon. The 'sensation,' which it is the design
of Mr. Wilkie Collins to raise in our monotonous bosom, is—
horror." Her high opinion of Collins fades, however, when she
reaches *Basil,* subtitled "A Tale of Modern Life." She writes that,
as the tale "progresses artfully towards its concluding horrors, and
is nothing without them, we conclude that the object of the author
is simply to excite those feelings of abhorrence and loathing with
which we are compelled to regard his catastrophes. Modern life,
no doubt, like every other, has great crimes, calamities, and mis-
eries hidden in its bosom." But, she cautions, a person who judges
modern life by Collins "will form a very inadequate opinion of
the life which, even in London, is made up of everyday and small
events, and is by no means a series of catastrophies."

I had found evidence that the "Sensation" controversy had an-
tedated *The Woman in White* by six years. I had reinforced my
sense of the literary application of the term. And then—quite by
happenstance, when I was browsing through the previous number
of *Blackwood's* in the 1855 bound volume—discovered something
much more interesting. There, Mrs. Oliphant had penned a
lengthy review of a book called *Psychological Inquiries* by Sir
Benjamin Brodie. First published anonymously in 1854, Brodie's
compilation of the observations of his long, eminent career in
medicine—especially as seen from the conservative *Blackwood's*
admiring point of view—enabled me to better understand and
illustrate the deepest subversive threat of "Sensation" to Victorian
society.

I did not infer Brodie's position as a representative of the Victorian medical and political establishment merely by his title and
Oliphant's glowing approval of his message. Brodie served as surgeon to the Queen and was President of the Royal Society from
1858 until his death in 1862. In one of the fascinating coincidences
that seem to characterize the world which a study of Sensation
illuminates, Brodie gave important testimony at the trials of both
Palmer and Smethurst. In Palmer's trial, he distinguished himself

by his unwillingness to admit that the examination of Cook's internal organs had been so badly mishandled by the authorities that any certainty of poisoning was impossible. In the Smethurst case, Brodie, deeply concerned over the bad reputation medical witnesses in these poisoning trials were acquiring, actually consulted with the Home Secretary before lending his authority and taking a chance on contributing to the mistrust brought about by the testimony of Taylor, et al. When he finally did take the stand, it was for the purpose not of furthering forensic knowledge but of defending the image of the Royal Society. As a sardonic tribute to the Queen's doctor's ardent support for the establishment, Miss Braddon refers to him in her first novel, *The Trail of the Serpent,* as a "surgeon *par excellence.*"

In any event, Brodie's work was certainly popular. At the beginning of her review of *Psychological Inquiries,* Mrs. Oliphant assumes that "everyone" is familiar with it. Her review is not so much criticism as advocacy journalism, summarizing Brodie's theories on the mind-brain dichotomy in human awareness, accompanied by interlocutory remarks overwhelmingly supportive of the author's position. What becomes immediately striking to the reader is the pejorative connotation which the term "sensation" has taken on in the context of official psychology. Oliphant gently upbraids Brodie for looseness in terminology because he comes close to misassigning Sensation to a loftier perch than it deserves in the hierarchical system of cognition:

When we describe an organ or nerve as the "seat of Consciousness,"—or of sensation, which is one form of consciousness,—we might, if literally interpreted, be supposed to assign to the physical organization psychical properties which belong (in man) to that spirit which has taken up its residence, and manifests its high activities, in the body. But in fact when we speak of the nerve being the seat of sensation, we are not at that moment, viewing it with relation to the mind, but comparing it with other parts of the vital organism. Compared with a bone or a blood vessel, it is the seat of sensation. The author before us occasionally uses this very form of expression, and, if we mistake not, has, in one place, designated the brain as "the sole seat of consciousness. . . ."

Still, Oliphant is able to overlook this minor delinquency of Brodie's because otherwise "no one could be more precise and emphatic in his strict maintenance of the dualism of mind and body." Mrs. Oliphant here wants to clearly establish that bodily functions are separate from the functions of the mind; and that mental functions have "psychical properties" which, in fact, belong to the soul, thus constituting the spiritual legacy of an orthodox deity. In other words, she states, the "contents of the human consciousness may be divided into two great classes—Thoughts and Sensations." The former represent man's link with God and afterlife; the latter are but the manifestation of man's lower, or animal, nature. The seat of the sensations, according to Oliphant's paraphrase of Brodie, is the "brain," as opposed to the "mind," thus establishing another dualism of the physical and psychical. The brain is "the organ of our instincts or appetites. . . . As to our feelings, they are, so far as the brain is concerned, resolvable into memories and sensations, to be distributed accordingly; or they must be placed altogether out of the brain, having their seat only in the spiritual essence." It is, therefore, those feelings which reside in the "brain" and not in the "spiritual essence" which are "sensation."

Some of these states of consciousness I realized would be especially meaningful to my unfinished etymological pursuits. Oliphant quotes Brodie on "animal appetites and instincts." He sees them as

being intimately connected with the nervous system and as having their special places allotted to them in it. But we are not warranted in having the same conclusions as to the emotions and passions, properly called. Hope and fear, joy and sorrow, pride and shame, these and such as these are conditions of the mind which have abstract or independent existence; but which, as they may be superadded to our perception and thoughts, admit of being excited and acted on through the medium of the nervous system. At the same time, as far as we can see, they have no specific locality in it.

Brodie is here attempting to relegate the most benign of the "uncontrollable," therefore, threatening, states of consciousness to the inferior "brain" and, at the same time, he is groping with what today is known as the "subconscious," the "no special locality" from which irrational feelings emerge. The eminent surgeon is looking for a map of the emotions and has understandably become lost, a sort of Dr. Livingstone of the spiritual anatomy.

In regard to more threatening states, Brodie is, in spite of the obscurity of the terrain, quite emphatic. Loss of memory must be a physical problem, deriving from injury to the brain. Dreams "present many curious perplexities, but the broad correspondence between the imperfect and tangled memories of which they are composed, and the imperfect sleep, or rather the imperfect wakefulness in which they occur, cannot be mistaken. Neither can we fail to observe the manner in which the cognitive action of the brain is connected with the impressions from the senses."

Oliphant, then, in support of Brodie's grand hypothesis, doubles his theory back to the more solid ground of strict Associationism. She cites, from her own experience, a case of a woman whose bad dreams were caused by the aggravation of a tumor on her leg. Her conclusions on the subject provide insight into the curious Victorian rationalizing of the unacceptable threats of the "abnormal":

> Happily, in our waking hours, there are other causes to counteract this operation of painful and uneasy sensations on the current of thought; but, even in our most wakeful hours, such operation is indisputable; it is the subject of daily observation: the morbid condition of our blood gives rise to morbid feelings, irrational fears or suspicions, anger, or despondency. It is a general law, though, as we have said, counteracted by higher psychical laws, that painful sensations introduce distressing or angry thoughts.

Once again we encounter the desire to displace or externalize psychological disturbances to physical causes. And the speciously empirical conclusions of medical moralists are again illuminated. Oliphant tells us of Brodie's "stringent observations . . . on the moral duty that lies on every man to sustain by temperance and every means in his power a fair condition of health." In short, this "empirical" study is again ideological, representing, to reparaphrase Steven Marcus, thought which is socially determined but unaware of its source.

Returning to the subject of the "sensations" and their connection with the passionate and bestial, Oliphant dispenses with them as she does dreams. They are simply *unacceptable* because they are incompatible with the spiritual aspirations of man:

> We indeed hope that dreams are no specimen of what the mind can accomplish when she thinks alone, or without the instrumentality of the body. If we strove to catch some glimpse of her in her own solitary state, we should choose those periods when she is absorbed in her highest efforts of reason and reflection. . . . But so far as we can comprehend so obscure a subject, there is no material organ for the exercise of Reason: it is the energy of the soul itself exercised on, and in companionship with, the organs of memory and perception.

Oliphant then turns to Brodie's handling of the original distinction between consciousness in man and in animals. First of all, she tells us that the "vital organism" of animals is merely "sensitive or conscious." In man, on the other hand, "an immaterial spirit, a higher principle of consciousness, assumes or takes upon itself . . . what in other animals is the sensitiveness of the vital organism." Here we see the Cartesian split in subject and object refined (or simplified) in a further stance, one closer to the anthropological than the philosophical. By splitting off the vital passions from the soul, it is relatively easy to split men from animals. The next step in this logical progression is to make some people—specific genders, classes, races—more equal than others.

But at this point, faced with the "instincts and appetites which we possess in common with others," Oliphant first backs off, almost as if she had a Crim. Con. or murder trial flash through her own "higher principle of consciousness," and worries for a bit over "whether we have no cerebral organ for *amativeness, alimentiveness, combativeness, destructiveness,* and the like." Her curious answer is that instinct "is a stumbling block that must be removed from our path. It lies there, a mysterious something between sensation and thought."

The sexual and Darwinian implications here are obvious. Violence and sexuality are unacceptable because they represent animal behavior. They must be separated from rational "human" endeavor in order that the theories of evolutionary biology can be opposed and defeated. (It is essential, of course, to remember here that *Origin of Species* was the landmark work of evolutionary study, but by no means the first; scientists had been nibbling at the idea throughout the nineteenth century.) In any case, Oliphant asserts, the "simpler type of animal embraces this circle only—irritability, movement, and sensation; sensation or so much pleasure, being, as far as that animal is concerned, the end of all its vital mechanism." Rather than evolution, a static hierarchy is established, the elevated human status being inversely proportional to the strength of the "sensations." "In a higher type [of animal], memory is introduced but it is still quite subordinate to sensation. In man the memory or that still loftier spirit of intelligence which acts on the memory, becomes predominate."

It is clear that the ultimate purpose of Brodie's book and Oliphant's proselytizing review is to use what appears to be a neuropsychological study to defend the religious and philosophical status quo. All responsibility for existence is left, in Oliphant's words, echoing the Church of England position, to "the great Author of nature." In any inquiry, she goes on, one must avoid "infringing on the prerogatives of the immaterial spirit."

Of course, it is not at all remarkable to find such a work with such a purpose in such a magazine in the middle of the nineteenth century. What is striking is the way Brodie's argument clarifies—by its resemblance to that body of work—much of the criticism of the Sensation novel and of news coverage of sexual and criminal prosecutions. As Arnold's essay delineates the implicit threat of crime stories to the politics of public administration and legislation, so this review reveals behind the scenes a kind of metaphysical politics which was equally subverted by the threat of Sensation, both in psychological terms and in the specific literary sense. The Sensation novel was the novel of unacceptable "brutish" feeling and behavior, unacceptable because it was "infringing on the prerogatives of the immaterial spirit."

The value of this connection cannot be overstated. In the words of one modern historian of science, Robert M. Young, the theory of evolution, to the Victorians,

> meant that the origin of man occurred by means of the continuous operation of natural laws and not by special creation. This, in turn, implied that it was no longer possible to separate mind and culture from the domain of scientific laws. Man and all his works—body and mind, society and culture—become, in principle, part of the science of biology. The continuity of types was based on the continuity of natural causes, and discontinuities between body and mind and between nature and culture became untenable. God did not act by isolated interpositions, and moral responsibility no longer had a separate, divinely ordained basis in the freedom of the will.

However, Young adds, the relevance of these implications to the "three themes in the history of psychology—associationism, neurophysiology, and phrenology," was "not widely grasped." At the time, in fact, he concludes, even the new discoveries in psychophysiology in the seventies failed to be taken up in the debate on Darwinism, and "the failure of the evolutionists and anti-evolutionists to exploit them becomes astonishing."

Of course, this failure is not so astonishing if one projects oneself, however temporarily, into the world of mid-Victorian popular culture. Even the Darwinists seem reluctant to make the necessary connections which are manifest in Sensation literature. Another instance of the right hand not knowing—or not wanting to know—what the left is doing seems to surface here. This in turn raises again the issue of the extent to which many Victorian thinkers suffered from a dimmed consciousness, to repeat Steven Marcus's assessment of the intellectual capacities inherent in much of the sexual material he encountered in his research into pornography and sexology for *The Other Victorians*.

The paradox is that we have found in our own consideration of Victorian underworlds or countercultures numerous instances of critical commentary which are extraordinarily insightful, standing happily alongside those which are quite dim. The *Saturday Review*'s assessment of the special correspondence on William Palmer in

The Leader is essentially accurate—if we take out the moralistic impulse. Dean Mansel's piece in the *Quarterly Review* is eloquent about the threat of newspaper novels to the rigidly submissive mind-set of orthodoxy—if we forget the morality. We know that the official consciousness well knew that the likes of Whitty and Collins and Braddon *were* unabashedly bashing sacred cows and attracting large followings in the process. Yet, somehow, the intelligent awareness manifested by the defenders of the faith when dealing with what they perceived as emanating from that lowland "no special locality" where the irrational and instinctive is produced, never seems to make a connection with the critical faculties as applied to what they perceive as emanating from the higher elevations of the soul. They don't ever put two and two together, and this *divided* (rather than completely dimmed) consciousness is the legacy they leave to conventional history in their own memoirs, biographies, and studies of journalism.

Nor is this an exclusively Victorian phenomenon. A British scholar has recently published a supposedly comprehensive book-length study of *Victorian News and Newspapers* (1985). Much of the research for this work was done at Colindale over a period of many years. The bibliography suggests that the author, Lucy Brown, has consulted the same newspapers which I have—and more. Yet her lengthy index shows no listing for Crim. Con., Murder, William Palmer, Mrs. Robinson, Madeline Smith, or Dr. Taylor—to mention only a few of the omissions. Edward Whitty is mentioned, however, in one phrase which notes that his parliamentary sketches for *The Leader* in 1852–53 were "early examples" of the type. In fact, Brown seems to have decided that reportage of crime and bestiality are beneath interest. It is as if the blinders-on aspect of mind-body dualism not only was perpetuated in the cognitive awareness of the collective Victorian establishment but has continued its obscurantist influence right down to the end of the twentieth century. How can one write about news without acknowledging one of the largest segments of what the news covers?

This gap is nowhere more apparent than in a piece called "Our Female Sensation Novelists" which appeared in *The Christian Remembrancer* in 1863. Herein the anonymous spokesman for literate Anglicanism seriously attempts to plumb the meaning of "sensation"—a phenomenon which, he acknowledges, represents serious social and philosophical unrest. Sensation writing, he reflects, "is an appeal to the nerves rather than to the heart." More damning is the fact that the contemporary fiction writer "willingly and designedly draws a picture of life which shall make reality insipid and the routine of ordinary existence intolerable to the imagination." It does this "by drugging thought and reason, and stimulating the attention through the lower and more animal instincts . . . and especially by tampering with things evil and infringing more or less on the confines of wrong." Thus we see that the critic's negative evaluation coincides, again, with Brodie's vision of the mind-brain dichotomy. In "one and all" Sensation novels there is an "appeal to the imagination, through the active agency of the nerves." This, in turn, is "excited by the unnatural or supernatural."

The degree to which such a psychophysiological paradigm was able to pervade all aspects of thought is strikingly demonstrated in another passage: "There is nothing more violently opposed to our moral sense, in all the contradictions to custom which they present to us, than the utter unrestraint in which the heroines of this order are allowed to expatiate and develop their impulsive, stormy, passionate characters." The writer makes clear that this has universal implications. Such behavior upsets the orthodox hierarchical world view: "This lower level, this drop from the empire of reason and self-control, is to be traced throughout this class of literature, which is a constant appeal to the animal part of our nature, and avows a preference for its manifestation, as though power and intensity come through it." That this quality is at once sexual and subversive is clear. The reviewer cites the immoral power of "instinct" in these novels by quoting from *East Lynne*. Lady Isabel, the wronged heroine, "was aware that a sensation all too warm, a feeling of attraction towards Francis Levison [her seducer; she thinks her husband is cheating on her], was waking within her; not a voluntary one. She could no more repress it than she could her own sense of being."

Two dominant and related characteristics of the genre are noted. First is "the possession by one idea—an idea so fixed and dominant that the mind impregnated by it has no choice but to obey." The second is based on the reviewer's perception of "the very language of the school":

A whole new set of words has come into use, and they are caught up and slipped into, as a matter of course, to express a certain degradation of the human into the animal or brutal, on the call of strong emotion. . . . Thus the victim of feeling or passion sinks at once into the inspired or possessed animal and is always supposed to be past articulate speech; and we have the *cry,* the *smothered cry of rage,* the *wail,* the *low wailing cry,* the *wail of despair.* . . . It is man's privilege to walk; in novels men, or at any rate women, *creep.*

Looking back over our survey of the newspapers and novels, the subject, Sensation, is seen in a new light. One not only remembers the overwhelming passions of Isabel Vane or the "monomania" of Lady Audley, but a list of animal images comes to mind. In the newspapers, one recalls the pigeons lower on the scale of creation than Palmer, and the brutal schoolmistress alluded to earlier in this chapter who is described as a "female Yahoo." Lady Audley's passion tears at her "like some ravenous beast." Collins's *Woman in White,* Anne Catherick, is possessed by a "wild unnatural force" which makes her eyes dilate "like the eyes of a wild animal." In *Armadale,* Midwinter is advised against fatalistic despair (provoked by the threat of the tigress, Gwilt) through which man "lowers himself to the level of the brutes that perish." Dickens's Bradley Headstone, the sexually deranged schoolmaster of *Our Mutual Friend,* is compared to "an ill-tamed wild animal," while London's *demi-monde* is populated by "birds of prey." The villain of Bulwer's *Strange Stories* represents, in Bulwer's own explication (in a letter to Dickens), "the sensuous material principle of nature." And, in Reade's *Hard Cash,* asylum inmates "howl like wolves" and give off "the peculiar wild-beast smell that marks the true maniac." Finally, LeFanu's "Green Tea," in this light, reads as a direct response to Brodie's perception of consciousness. An eminently respectable and religious man is overcome by his irrational fears, which are symbolized by an hallucinatory monkey.

The Sensation novel, then, occupies a position not on a side path of "low" demonic literature, but in the mainstream of the intellectual change which was taking place. It was a time when, according to Lionel Trilling, "Less and less did it seem possible for the imagination to be at ease with the ancient picture of the universe that was essential to the literal plausibility of the Christian story. The traditional iconography of religion, whether it figures over the altar or in the mind, inevitably came to seem anachronistic, made so by the remorseless progress of science in establishing the scarcely imaginable vastness of the universe and the immutability of its laws."

At the same time, the quotidian social science of the newspapers opened a vastness of the psyche and contributed to an even more iconoclastic vision of established belief. An anonymous American contemporary of the Sensation novelists put it succinctly while discussing *Hard Cash,* observing that "philosophy has been so unsettled by modern speculation and unscientific theories, by phrenologists, psychologists, and spiritualists, that the medical profession have no definition of sanity or insanity which they all accept; and there is in the profession no agreement as to where is to be drawn the line between the two." Thus we observe from this perspective a culture whose epistemology was distinctly unsettled. The symbolic center of this confusion was the "no special locality" where mind and matter come together, which was rationalized by Brodie, embodied in a monkey by LeFanu, and largely repressed in discussions of High Culture by the very writers who squawked loudest about its enduring presence in the Low. One must assume that the cause of this intellectual chaos was the reluctance to let go of a reserved seat in the arena of the afterlife, a soul or spirit in man which would live into eternity, guaranteed, small moral deposit required. The explosion of real—and realistic—crime stories exploited the confusion. In *In Memoriam* (1850), often considered "the characteristic poem of its time," Tennyson prevails on man to

> *Arise and fly.*
> *The reeling Faun, the sensual feast,*
> *Move upward, working out the beast,*
> *And let the ape and tiger die.*

By insisting, in his Epilogue, on "a closer link / Betwixt us and the crowning race," and the fact that we are "no longer half-akin to brute," the poet laureate rationalizes his orthodox Christianity, specifically in terms of his doubt of ever meeting his beloved

Hallam again in an afterlife. The Sensation newspapers and novels were part of a larger process, inexorably grinding away at the foundations of that rationalization.

Nor has this subversive force ceased to function. One need look no further than one of the most recent and comprehensive summaries of the state of the art of literary studies. Shirley Staton, in 1987, lingering over the "post-structuralist insight into the primacy of language over subjectivity," remarks:

> Yet even before structuralist and post-structuralist views disrupted our common-sense notions about knowable objects, unified texts, and subjective identity, Freud's psychoanalytic theories had jolted belief in the unified self. The comforting nineteenth-century image of ourselves as individuals controlling our destiny was, as Freud had insisted, illusion. . . . [Psychoanalysis] depicted the human psyche as a fragmented, multi-layered, largely unconscious, and hence, largely unknowable process.

It should be added that Freud also contended (in "The Future of an Illusion") that this unknowability in many ways led to man needing to create a God in the first place—as defense, protection, security. In any case, as Staton concludes, even today, "the general paradigm for 'reality' is shifting from an essentialist, static, unified, closed self and world to a relativistic, in-process, decentered, open universe."

It seems to me now that when I stumbled into the world of Bell Macdonald's clippings sixteen years ago, I stumbled into one of the most dramatically illustrative phases of this process of the "decentering" of the universe. The fact that I have had to write this book to recall that phase in the evolution of human awareness is in itself a prime example of the intensity and endurance of the denial built into the conflict.

❖

Black Swine in the Sewers of Hampstead

In August of 1859, the Bishop of London received two letters—signed only "A Parishioner"—accusing a clergyman of "disgracefully immoral conduct." The Reverend James Bonwell, rector of St. Philip's Parish in the East End slum of Stepney, was alleged to have seduced one Elizabeth Yorath, the daughter of a respectable physician in Monmouthshire. The young woman had recently turned up in Stepney, visibly pregnant, where Bonwell provided her housing in the master's apartment of the disused boys' parochial school, and visited her there for extended periods. As Bonwell was supposed to be happily married to the headmistress of a boarding school for young ladies at the family residence in Islington, this was considered a particularly shocking matter. Moreover, Yorath had since given birth to a child—delivered by the notorious Dr. Godfrey, who had recently been the focus of a prominent criminal case when he was charged with seducing a pubkeeper's daughter and fathering her bastard. (He was also suspected of seducing his patients.) At any rate, Yorath and the newborn, the letters went on, "had mysteriously disappeared a few nights later from St. Philip's." It was hinted that there may have been foul play.

As a consequence of the gravity of the charges, the police were called in. Inspector Whicher, who was later reputed to be the model for Sergeant Cuff in *The Moonstone,* was put on the case, and his subsequent investigation was responsible for several disclosures. It appeared that Bonwell had first represented himself to Yorath and her family as a widower when he had been sent to Monmouthshire on an ecclesiastical mission. Therefore he had used the cover of the Church of England to execute both an act of deception and the disgraceful seduction.

Elizabeth Yorath and her son were also traced forward in time by Whicher from their departure from the boys' school lodgings. Bonwell had taken them to Bolton's Sussex Hotel in Tooley Street, just across London Bridge, not far from the Marshalsea prison which Dickens had made infamous in *Little Dorrit* (1857). At the hotel, the baby—who had had difficulty swallowing since birth—was again attended by Dr. Godfrey, who was called across the Thames from his offices near Stepney in Whitechapel, where Jack the Ripper was to distinguish himself thirty years later. Godfrey was still free to practice because he had been acquitted of responsibility in his own trial when the illegitimate child in question was found to be suffering from a congenital venereal disease which neither Godfrey nor the publican's daughter shared. The jury concluded there had to be at least one more (diseased) seducer in the case. At any rate, young Philip Yorath choked to death soon after arriving at the hotel in the Borough.

This presented Bonwell, Yorath, and Godfrey with some serious choices. After all, the child was gone; what was the harm in suppressing the entire series of incidents? No one would be the worse for the disinformation. So Yorath was sent away. Then Bonwell, presenting a certificate signed by Godfrey which attributed the child's death to "atrophy," engaged an undertaker named Ayres and asked him to take the tiny corpse from the hotel and bury it wherever he saw fit.

Ayres acted without hesitation (suggesting that he was practiced at this particular procedure). He simply put the baby in the coffin of an adult woman named Acock, sealed the coffin, and buried woman and infant together in Tower Hamlets Cemetery, having collected fees for each, and without bothering to inform either Bonwell or Acock's grieving relatives or the authorities.

Inspector Whicher, having traced the mystery this far, then ordered an exhumation and the story was confirmed by the discovery of the presence of two bodies in the grave. A coroner's inquiry was called, and Bonwell and Ayres were censured. It took another year—and many news updates—for the Church of England to dismiss Bonwell and hold him accountable for considerable costs.

In its initial stages, the case, which *Reynold's Weekly* dubbed "the surreptitious disposal of the dead body of an ilegitimate child," preoccupied the news media. This public fascination was no small thing, considering that the late summer and fall of 1859 were typically extraordinary mid-Victorian seasons of crime. Dr. Smethurst had just been pardoned on homicide charges and re-arrested for committing bigamy with the dead woman, whom he had apparently neither murdered nor married legally. In fact, since Palmer in 1856, villainous and lascivious medical men had become a staple of the police reports, Godfrey being only a minor—if high-profile—example. (He had been stoned by a mob after his acquittal.)

And illicit sexuality in general was rampant: there had been the notorious "courtship by a married woman in men's clothing"; there had been an epidemic of abductions of young women into white slavery (frequently to Germany); and two Midlands women had been gang-raped in a ditch by eight local "ruffians" (there were no street lamps or other amenities such as public transport in the countryside in those days) while walking home from a social event. Other children fared no better than poor Philip Yorath. Within a week that October of 1859, a skeleton of one child was found in a garden in Bayswater and a woman from Hackney was charged with hanging her three-year-old son from his bedstead.

But "delinquent clergy" appear to have captured an unprece-dented share of the public fancy. One reverend gentleman from Birkenhead had not only run off with another woman but left his wife and children to be fed and housed by the parish. Henry John Hatch, former chaplain at the Wandsworth House of Detection, became involved in a long-running case in which he was accused, convicted, and jailed for rape. Then he was released when the eleven-year-old girl who claimed he had climbed into her bed and forcibly engaged her and her eight-year-old sister in sexual inter-course recanted her testimony.

Of all these machinations and fornications and murders, how-ever, it was the collaboration of Bonwell, Yorath, Godfrey, and Ayres in the surreptitious disposal of Philip Yorath which produced the most memorable piece of journalism. This exemplary writing appeared in the form of a lengthy editorial which Macdonald clipped from *The Daily Telegraph* of Monday, October 10, 1859. It begins:

It is a trite story, that of the exquisite who, being told by an acquaintance that he was about to visit a friend in Bloomsbury Square, asked whereabouts on the road he changed horses. Yet such is the immensity of this metropolis, so innumerable are its thoroughfares, and so widely separated its districts, that one who had passed half a lifetime at the westend of London might well be excused for entire ignorance as to the situation of Bethnal Green, Jacob's Island, Mile-end, and Stepney. They are as vaguely remote to many as the Ultima Thule of Orkney or Shetland. It is exceedingly probable that we have among our readers thousands who, with or without a map, would be utterly unable to point out the localities of Piccadilly Square, Honey-lane Market, Hay-Hill, Little Britain, Cloth Fair, Cock-lane, Bell square, Long-alley, and Bleeding-heart-yard; and people are born and run their race of life, and die within a mile or two of one another, and are as completely estranged from their neighbours as though they were separated from them by rocky mountains, by unfordable streams, by stormy seas.

This London is an amalgam of worlds within worlds, and the occurrences of every day convince us that there is not one of these worlds but has its special mysteries and its generic crimes. Exaggeration and ridicule often attach to the vastness of London, and the ignorance of its penetralia common to us who dwell therein. It has been said that beasts of chase still roam in the verdant fastnesses of Grosvenor square, that there are undiscovered patches of primaeval forest in Hyde Park and that Hampstead sewers shelter a monstrous breed of black swine, which have propagated and run wild among the slimy feculence, and whose ferocious snouts will one day up-root Highgate archway, while they make Holloway intolerable with their grunting. Seriously that may be said of the Londoner, who prides himself on his accurate topographical knowledge, which was said in modesty by the great philos-

It is a trite story, that of the exquisite who, being told by an acquaintance that he was about to visit a friend in Bloomsbury-square, asked whereabouts on the road he changed horses. Yet such is the immensity of this metropolis, so innumerable are its thoroughfares, and so widely separated its districts, that one who had passed half a lifetime at the west-end of London might well be excused for entire ignorance as to the situation of Bethnal-green, Jacob's Island, Mile-end, and Stepney. They are as vaguely remote to many as the Ultima Thule of Orkney or Shetland. It is exceedingly probable that we have among our readers thousands who, with or without a map, would be utterly unable to point out the localities of Piccadilly-square, Honey-lane market, Hay-hill, Little Britain, Cloth Fair, Cock-lane, Bell-square, Long-alley, and Bleeding-heart-yard; and people are born, and run their race of life, and die within a mile or two of one another, and are as completely estranged from their neighbours as though they were separated from them by rocky mountains, by unfordable streams, by stormy seas.

This London is an amalgam of worlds within worlds, and the occurrences of every day convince us that there is not one of these worlds but has its special mysteries and its generic crimes. Exaggeration and ridicule often attach to the vastness of London, and the ignorance of its penetralia common to us who dwell therein. It has been said that beasts of chase still roam in the verdant fastnesses of Grosvenor square, that there are undiscovered patches of primeval forest in Hyde-park, and that the Hampstead sewers shelter a monstrous breed of black swine, which have propagated and run wild among the slimy feculence, and whose ferocious snouts will one day uproot Highgate archway, while they make Holloway intolerable with their grunting. Seriously that may be said of the Londoner, who prides himself on his accurate topographical knowledge, which was said in modesty by the great philosopher of light. He is but picking up shells on the shore, while all before him lies a vast and undiscovered ocean.

It has seemed, however, fated, of late days, that the London public should hear enough—if not, indeed, too much—of the remote and uncgenial region at the east end of the metropolis. Murders, actions for seduction, fierce theological dimensions, followed by alarming riots, robberies, and murderous assaults—such eventualities as these have formed the staple of our most recent tidings from the outlying faubourgs of Whitechapel, Spitalfields, Mile-end, Bow, Stepney, Wapping, and Rotherhithe. The most appropriate name for St. George's in-the-East would seem to be "St. Giles's-in-the-East;" and to the scandalous accounts of church brawls have been lately added the ghastly revelations of the charnal house. The last importation from the East-end is the revolting story of the surreptitious disposal of the dead body of an infant, the illegitimate child of one ELIZABETH YORATH, and which was smuggled into the earth in the coffin of an adult person, under the auspices of an undertaker in the Borough and a clergyman of the Church of England. We have already given an outline of the case, by which the Reverend Mr. BONWELL, the incumbent of St. Philip's, Stepney, and Mr. AYRES, the undertaker of Redcross-street, appeared to be so strangely compromised; and we have published from day to day full details of the evidence tendered at the Coroner's Inquest set on foot at Governmental instigation, and after an order from the Secretary of State for the dis-

interment of the child, to discover whether any foul means had been made use of to procure its death. So far as medical investigation can prove, there is nothing to show that the child of ELIZABETH YORATH, confined on the 12th of August last, in a certain schoolroom occupied by the Reverend Mr. BONWELL, and lying in there with his connivance and consent, the noted Doctor GODFREY of Finsbury and Whitechapel being the accoucheur, and which child—died at BOLTON'S Sussex Hotel, had been murderously dealt by. Dr. GODFREY, who gave the certificate of death, stated that the infant died of "atrophy," or "inanition," in other words by exhaustion, brought on by want of food; but witnesses were present who saw it fed, and moreover reject the food presented to it. Certain obstetric difficulties, amongst others that of a cross presentation, had attended its birth. It had been weakly and ailing from the beginning—"more dead than alive," according to Dr. GODFREY. Its digestive powers were not strong enough even for the consumption of milk. It had chronic diarrhoea during its short span, and it died. Hundreds of children die thus every day. Almost every healthy infant is the result of a "triage," and the unsuccessful candidates, of which it is the picked one, are buried quietly out of the way. The verdict of the coroner's jury is, as seems becoming more and more frequent, exceedingly vague and unsatisfactory. They found that the child was in the care of its mother and of the Rev. Mr. BONWELL; that it died of one of two causes, either that it did not or could not swallow food; that it was nevertheless able to swallow some, though in what quantities the jury were unable to tell; and finally, it seemed to the gentlemen of the jury that the conduct of ELIZABETH YORATH, the Rev. Mr. BONWELL, and Mr. THOMAS AYRES, the undertaker, was "highly censurable." Censurable in what particular? Did the jury mean to reprehend the wretched girl YORATH, who gave way to the lust of a villain and bore a bastard child? Was the incumbent of St. Philip, Stepney, who, of course, could have had no active participation in the seduction of his protégé, to be censured for harbouring her in a school-room which he occupied, and in which he often himself slept; for causing her removal, with the offspring of her shame, to a mean inn in the borough; for casting about for the first undertaker he could find, and bargaining for the hugger-mugger burial of the dead child with the ghoul AYRES? For what, too, was the undertaker blamable? For carrying infant shells about in bags, cramming infant corpses into them, nailing them down with a few tacks, and afterwards shifting them coffinless to the biers of adults?, for suffering his children to tear up the certificate of death, and cosening the Tower Hamlets Cemetery Company by interring two corpses and paying the dues for only one?

Beyond the ascertained fact that the child of ELIZABETH YORATH died from natural causes, the whole of this dismal affair is enveloped in doubt and mystery. For all the light the coroner's jury have thrown on the case, they might as well have returned a verdict of "Ignoramus," "we know nothing at all about it;" and it seems curiously to have been the wish of those whose duty it was to guide their labours and elucidate the evidence to keep them as much in the dark as possible. Why was the Coroner so anxious that no extraneous questions should be asked of the Reverend Mr. BONWELL?

A facsimile page from *Various Trials*.

opher of light. He is but picking up shells on the shore, while all before him lies a vast and undiscovered ocean.

It has seemed, however, fated, of late days, that the London public should hear enough—if not, indeed, too much—of the remote and ungenial region at the east end of the metropolis. Murders, actions for seduction, fierce theological dissensions, followed by alarming riots, robberies, and murderous assaults—such eventualities as these have formed the staple of our most recent tidings from the outlying faubourgs of White Chapel, Spitalfields, Mile-end, Bow, Stepney, Wapping, and Rotherhithe. . . . [To] the scandalous accounts of church brawls have been lately added the ghastly revelations of the charnel house. The last importation from the East-end is the revolting story of the surreptitious disposal of the dead body of an infant, the illegitimate child of one Elizabeth Yorath, and which was smuggled into the earth in the coffin of an adult person, under the auspices of an undertaker in the Borough, and a clergyman of the Church of England.

As we consider this editorial commentary from *The Daily Telegraph,* its multi-layered relevance to any study of the popular culture of the mid-nineteenth century should be manifest. The newspapers are bringing bad news, news which at once binds the city together and fragments it. The papers seem to have evoked in the public mind a kind of fearfully decomposing symmetry. The beasts attacking from beneath the surface suggest an awareness that *Origin of Species* would be published that month; or it calls up a pre-Freudian vision of the "seething cauldron" of the subconscious. Certainly the editorial anticipates the imagery of "creeping horrors underground" which Mrs. Oliphant used to condemn the implications of the Sensation novels a few years later. The litany of place names—at once homely and exotic—reinforces the sense of mystery in familiar places. The city is a kind of puzzle, a mystery story of its own, without an ending, certainly without a *happy* ending—which cries out to be interpreted (or, more precisely reinterpreted). Looming over this surreal landscape is the Unholy Trinity (doctor, preacher, undertaker), which has neglected its custodial duty to shepherd Victorians from birth through respectful life to respectable mortality. If God is not dead, He is deathly ill.

Every day for almost a year—from September 1984 through the following summer—I made the mile-long trek from the weathered pink villa we had rented on a hill in Provence down to my tiny "office" over the café in the village. Of course, there were the research trips I have described to London and Scotland (among others less fruitful to Continental libraries) which broke the routine, but—basically—I had given myself up for a year to a single-minded endeavor. I had received a grant and I was determined to give the National Endowment for the Humanities its money's worth. I had promised to track down relevant library connections to Bell Macdonald's clippings and to visit the very room where that clipping had been done, but I had also committed myself to enrich whatever nineteenth-century background I already possessed, to amass sufficient detail to be able to see the period plain, and then—it was assumed—write about what I had found out. If I were able to make at least significant strides in this direction I should be able to answer the essential question which Neil McKendrick had raised in January 1984, in his front-page *New York Times Book Review* essay on Peter Gay's much-heralded *Education of the Senses.* I wanted to answer "why, amid all the rich evidence of sexual [and, of course, criminal] information amply available to those with eyes to see in Victorian England, those providing it still had to adopt an acceptable moral disguise." If I were able to formulate a reasonable response, then I would perhaps become the "someone" McKendrick said was still needed, in spite of decades of pointed and uncensored inquiry into the "other" lives of proper Victorians, "to explain why that code [of respectability] was defended and justified with such passionate anxiety and such distinctive zeal." And even if I came up with no one comprehensive answer, I could at least say that I had fully taken advantage of my singular opportunity to survey all (or most) of the possibilities.

The office I rented to do my work functioned one night a month as the meeting room of the local football club. It was windowless— hot in summer and cold in wintertime—but it did very nicely for my purposes. There was a large table, half of which I covered with notes and documents. There were shelves, on which I made room—next to photographs and trophies commemorating a half century of the local soccer history—for the fifty-odd books I had had shipped over from the States to greet me: the library which was supposed to contain more or less all that one could possibly know about the role of criminal and sexual knowledge in the Victorian age. I arranged these books in a tentative order, so that I could methodically attack them, as it were, one by one, taking notes all the time, until all the soldiers were fallen.

My research, I came to realize more and more, was in fact an attempt to visualize an historical process of coping with a social, intellectual, and spiritual revolution which no one had anticipated as Britain moved from an agrarian manorial system to a mechanized urban one. The Industrial Revolution had become a concrete reality to me and a recurring background theme was growing more and more central to this vision: the Victorians were playing catch-up ball.

I was demonstrating by my reading and writing that brooding protest was not merely a fringe element in an "age of equipoise." Perhaps Palmerston, the Prime Minister, had begun to reconcile the new doctrine of "self-help" and the older ideal of the gentleman in a burgeoning middle-class political constituency, but new problems were appearing as quickly as the old seemed to go away. Since sensationalism tolerated neither ideal nor compromise, I had found ample evidence to controvert Macaulay's claims (in 1861) that recent progress had, in the course of advancing medical science, improving agricultural efficiency, and inventing new weapons for the military, also "lightened up the night with the splendour of the day" and "extended the range of human vision."

I was indeed becoming aware of something quite different. Human vision was extending into the darker and deeper regions which have become the province of psychoanalysis. And of course psychoanalytic critics have feasted on the crime story (although without necessarily relating it to the actual historical evolution of the Sensation controversy in the nineteenth century). These critics emphasize, for instance, that detective fiction can symbolize—among other primal concerns—a search for a lost parent. The reader identifies with the detective. The reader may also—in this vicarious pursuit—get tangled up in the underbrush of his own neurosis. As Geraldine Pederson-Krag has put it, the reader of mystery stories, in collaborating in the solution to a crime, "gratifies his infantile curiosity with impunity, redressing completely the helpless inadequacy and anxious guilt unconsciously remembered from childhood."

There has also been a surge of interest in the intrinsic qualities of mystery stories themselves, studies which often touch as well on the concerns of psychoanalysis. Geoffrey Hartman has called the detective form a "whodonut," a story with a hole in it; one attempts to fill the void in oneself. The socio-historical implications of this line of thought were potentially quite rewarding when I encountered it: the nineteenth century, confronted with void, had invented the detective story as a means of acting out its obsessive quest to fill the emptiness of an afterlife without the promise of heaven as a tradeoff for mortality.

Nevertheless, these psychoanalytical and structuralist and post-structuralist modes of literary inquiry—along with many other worthy theories—did not quite fit into the book that was shaping in my mind. So, as I went along, these various discards of skeins of thought came to compose themselves as a form of countertext, functioning not as a work in progress but as a cautionary definition of limits beyond which I could not maintain a coherent course.

There were other details and ideas I encountered, none requiring for my purposes extended treatment, but which not only reinforced the tendencies of my thinking but led me back to my central vision. For example, I read in one essay on Victorian city life that there were pubs in midcentury which featured an entertainment in which men dressed up as women and pretended they were giving graphic sexual testimony in court. I also gradually became aware that denial of crime on the part of the middle class was not just an abstract concept, a fear of regression; it was *real* fear of being mugged or murdered in their own beds. Moreover, some degree of the aura of gloom and doom we find in the papers and reviews had to result from the general fear of disease and criminal contamination (described compellingly in Bruce Haley's *The Healthy Body in Victorian Culture,* 1980) brought on in Britain by lack of sanitation and also by the massive Irish immigration of the 1840s—

the same immigration which brought my own ancestors to America, fleeing famine.

There was the insight, garnered from H. J. Dyos and Michael Wolff's collection, *The Victorian City,* into how photography (refined during the same period) had led artists first into, then away from, naturalism. That is, the shocking realism of detailed news reports was paralleled by the often unsettling reality of early photographs. Real artists were fascinated by cameras, then driven by them from the conventions of representationalism to the fragmented vision of Impressionism and Post-Impressionism—into abstraction, in short—in pursuit of a deeper truth than that found on the surface of a glossy photo.

In any case, all of this reading, all of these false starts, all of these lost opportunities for elucidation (or pedantry), enabled me to sharpen my focus, concentrate on what I took to be the Victorian primal scene. And that scene was the vision evoked by *The Daily Telegraph* commentary on the surreptitious disposal of the illegitimate child: of the people of London divided by metaphorical mountains; in fear of monstrous swine who would one day uproot their monuments; sufficiently confused by the news that the universe they once thought they knew so well had become a "vast and undiscovered ocean." By knowing so much, the Victorians were in the process of discovering how little sense it all made; they had taken on the knowledge of no knowledge.

As this scene took hold in my mind's eye, it began to people itself, fill in details, interweave with my own sense of reality. But the subject remained the same: the city streets, the wild beasts underground, the multitudinous shells (fossils?) on the horizonless shore. Of course, I was aware, the beasts under Hampstead were both unreal and real: metaphors, but metaphors for the real city. In order to understand their significance I had to better articulate to myself and others what was happening to the city in general in 1859.

It is not that easy, even after extended study, to imagine daily life and attitudes in any period of the past. It seems to me (perhaps from overexposure) that the mid-Victorian era is particularly slippery. It is, for instance, well known that Englishmen were unsettled by the threat of revolution from the Continent in 1848; and that, consequent to that revolution never occurring, the British were full of the pride and self-satisfaction that is symbolized in their triumphant display of mechanical superiority to the rest of the world at the Crystal Palace Great Exhibition of 1851. Beneath this neat juxtaposition of British feast and foreign famine, however, society was undergoing other immensely subtle changes, changes which qualify even the most obvious interpretations of events. Asa Briggs has pointed out—by way of demonstrating the pitiful condition of roads in eighteenth-century England—the testimony of one gentleman to the effect that living in Kensington (on the western edge of Hyde Park, well within the central part of metropolitan London today) felt like living on a rock in an ocean. One would then assume that the spread of the city to Kensington and the growth of railroad and communication networks not only to Kensington but throughout the land would have an immensely salutary effect—particularly to the person on the rock. The statistics of this growth are indeed impressive and do tend to be cited as examples of progress. Consider: there were 500 miles of railroad track laid in 1838 and 2,000 in 1843. By 1855, there were 8,000 miles of track *in use* and all the major cities in England were connected.

The communications media experienced a parallel expansion. The weekly *Illustrated London News* had a circulation of 60,000 in 1842, its first year. In 1851—in part because of features on the Great Exhibition—it had grown to 150,000. By 1855, boosted by the wire reports from the Crimean War, it reached 200,000. Its circulation of 300,000 in 1863 was the same as Dickens's *All the Year Round,* which of course included a number of the prominent Sensation novels.

Dailies moved apace. In 1855, there were 700 newspapers in the United Kingdom; in 1860, there were 1,100. In the latter year, *The Times,* with 60,000 readers, had been passed as leader in circulation by the relatively sensational—and cheap—*Daily Telegraph.*

Superficially, these details suggest progress; indeed, it was progress. But the sense conveyed by the image of black swine in the sewers of Hampstead conjures up nothing of the kind. Perhaps the advances in travel and communication *had* materially joined together the entire country (not to mention the separate villages cited in the editorial which by now had become part of one largely barren urban sprawl), but these phenomena were certainly at best a mixed blessing. The city was also clearly growing out of hand. London had one million residents in 1801; two million in 1841; three million in 1861; and four million in 1871. But the density taken on by the city was in no way accompanied by a parallel development in general availability of absolute necessities to much of the populace. News was cheaper, trains were available, the middle classes had staked a financial claim in the country, but little or nothing had been done for those who needed it most. This paradox is epitomized in the amount of crime, poverty, and disease encountered in the newspapers. In fact, the London Underground railway was being built at the same time as the drainage system necessary to subdue cholera in the fifties and sixties, but the architectural triumph of Victoria Station (1860) was completed long before an adequate sewage system was available to the poorer sections. There must have been among thoughtful Victorians a chronic—if often inarticulate—"sensation" of the ironic connotations of progress.

One way of seeing this clearly is the example of the railroads. While they brought prosperity, convenience, and knowledge to many, they also—as H. J. Dyos has pointed out (1973)—cut up the city like so many slices of a pie. Various lines of track spread out of central London like the spokes of a wheel. In order to build this track, entire neighborhoods were relocated to already overcrowded adjoining areas which created filthy, dangerous slums. People were also forced to the suburbs (which were often, as we have seen in Braddon and Collins, even worse hellholes than the "rookeries" they had left, in part because these displaced persons were not only deprived but lost, without community support). Moreover, the communities which were left intact were now cut off from one another by the tracks. This process left the city an "apparently incoherent, almost unintelligible, tangle of incidental shapes." Citizens of London were left with a sense among them of *anomie,* or breakdown in norms and values, with which it has become fashionable to characterize the avant-garde artistic expressions of much more recent times.

It is, at any rate, this sense of uprootedness which is explicitly communicated in the editorial on Bonwell, Yorath, Godfrey, and

Ayres. The writer is aware of the contradictory aspects of progress as exemplified by the growth of the news media. He also seems to have intuited another paradox: that the quaint and once intimate communities (even if they had always been down-at-the-heels or dicey) like Little Britain and Bleeding-heart-yard, have almost simultaneously been assimilated into the larger metropolis and then split off from it again by the very technological and economical developments that brought them together in the first place: "improvements" in travel and communications, and the consequent expansion of London into the greatest and most prosperous city in the history of the earth.

This image of the mythological "penetralia" lurking in the depths of city life is ambivalent in ways which connect with virtually all areas of Victorian culture. For example, one of the most famous of mid-Victorian narrative paintings is Ford Madox Brown's *Work* (begun in 1852, completed in 1865). Rather than describe this immensely busy work in my own words, I would like to quote at length Christopher Wood's 1976 commentary on Brown's picture, which includes extended portions of the artist's own description of his work:

> God and work were the catchwords of the age. The Victorians' passionate belief in the gospel of work led them to despise idleness as a social and economic sin. And they worked incredibly hard, in both office and factory. Twelve hours a day, six days a week, was common for most workers, until Saturday half-days began in the 1850's. The doctrines of work, self-help, discipline and thrift were held to be the root of England's greatness, the justification of her position as the first and the greatest industrial nation in the world.
>
> The gospel of work inspired Ford Madox Brown's "Work" . . . remarkable in that [it] not only [shows] people at work, but that . . . [it attempts] to symbolize the industrial revolution and the new industrial society that emerged from it. Brown's picture was begun in 1852, and is set in Heath Street, Hampstead, not far from where he lived. Excavations were going on there, and he admired the British excavator, or navvy . . . "in the full swing of his activity," thinking him just as fit a subject for painting "as the fisherman of the Adriatic, the

peasant of the Campagna, or the Neapolitan Lazzarone." Although it was recognized that the British navvy was the best in the world (he built most of the world's railways) no one had thought seriously of painting him. Even photographs of navvies at work are rare. Brown, however, found their costume "manly and picturesque," and made them the centrepiece of his picture "as the outward and visible type of Work." The carpenter, with his bow-tie, fancy waistcoat and copy of *The Times,* represents the craftsman class, superior to the ordinary labourer. The other figures in the crowded composition are intended to symbolize the classes of Victorian society. In the background are a gentleman and his daughter on horseback, representing the leisured classes. The man (the model was the painter R. B. Martineau) is according to Madox Brown "very rich, probably a colonel in the army, with a seat in Parliament, and fifteen thousand a year and a pack of hounds." It was difficult for the artist to include the most vital element of Victorian society, the urban middle classes—industrialists, merchants and bankers. They are perhaps represented by the two crinolined ladies on the left, one of whom is entirely decorative, while the other distributes Temperance tracts, a favourite pastime of non-conformist ladies. The tract reads "The Hodman's Haven, or Drink for Thirsty Souls." The thirsty hodman in the centre is unrepentantly throwing back a pot of ale. The lady with the tracts was included at the request of Thomas Plint of Leeds, Brown's patron, and a fervent Evangelical. On the right, leaning on the fence, are the intellectuals, Thomas Carlyle, critic and prophet of the new society, and F. D. Maurice, Christian Socialist and founder of the Working Men's Colleges, a poster for which is on the wall to the left. Beside the poster is a girl flower-seller, ragged and barefoot; in the road to the right is an orange-seller and sandwich-board men; all representatives of that vast tribe of street traders so assiduously catalogued by Mayhew in his historic book *London Labour and the London Poor.* The sleeping tramps, the lounger leaning against the tree, the ragged children, even the pampered whippet eyeing a sleeping mongrel, are symbols of idleness. The whole picture is packed with moral innuendoes—it is the most intensely symbolic narrative picture of the Victorian period, as well as being Madox Brown's masterpiece. Even the frame is inscribed with biblical texts justifying the gospel of work: "In the sweat of thy face shalt thou eat bread," and, "Seest thou a man diligent in his business? He shall stand before Kings."

We have under consideration now at least three artifacts: a painting, an artist's explication of that painting, and a modern critic's analysis of what painting and explication signify in the mid-Victorian world view. God is Work, says the latter. But I have already argued that a fourth artifact from a daily newspaper—roughly contemporary to the act of the painting and the composition of the explication of that painting—suggests that such an uplifting vision of God is untenable.

Moreover, the inspiration for the two apparently contradictory images—of the happily toiling laborers and the ominous grunting swine—is identical. Each is not only explicitly located in the prosperously genteel neighborhood of Hampstead but has on its mind the same examples of progress. The excavations in Hampstead (unidentified specifically anywhere I have looked) are taking place during the period when streets were paved and sewers, track bed, and underground railways were being built. Indeed, Ford Madox Brown admits that excavation was general in Hampstead in the early fifties. What this means, then, is that the very activity to which Brown and Wood attribute spiritually edifying qualities was perceived by others—with considerable justification—as basically threatening; threatening, that is, to both the memory (however misconceived) of the blissful rustic past and the "vast and undiscovered ocean" of the future. These contradictory responses reveal the degree that material scientific improvements could be either seriously disruptive (as in the case of the railroads) or impotent (as in the case of the sewers, whose success at eliminating cholera was still distant). In this sense, the painter's explication of what *everything* (and there is a lot more explanation, which Wood does not quote) means in his work can be seen not as an act of confidence or professional thoroughness, but as an obsessive nervous fidget (which it certainly is): a neurotic attempt to control an environment which is rapidly getting out of control.

I am reminded at this point of the first trip I ever took far from home—from a coal-mining town in Pennsylvania to northern California, where my mother's family had relocated (or dislocated) when the mines closed after World War II. I was about twelve, quite impressionable, and overwhelmed by both the natural abundance and the wealth of the Bay area south of San Francisco; but I was also mightily distressed by my own sense of *anomie*. I had lived my entire life in one town, to which no one ever moved and in which there was no construction of new houses. Generations of families inhabited the same block, if not house. Yet here in San Mateo and environs I found communities of ten thousand which had not even existed a couple of years before. Everyone was from somewhere else. Neighbors barely recognized each other. The street plans of the housing tracts wiggled and curved like lines in a maze, and the houses were indistinguishable from one another. I often felt lost.

On that visit just one hundred years after the first Crystal Palace Exhibition, my most memorable side trip was to a mansion near San Jose which had been inhabited for some years by the recently deceased widow of the founder of the Winchester Rifle Company. This mansion was called the Winchester Mystery House because the widow—alone and apparently afraid of evil spirits—had chosen to ward off her private demons by supporting a never-ending construction process. So long as she could hear the sound of hammers, of men working, the story went, she felt secure and at peace. The consequence of these decades of activity was fascinating to my twelve-year-old eyes: an enormous rambling house full of functionless remnants of the widow's expensive obsession. There were doors which opened onto blank walls; staircases which led nowhere; bathtubs and toilets without plumbing; entire wings unused. This—and California in general—was the first truly "decentered" universe I had entered.

So, studying in France, contemplating the editorial about the black swine and examining Brown's bright canvas of Hampstead, I was able to imagine a Victorian person feeling, in the face of the changing, torn-apart city, the same loss and fascination and confusion I had experienced in the Winchester Mystery House. And the unknowable was certainly more scary to our ancestors. I could always go home again, and I was too young to have begun to fuss about the metaphysical implications of social disjunction. Ironically, I well knew because of my participatory research that Hampstead—unlike California—had resisted change. The Heath Street in Brown's painting is still recognizable today; and a large part of Hampstead's chic derives from the maintenance of a preservationist spirit.

In any case, the apparently isolated *Daily Telegraph* editorial—isolated in the sense that it appears at first to be merely a protest against a specific crime wave in the slums—can be seen now as a glass under which we can more closely examine many aspects of Victorian culture. This editorial confirms as well as anything I have encountered in Victorian newspapers Dyos's observation that the "true verbal and graphic equivalent of urbanism is journalism proper, the best lens we have for a close-up of the Victorian city, of its disconnections, intimacies, conflicts, aberrations, incidents—of its whole symbiotic continuum and style."

19

❖

Happy Endings

The snouts of the swine—and the influence of Sensation stories—reach far and wide beyond mid-Victorian Hampstead (or England). In the history of literature, for example, we might talk about the disruptive force which news of "reality" had on "realism." George Levine's *The Realistic Imagination* (1981) neatly summarizes the transitions one can discern when taking a long view of nineteenth-century prose fiction:

> If we move from Austen [in the early nineteenth century] to Conrad [at the end of that century], we can watch the implications of reversals within Austen's *oeuvre* and within particular texts. . . . Things become animate, as in Dickens, or they leap, as in Conrad, into a chaos of conflicting passions. The implicit contention between the disorder of reality and the order of comedy becomes explicit. Desire and disorder contend and flow together. The vivid imitation of the common walks of life becomes a nightmare or a game.

After the 1850s, Levine says, George Eliot's works "indicate if not the collapse of a faith in the meaningfulness of the real world, at least a collapse of faith in the dominant reality of the empirically verifiable." In *The Mill on Floss* (1860), for example, reality is a "destructive and formless flood." In Conrad, beginning near the turn of the century, "Everything external—seen with a Dickensian madness of clarity—becomes psychological and disruptive."

In fact, it is in Conrad's *Heart of Darkness* (which first appeared in *Blackwood's* in 1899 and then was revised for book publication in 1902) that we find a story which is not only one of the preeminent examples of the transition from the nineteenth century to modernism, but a tale which best illuminates the significance of Victorian sensationalism in twentieth-century high art.

Readers will perhaps remember that *Heart of Darkness* opens with five men socializing on board a yacht in the Thames estuary. One of them, Marlow, then spins a yarn. His story traces his experience as a ship's captain for a European corporation which collects ivory in Africa and exports it back home. (The assumption is that the African country—and river—is the Congo, and the European nation is Belgium.) Marlow arrives at the station on the coast to find murmurings of weird doings at the company's furthest outpost, deep in the jungle. He embarks with a company of "pilgrims" to steam upriver and find out what has happened to Kurtz, the company's agent there, and, of course, to lay claim to the precious ivory. Marlow and his band are ambushed by natives but finally they penetrate to Kurtz's compound. They find this cleared outpost of civilization ornamented only by slim standing posts onto which are impaled human skulls. Kurtz, seriously ill, has apparently fallen under the spell of the savages among whom he has been living—in particular a "wild and gorgeous apparition of a woman," a sensual black priestess draped in animal furs.

These details are particularly ironic because, Marlow tells us, Kurtz's "mother was half-English, his father half-French. All Europe contributed to the making of Kurtz, and by and by I learned that most appropriately the International Society for the Suppression of Savage Customs had entrusted him with the making of a report for its future guidance."

Finally, Kurtz dies, but not before confiding in his last words (to Marlow) what he has learned from his sojourn into the heart of darkness. "The horror! The horror!" he exclaims.

Marlow manages to escape back to the coast. His report on Kurtz (along with Kurtz's own report on savage customs) is considered quite unsatisfactory by his employers. He is sent back to the "sepulchral city" in Europe which is the company's headquarters. There he feels obliged by custom to visit Kurtz's fiancée. She asks what her dead lover's last words were. Marlow hesitates, then tells a lie: "The last word he pronounced was—your name."

The story switches back to the yacht near London. Marlow, having concluded his memoir, worries aloud to his friends whether he had "rendered Kurtz that justice which was his due. Hadn't he said he wanted only justice? But I couldn't. I could not tell her. It would have been too dark—too dark altogether. . . ."

Heart of Darkness is a story which lends itself to a multitude of interpretations, many of them consistent with the pervasive influence I have already claimed for the sensationalism of almost half a century before. Conrad uses the contrast of the modern city and the primitive jungle to construct a sardonic fable about the exploitive moral emptiness of capitalistic colonialism. Marlow looks back before commencing his narration at London and sees "the mournful gloom brooding motionless over the biggest, and the greatest, town on earth." Then he acknowledges that the area he sees from the Thames "also has been one of the dark places of the earth." He contemplates what he imagines a Roman settler might have found there: "utter savagery"; the "incomprehensible which is also detestable"; and the "fascination of the abomination." These foreshadow his adventure in central Africa, which happens to be one of the blank spaces on the map that his nineteenth-century controlling imagination had always wanted to fill in. And the recounting of that adventure evokes again and again the attempt at a "triumph of the wilderness" over civilization. *Heart of Darkness* is then implicitly related to the *Daily Telegraph* editorial in 1859 which portends much the same sort of trampling of urban rationality by wild beasts. Moreover, we need not only read into the story its significance for twentieth-century literature; this influence is openly acknowledged by T. S. Eliot's archetypal modernist poem of futility, "The Hollow Men" (1925) which uses as its epigraph a line from Conrad's story (spoken in the story with "scathing contempt" by a black servant at the company outpost): " 'Mistah Kurtz—he dead.' "

Peter Brooks's *Reading for the Plot* (1985) understands *Heart of Darkness*'s tie to past and future and penetrates Conrad's fiction even more deeply. Although Brooks is not writing about nineteenth-century social history or crime literature per se, he does acknowledge the essentially Victorian quality of the detective story, traces of which are quite evident in *Heart of Darkness*. For me, Brooks's analysis also reinforces a sense of alliance between Conrad's text and the subversive posture toward orthodoxy I have found in Victorian sensationalism. Reading Brooks for the first time, I began to see Marlow's journey as a parallel—if more perilous—version of Bell Macdonald's paper chase through the police reports. After all, Marlow's trek upriver is not only a mission to bring back Kurtz, his report, and the ivory, but it functions, according to Brooks, as a fictional "unravelling of the threads of civilization," an investigation of "a very lack of the possibility of order."

Marlow, therefore, while confronting the conflict between savagery and civilization (like a detective trying to extract order from disorder, a real nineteenth-century gentleman) must ultimately try to face up to the real significance of Kurtz's last words. "The horror! The horror!" as Brooks says, are "about as close as articulate speech can come to the primal cry." They represent "minimal language, language on the verge of reversion to savagery, on the verge of a fall from language." We are reminded here once again of many of the essentials of the Sensation controversy, particularly of *The Christian Remembrancer*'s 1863 denunciation of the animalistic language of Sensation novels.

But Brooks of course is not interested in prescribing morality. He wants to demonstrate that *Heart of Darkness* is not only about society and psychology but about language, and about telling tales, about how "the very start of Marlow's narrative suggests an infinite possibility of repetition when he reaches back nineteen hundred years to imagine the Roman commander navigating up the Thames, into a land of savagery: a further level of *fabula,* an ancient historical story that all modern stories must rehearse."

Brooks's approach to language and narrative structure is fascinating, but I must reluctantly draw back from it here, because for the purposes of my study I want to keep my focus on the specific role of savagery in the mistellings of truth encountered in Conrad rather than on the "infinite possibility of repetition," though this latter insight is as clearly relevant. Here Brooks is moving into one of the areas beyond the limits I had to set for myself back in the dark room in sunny Provence. The many able and willing practitioners of the newer forms of literary criticism—of deconstruction, of narratology, of semiotics—I hope will be able to apply their theories to these forgotten police reports and neglected crime novels and harvest an abundance of indeterminacy. I must resist the temptation to anticipate them. My chosen task is to continue to sort out the relationship between certain criminal and sexual aspects of the printed word and particular events which occurred in the nineteenth century.

This places me, I am aware, in something of a precarious situation with my colleagues. For decades, after all, literary critics have divided themselves into two general groups: those who, as articulated by G. Thomas Tanselle, regard works of literature as "verbal icons" or "linguistic moments" and feel that they have freed themselves of historical restraints; and those others who hold that the meaning of literature emerges from a knowledge of its historical context. In this respect, I am sure, there are those who will think I have been playing both sides of the street. On the one hand, throughout this book I have attempted to pay close attention to the intrinsic values of the texts I have confronted. In this sense I have considered them out of time, as it were, when it was convenient. I also have acknowledged that many of my interpretations are indeterminate and may well fluctuate from moment to moment, from reader to reader. These readings also incline to the ahistorical. On the other hand, I have clearly not abandoned history. It seems to me that, without understanding the "facts" of Victorian progress, not to mention the "ideology" of that progress, we will never fully appreciate the multiple ironies of terms like "Sensation" or images like that of the black swine. I would like to think that I have profited from my acquaintance with both sides of the question. Perhaps, indeed, Bell Macdonald's clippings have enabled us to contemplate the convergence of these often incompatible points of view.

A reading of *Heart of Darkness,* then, can move us back and forth from the intricacies of ahistorical narrative analysis to ideas which derive from "the facts" of actual Victorian people and events. Consider the title of Brooks's chapter on *Heart of Darkness:* "An Unreadable Report." Here Brooks, as in his discussion of telling and retelling, is calling attention to the infinite possibilities, and impossibilities, of language. Marlow's story is "unreadable" to

Kurtz's fiancée (in the first and last place) because she stands for, as do Kurtz's origins, bourgeois European culture. The truth, Marlow tells his friends, is therefore "too dark" for her. (Remember Thackeray's comment that the Northumberland Street affair would be "too dark" for a street preacher's sermon!) So Marlow lies. Kurtz's original report is also an untruth because the basic text whitewashes conditions in the jungle. The postscript Kurtz added to the report on his deathbed—a scrawled order to "exterminate" savage customs and, presumably, savages themselves—is not only indiscreet but makes less sense than the whitewash in light of Kurtz's seeming immersion in these very customs. So Marlow prevaricates again—by actually removing the postscript before turning in the report to the company. One could say that virtually everything in the story is unreadable. The prehistory is unreadable. The primitive is unreadable. The unconscious is unreadable in and of itself. However, besides all the unreadability and necessity for retelling, there still remains the actuality of the Victorian temper—and the language expressing that temper—which Conrad's story appears designed to subvert. This is the infinite potential for not telling the whole truth, for suppression and distortion of distasteful fact.

As I have already demonstrated throughout my own story, this distorting tendency was particularly remarkable in the middle years of the nineteenth century because newly popular newspapers and crime novels suggested implicitly and explicitly that buried "savage customs" might well be re-enacting themselves in the greatest city, and country, on earth, in an age that had become "pure." In *Heart of Darkness* this defensive instinct has become also aggressive, exploitive. Marlow's lies (and those of the company, among others) at virtually each step tend to confound, to make it easier to displace and deny the horror that Kurtz has discovered and Marlow has discovered in Kurtz. These selective alterations of reality also conveniently (against the avowed drift of Marlow's intelligence, by the way) serve to allow the perpetuation of the exploitation of the non-white world in the service of ideology—religious, economic, racial.

Just remember: Africa is "darkness"; Kurtz's last words are "too dark" for European civilization; the swine threatening to uproot Hampstead are "black." (Freud referred to woman as the "dark continent," which suggests a sexist component as well.) These images suggest that sensationalism illuminates the libidinal inheritance from the past the Victorians worked so hard to suppress, as well as the murderously oppressive and discriminatory future which they were to impose (with self-satisfied "justification") on others whom they did not or could not understand or control—ostensibly in the service of "God." History is not only a story of people retelling stories which are not exactly true, but a story of defensive wish-fulfillment overlapping with self-serving and self-righteous greed. And this racialist component—as we near the conclusion of our survey of multiple understandings and misunderstandings of the savage breasts of other Victorians—cannot be passed over.

In fact, there is a racial undercurrent near the surface of many of the discussions of sensationalism throughout the 1860s. Images of disease, bestiality, and sex occur and recur in the context of "blackness," and not only in the peculiar blackness assigned to the swine under Hampstead. A ready example not previously examined can be found in a *Westminster Review* attack on *Armadale* in 1866: "There is no accounting for tastes, blubber for the Esquimaux, half-hatched eggs for the Chinese, and Sensational novels for the English." The writer recalls the Middle Ages when "afflicted" people barked like dogs and mewed like cats. Now, he goes on, "as those diseases always occurred in seasons of death and poverty, so does the Sensational Mania in Literature burst out only in times of mental poverty and afflict only the most poverty-stricken minds." Now the "mania" for Sensation seems to have changed from "epidemic" to "endemic." Its "virus" is spreading in all directions. The reviewer alludes to a showman who once traveled the country with a menagerie including "a big black baboon, whose habits were so filthy, and whose behaviour was so disgusting," that "respectable" people complained. The showman responded that without the big black baboon his show would be ruined because the ape attracted all the young girls in the country. In a like manner, the review continues, by 1866,

bigamy has been Miss Braddon's big black baboon, with which she has attracted all the young girls in the country. And now Mr. Wilkie Collins has set up a big black baboon on his own account. His big black baboon is Miss Gwilt, a bigamist, thief, gaol-bird, forgeress, murderess, and suicide. This beats all Miss Braddon's big black baboons put together. . . .

This is a review which seems to have evolution and cultural relativism on its mind as much as popular storytelling. And, indeed, in the last stages of my research I was lucky enough to encounter a newly published book which demonstrates the intense impact awareness of other races had on thought and life in the mid-Victorian era. In *Victorian Anthropology* (1987), George W. Stocking composes a densely comprehensive history of the study of mankind. Like Peter Brooks's analysis of Conrad (not to mention Brooks's chapters on Dickens and Freud), his work is particularly helpful in drawing conclusions about the peculiar relationship between the Victorian official consciousness and sensationalism. One gets from Stocking a clear articulation of the general racial and evolutionary implications of *The Daily Telegraph's* black swine or the *Westminster Review*'s big black baboon or LeFanu's satanic monkey. Seeing the world from the point of view of the Victorians, Stocking manages to effectively fill in the cultural background against which the news reports and crime novels themselves evolved into the higher species of Conrad's fiction.

Stocking, beginning with the Crystal Palace Exhibition of 1851, examines the contents of that predecessor of our World's Fairs. The fact was that the major exhibit categories—Raw Materials, Machinery, Manufactures, and Fine Arts—tended to emphasize the development of industrialized nations at the expense of those which were not industrial. It was difficult for "less advanced aborigines" to participate at all, and contributions from British colonies usually found themselves in the Raw Material category. There were pandamus mats from Tahiti, and a large stuffed elephant from India; but, Stocking writes,

Appropriately, the fullest expression of the European spirit of civilized industry was found in the west wing. There, in the rooms filled with machinery in motion, one could watch the power looms, the model locomotives, the centrifugal pumps, the vertical steam engines. . . . [The] British Industrial

Revolution, pandemonic in its noise, but cleansed for the moment of its pain, went twirling and thrusting away. . . .

Here in the west wing, the "most obvious lesson of the Exhibition" was drawn: "that in pursuing their sacred mission not all men had advanced at the same pace, or arrived at the same point." The white European races, particularly the Anglo-Saxon, had established—or invented—a moral and genetic hegemony out of the technological imbalance.

The ethnocentrism, or outright racism, implied in this lesson set the stage for decades of indifference to, and justified aggression against, the essential humanity of people of other cultures, culminating in full-scale extermination of populations. One of the many ironies embedded here is that establishment scientists and critics who at first resisted the implied connection of mankind to animals in Darwin now managed to use *Origin of Species* to their own purposes. They turned the tables, justifying colonialism by citing the backwardness of others on the evolutionary scale. Darwin's work was further perverted by the notion that "savages" were not even human, but products of different geneological systems. Stocking cites our old friend Henry Thomas Buckle on the problem of "national character." In Buckle's *History of Civilization,* we may recall, the subjectivity of murder and suicide was seen as misleading, the acts having actually been dictated by fixed environmental laws—always in the services of English Protestant civilization. Stocking points out that Buckle also felt that "savages" had no national character. This logic of Buckle's then determined that civilization was divided into two parts: "European, where the tendency was 'to subordinate nature to man'; and the non-European, 'where it was to subordinate man to nature.' " Places like India, Egypt, Mexico, and Peru, for example, merely illustrated the "immense mischief" of the powers of nature over man, and thus were not worthy of consideration as progressive cultures.

We are, in short, back to the argument frequently rehearsed by critics of sensationalism, who dismissed accounts of court proceedings and fictional thrillers (not to mention one half of consciousness in the psychological concept of "Sensation") as subhuman or uncivilized. As I was reading Stocking, in fact, I recalled an essay I had encountered years before, at the time I was spending my days in the New York Public Library looking up all the listings for "Sensation" in various bibliographies. This was Laurence Oliphant's "Sensation Diplomacy in Japan" which appeared in *Blackwood's* in 1863. In that piece, Oliphant argues that the penchant of the Japanese for beheading one another and committing hara-kiri—these were the acts considered "Sensation Diplomacy"—disqualified Orientals from either sympathy or the benefits of a democratic political system. (Much the same argument was used by others—James Fitzjames Stephen, who was Virginia Woolf's uncle, among them—to justify the continuing oppression of the Indian subcontinent.)

Stocking says that this sort of relegation of exotic cultures to inferior or alien status became more common after the Crystal Palace, enabling British imperialists to discourage democratic institutions or humane treatment for the lesser races of the colonies. He also manages to shed even more light on London's own "black swine" who were, of course, usually of Anglo-Saxon or Celtic stock. Contemporary middle-class observers distinguished—as did, we remember, H. A. Page in "The Morality of Literary Art" (in the *Contemporary Review* in 1867) on the pretext of establishing contemporary guidelines for creativity—between the "rural primitivism" of pre-industrial "Merrie England" and the "disturbing and alien phenomenon" of contemporary city slums. Even for Engels and Mayhew the slumdwellers were a "race apart." By and large the Victorians—all exceptional reformers admitted—attempted to keep this enemy within, and its savagery, at a distance, or to rationalize it into a non-threatening or irrelevant status.

In any case, we find in Stocking's *Victorian Anthropology* further illumination of the midcentury anti-Enlightenment which denied so vigorously the presence of crime and sex in British society and—as a related phenomenon—promoted the inhumane exploitation of other nations and races in the name of progress. These paradoxes—at once insanely comical, sex-ridden, and perversely barbaric—are the subject of the police reports, the Sensation novel, and *Heart of Darkness*. And, in the end, the response of Victorian anthropologists to the unpalatable realities they discovered was not unlike that of their contemporaries, the critics confounded by sensationalism. George Levine, reviewing Stocking for *The New York Times*, eloquently articulates the parallel between the ideological obligations of science and literature in Victorian England:

> The end of Mr. Stocking's story is not, of course, an end. He shows how Victorian anthropology became part of the deep passion of the Victorians for replacing their lost religion with a human culture that was both rational and progressive. It made the irrational comprehensible by subjecting it to science. "By equating the irrational with the primitive, it was possible to bring it under the control of cultural progress." That is, anthropology became another great Victorian fiction with a happy ending.

The happy ending then was the singular element the Victorian establishment demanded, and it is what news reports like those on the Rugeley poisonings did not give it. It is what novels like *Lady Audley's Secret,* with its sly sardonic inversions of peaceful closure, refused to serve up. The natural antagonism between unpalatable verisimilitude and the happy ending is indeed the overriding subversive concern of *Heart of Darkness.* When the act of telling the whole truth is to also admit "the horror," the mind cannot bear but to retreat into selective or incomplete memory.

In attempting, then, to explain the Victorians' inclination to suppress their open secrets, I would say that perhaps it was because they had more to forget; more precisely, it was because they were *afraid* they had more to forget. Their passion for this forgetting (or code of respectability) provides one of the more chilling implications of our readings in Victorian sensationalism: that selective memory can slip into a self-righteous and selective discrimination which in turn provides a reinforced ideological base from which wholesale exploitation, even slaughter, can be justified as a necessary adjunct to progress. This is the ultimate horror.

A Brief and Idiosyncratic Chronology of England: 1832–71

1832 First Reform Bill moves political power to sections of middle class. Whigs control Parliament.

1834 New Poor Law, at least in short run, leads to callous treatment of unemployed and homeless. Peel's Tory government replaces Whigs. Criminal Law Commission initiated.

1835 Whigs return. Municipal Reform Act gives newly developing cities increased national political clout. Railway boom.

1837 Accession of Victoria as Queen of England and of William Bell Macdonald as Laird of Rammerscales, near Lockerbie, Scotland. Publication of *Oliver Twist*, at once a "Newgate novel" and a vicious attack on heartlessness of Poor Law and conditions in slums. Collapse of railway boom.

1838 Negro Emancipation. *Sirius* is first steamship to cross Atlantic.

1839 Daguerreotype photograph introduced. Postage reduced to a penny. Bell Macdonald begins his collection of clippings of criminal reports from newspapers.

1841 *Punch* introduced. Whigs fall. Peel is P.M. again.

1842 Chartist riots. Hong Kong annexed. Daniel Good, a London coachman, tried and executed for murdering his mistress. Detective Department created in London Police. Income tax introduced. First illustrated news magazines appear.

1845 Railway mania. Failure of potato crop.

1846 Lord Russell becomes P.M., beginning two decades of ever more frequent—almost annual—changes in government. Repeal of Corn Laws. *Daily News* begins to publish, adding commentary to news.

1847 *Vanity Fair, Wuthering Heights,* and *Jane Eyre* published. Chloroform first used. Potato famine.

1848 European revolutions bypass England. Cholera epidemics.

1849 Dickens's magazine *Household Words* begins publication, as do Henry

231

Mayhew's muckraking columns on poor and criminal classes for the *Morning Chronicle*. Tenant farmer James Rush murders his landlord at Stanfield Hall, Norwich. G. P. Manning and his wife Maria murder Patrick O'Connor in their Bermondsey, London, house and bury him in the basement. Telegraph system in place. Punjab annexed. Gold discovered in California.

1851   Crystal Palace Exhibition shows Britain to be the workshop of the world in the age of the machine. Dr. Livingstone reaches Zambesi. Dickens begins *Bleak House*.

1852   Ford Madox Brown embarks on his allegorical painting of excavations in Hampstead: *Work*. Government produces Sewerage and Cholera reports.

1854   More cholera outbreaks. Crimean War: first "Special Correspondent" dispatched by *The Times* to cover debacle there. Working Man's College founded.

1855   Abolition of Stamp Duty on newspapers. Special correspondents abound. Railway system in place. London connected by telegraph to the Black Sea.

1856   Emergence of *Daily Telegraph*, leader of new penny dailies. Peace of Paris. Holman Hunt paints *The Scapegoat*. Bombardment of Canton. The Rugeley Poisoning Case: surgeon William Palmer tried and executed. Outrage over extent and detail of news coverage.

1857   Indian Mutiny. Glut of adultery suits in newspapers. Thomas Hughes's *Tom Brown's Schooldays* spreads doctrine of "muscular Christianity." Trial of Madeline Smith for poisoning her French lover ends with verdict of "not proven."

1858   Conspiracy to Murder Bill. India taken over by the Crown from East India Company. Jews admitted to Parliament. Divorce Act becomes law. Mrs. Robinson sued for divorce on the evidence of her diary. Dickens publicly separates from his wife of twenty-two years.

1859   Darwin's *Origin of Species* published. Beginning of serial run of Wilkie Collins's *The Woman in White* in Dickens's new magazine, *All the Year Round*, following *A Tale of Two Cities*, initiates craze for Sensation fiction. Livingstone reaches Lake Nyasa. Prosecution bungles case against Dr. Smethurst for poisoning his wife, but convicts him of bigamy. Surreptitious disposal of illegitimate child by doctor, clergyman, and undertaker.

1860–61   *Great Expectations* and Bulwer-Lytton's *A Strange Story* follow *The Woman in White* in *All the Year Round*. Victoria Station completed. Serialization of *Lady Audley's Secret* begins. *Cornhill Magazine* founded by Thackeray. Repeal of Paper Duty. *Daily Telegraph* overtakes *The Times* as daily circulation leader. Population of London reaches 3 million, triple the number of 1801.

1862   William Bell Macdonald dies and clipping of court reports at Rammerscales ceases. Controversy over fictional sensationalism erupts in critical journals.

1863   London Underground opens. Taiping Rebellion.

1865   *Our Mutual Friend* and *Alice's Adventures in Wonderland* published. Antiseptic surgery introduced. Sanitation system almost general, but cholera persists in undrained slums. Ford Madox Brown's *Work* is completed.

1867   Second Reform Bill further extends franchise.

1870   Dickens dies, leaving *Mystery of Edwin Drood* unfinished.

1871   First Impressionist Exhibition in France.
         Population of London reaches 4 million.

Notes

Bell Macdonald's clippings are referred to as *Trials* throughout.

Prologue: A Lost Archive of Crime

p. 4   Humphrey House, *The Dickens World*. 2nd ed. (1942; London: Oxford University Press, 1971), p. 211.

Chapter 1: Bawdy Victorians

p. 11   John Challis: *Trials*, III, 164.

p. 12   "Melancholy Death": *Ibid.*, III, 128, p. 101.

p. 13   Steven Marcus, *The Other Victorians* (1966; New York: NAL, 1974).

p. 13   "Indecent and most extraordinary conduct": *Trials*, IV, 150.

p. 14   "More Zeal Than Discretion": *Ibid.*, IV, 139.

p. 14   "Chacun à Son Goût: *Ibid.*, IV, 375.

p. 16   "A Merry Tale from Croydon": *Ibid.*, IV, 61–62.

p. 16   "The grotesque character of the details": "Life in London," *Ibid.*, IV, 64.

p. 17   Marquess of Lansdowne. Quoted (pp. 4–5) in a curiously prurient compilation of infidelities—perhaps produced in the underground of soft-core and hard-core pornographic presses—called *Crim. Con.: Actions and Trials and Other Legal Proceedings Relating to Marriage before the Passing of the Present Divorce Act*. The book describes the Divorce Act as occurring "thirty years ago" (p. 1), which would establish the publishing date as 1887 or 1888.

p. 17   *Ling* v. *Croker*: "Extraordinary Trial for Crim. Con.," *Trials*, IV, 11.

p. 19   "It is impossible to look": *Trials*, V, 349.

p. 19   "Confessional in Belgravia": *Trials*, IV, 139–40.

p. 20   Breach of promise: *Trials*, III, 27.

p. 20   Hugh Rowley: *Trials*, V, 20–21, 58–68.

Chapter 2: Seeds of Paradise

p. 21   "The Outrage at the War Office": *Trials*, III, 2.

p. 22   Ignorance and depravity: *Trials*, IV, 66.

p. 23   Marcus, *The Other Victorians*, p. 11.

p. 24   Marcus on Ashbee: See *The Other Victorians*, pp. 54–55.

p. 24   Elton and Crawley: *Trials*, IV, 138.

Chapter 3: Brutal Victorians

p. 27   "Murder by Starvation": *Trials*, III, 13.

p. 30   "The Horrible Case of Child Murder": *Ibid.*, III, 155.

Chapter 4: Sensuality and Slavery

p. 35   The Sloanes: *Trials*, II, 104–08, 117–19.

p. 37   J. H. Plumb, "The Victorians Unbuttoned," *In the Light of History* (Boston: Houghton Mifflin, 1973), pp. 244–46.

Chapter 5: Newgate to Newspapers

p. 41   Statistics: There are many sources but I am particularly indebted to Raymond Williams's *The Long Revolution* (London: Chatto & Windus, 1961) for my perspective here.

p. 42   Richard Altick, *Victorian Studies in Scarlet* (New York: Norton, 1970), pp. 43–44, 56. It should be noted that Altick has less enthusiasm than I for the significance of Victorian police reports as research sources, worrying about their "unreliability" (p. 11) and their "necessarily evasive language" (p. 36). Of course, reliability is not my primary concern here—though the reports in *Trials* seem as factual as any other comparable annals—and I believe I have clearly established that the language is less evasive than even that of our own liberated times.

p. 42   Luke Heath: Andrew Knapp and William Baldwin, eds., *The Newgate Calendar* (London: J. Robins, 1828), IV, 123–25.

p. 42   John Thurtell, et al.: *Ibid.*, 353–74. The last case in this volume deals with the hanging of William Probert, chief witness against Thurtell and Hunt, for horse stealing.

Chapter 6: A Pre-Victoria Media Murder

p. 48   *The Morning Chronicle*, October 31, 1823, p. 3, cols. 4–5. The quote about murder speaking with "most miraculous organ" is from *Hamlet*, and the symbolic significance of that play to Victorian crime writers—allusions recur consistently—is worth a monograph of its own.

p. 50   Pierce Egan interviews Thurtell: *The Times*, December 9, 1823, p. 2, col. 5. There is also here an interview with the prisoner conducted by Sir Edmund Nagle, who had been Thurtell's commanding officer in the Navy.

p. 50   "A run-of-the-mill affair": Altick, *Victorian Studies in Scarlet*, p. 23.

p. 51   Editorial in *Morning Chronicle* of December 17, 1823, is on p. 2, cols. 3–5. The 1772 monograph cited appeared in a volume titled *Joineriana*.

p. 52   Fewer than twenty murder convictions per year: The "Postscript" to Knapp and Baldwin's 1828 volume of *The Newgate Calendar* claims that 579 people were executed in England between 1819 and 1825. One hundred and one of these had been convicted of murder; the rest included arsonists, burglars and other thieves, forgers, rapists, sodomites, traitors, and perpetrators of "sacrilege." There were at the time, according to the editors, "about 223" offenses "made capital by the laws of England," two thirds of which were introduced during the reign of George III (1760–1820).

p. 53   Wordsworth: In "Preface to Lyrical Ballads," see *Prose of the Romantic Period*, ed. Carl Woodring (Boston: Houghton Mifflin, 1961), pp. 53–54.

Chapter 7: Bell Macdonald's 1840s

p. 55   On Daniel Good: *Trials*, I, 69. Macdonald clipped this from *The Times*, May 6, 1842, p. 6, col. 1.

p. 56   On the Mannings: "Execution of the Mannings," *Trials*, I, 380.

p. 57   Preface: *Illustrated London News*, I (1842), n.p.

p. 58   On Daniel Good: *Ibid.*, p. 32.

p. 58   On Mannings: *Ibid.*, n.v. (Sept. 1, 1849), pp. 150–51.

Chapter 8: The Devil in Patent Leather Boots

p. 63   James Hannay, "Letter from Britain," *New York Daily Tribune* (June 21, 1856), p. 6.

p. 64   Dr. Jones's testimony: "Supposed Murder by a Surgeon," *Trials*, III, 302.

p. 65   Chambermaid's testimony: *Ibid.*, 303.

p. 66   Dickens's letter to John Forster in Sept. 1857. Cited by Edgar Johnson in *Charles Dickens, His Tragedy and Triumph* (New York: Simon & Schuster, 1952), p. 880.

p. 67   Walkenden's testimony: "The Third Coroner's Inquest: The Deceased's Intemperance," *ibid.*, 315.

p. 68   Taylor's testimony: "Supposed Murder by a Surgeon," *ibid.*, 303.

p. 70   Taylor's report: "Latest Particulars: Professor Taylor's Analysis," *ibid.*, 310–11.

p. 70   *Medical Times and Gazette*: *Ibid.*, 323–24. *Household Words* is quoted in the same volume, p. 361.

p. 70   Coroner's inquiry into deaths of Anne and Walter Palmer: "The Exhumed Bodies," *ibid.*, 308.

p. 71   Wife to housekeeper: "Expected Fresh Disclosures," *ibid.*, 308.

p. 72   Horse named Strychnine: "The Suspected Poisoning Case," *ibid.*, 308.

p. 72   Criticism of Taylor's analysis: "The Adjourned Inquest," *ibid.*, 307.

p. 73   Verdict gives satisfaction: "Conclusion of the Inquest on Mrs. Palmer," *ibid.*, 312.

p. 74   "Utter impossibility to form a correct diagnosis": "Exhumation of the Body of Cook," *ibid.*, 328.

p. 75   Taylor dogmatical yet contradictory on Smethurst: *Trials.*, IV, 349–50.

Chapter 9: A Very Special Correspondence

p. 78   "Let us imagine a . . . Parisian": *Trials*, III, 324; *The Leader*, 7 (January 19, 1856), p. 52.

p. 80   Graveyard poets: *Ibid.*

p. 80   Palmer's personal appearance: *Trials*, III, 325; *The Leader*, January 19, p. 52.

p. 82   Courtroom satire: "The Rugeley Poisonings," *Trials*, III, 327; *The Leader*, January 26, 1856, p. 80.

p. 82   Pecksniff: *Ibid.*

p. 82   Victorian morality overblown: Angus Wilson, *The World of Charles Dickens* (New York: Viking, 1970), p. 177.

p. 82   Palmer's wife's upbringing: *Trials*, III, 326; *The Leader*, January 26, 1856, p. 78.

p. 83   All the incidents: *Trials*, III, 325; *The Leader*, January 19, 1856, p. 54.

p. 84   Paris danced: "Palmer at Stafford," *Trials*, III, 364; *The Leader*, June 14, 1856, p. 557.

p. 84   Description of Stafford: "Execution of William Palmer," *Trials*, III, 369; *The Leader*, June 21, 1856, p. 582.

p. 85   Evening at Cremorne: "Palmer at Stafford," *Trials*, 364; *The Leader*, June 14, 1856, p. 557. In *The Other Victorians*, Marcus quotes a remarkably similar passage on the Cremorne Gardens, from William Acton's 1857 study, *Prostitution*.

p. 87   "Walking slowly to the gate": *Ibid.*

p. 88   To the gallows: "Execution of William Palmer," *Trials*, III, 370–71; *The Leader*, June 21, 1856, p. 583.

p. 90   "[The] sensation is again indisputable": Margaret Oliphant, "Sensation Novels," *Blackwood's Edinburgh Magazine*, 91 (May 1862), p. 572.

p. 91   Summary of Palmer's career: "Execution of William Palmer," *Trials*, III, 372; *The Leader*, June 21, p. 583.

Chapter 10: Adventures of a Scholar-Detective

p. 94   Dissertation: Allan R. Brick, *The Leader, Organ of Radicalism*. Ph.D. Dissertation, Yale University, 1957.

p. 95   T. H. S. Escott, *Masters of English Journalism* (London: T. F. Unwin, 1911), pp. 222–23.

p. 95   Parliamentary columns: Edward M. Whitty, *St. Stephen's in the Fifties*, ed. Justin McCarthy (London: T. F. Unwin, 1906), p. xxxv.

p. 97   The Rugeley Edition of the *Illustrated Times* appeared February 2, 1856.

p. 97   Gay on *Saturday Review*: pp. 378, 406.

p. 99   "A kind of artistic Newgate Calendar": "Our Civilization," *Saturday Review* (June 28, 1856), pp. 195–96.

Chapter 11: "Morbid Depression Alternating with Excitement"

p. 103   Saturday Review on Mrs. Robinson: "The Purity of the Press," *Saturday Review* (June 26, 1858), pp. 56–57.

p. 103   Robinsons' marital history: "*Robinson* v. *Robinson and Lane*," *Trials*, IV, 137.

p. 104   Oct. 7, Sunday: *Ibid.*

p. 105   That evening, in the library: *Ibid.*

p. 106   Next day, on the hill: *Ibid.*

p. 106   Two days later: *Ibid.*

p. 107   In the cab; next day, Oct. 14: *Ibid.*

p. 108   "Morbid depression alternating with excitement": *Ibid.*, 138.

p. 111   "Clear water": "The Purity of the Press," *Saturday Review* (June 26, 1858), p. 657.

p. 112   Mesmer. See L. Chertok and R. deSaussure, *The Therapeutic Revolution: From Mesmer to Freud* (New York: Brunner Mazel, 1979).

p. 113   Hartman on "escapist fantasy": Mary S. Hartman, *Victorian Murderesses* (New York: Schocken), p. 257.

p. 115   Ralph Blumenthal, "Did Freud's Isolation, Peer Rejection, Prompt Key Theory Reversal?" *New York Times*, August 25, 1981, pp. C1, 2.

p. 115   "Being slowly destroyed": J. Hillis Miller, *Charles Dickens: The World of His Novels* (Bloomington: Indiana University Press, 1973), p. 169.

p. 116   Psychiatrist: Ralph Colp, Jr. See his essay, "Charles Darwin, Dr. Edward Lane and the 'Singular Trial' of Robinson v. Robinson and Lane," *Journal of the History of Medicine and the Allied Sciences*, 36 (April 1981), pp. 205–13. Dr. Colp encountered the Robinsons through the files of *The Times*. Many of Bell Macdonald's clippings on the case come from *The Times* as well.

Chapter 12: **Critical Passions: I. Connections**

p. 120   Thomas Hardy, *Desperate Remedies* (London: Macmillan, 1912), p. v.

p. 121   Walter Phillips, *Dickens, Reade and Collins: Sensation Novelists* (New York: Columbia University Press, 1918), p. 92.

p. 121   Braddon: See R. W. Wolff, *Sensational Victorian* (New York: Garland, 1979).

p. 122   *All the Year Round*: Dickens also frequently published topical non-fiction on criminal matters, and their literary and social implications.

p. 123   On Collins's ambiguous position in London society: S. M. Ellis, *Wilkie Collins, LeFanu and Others* (London: Constable, 1931), p. 28.

p. 124   Bulwer-Lytton: Robert Lee Wolff, *Strange Stories* (Boston: Gambit, 1971), p. 156.

p. 124   LeFanu: See Ellis, among others.

p. 125   W. F. Rae, "Sensation Novelists: Miss Braddon," *North British Review*, XLII (1865), p. 181.

p. 125   "Studiously, and of set purpose": "The Morality of Literary Art," *Contemporary Review*, II (June 1867), p. 164.

p. 125   "There is an aroma": "Orley Farm," *National Review*, XVI (January 1863), p. 30.

p. 125   Margaret Oliphant, "Sensation Novels," p. 566.

p. 126   Henry James, "Miss Braddon," *The Nation* 1 (Nov. 9, 1865), p. 593.

p. 126   "The Sensational Williams," *All the Year Round*, 11 (Feb. 13, 1864), p. 14.

p. 127   Henry James, "Miss Braddon," p. 593.

p. 128　H. L. Mansel, "Sensation Novels," *Quarterly Review*, 114 (April 1863), p. 261.

p. 129　Unroofing London: *Trials*, V, 33. This is part of an extended allusion to the demon Asmodeus in LeSage's *The Devil on Two Sticks* (1725). Asmodeus transports a young Spanish cavalier over the rooftops of Madrid, revealing all the goings-on inside.

p. 130　Plaistow murder: Review of *Uncle Silas* by J. S. LeFanu, *The Times*, April 14, 1865, p. 4.

p. 134　"Transform their real situations": Miller, *Charles Dickens: The World of His Novels*, p. 306.

p. 134　"On the threshold of the twentieth century": *Ibid.*, p. 293.

Chapter 13: Critical Passions: II. Missed Connections

p. 136　"Hybrid combinations": "The Philosophy of Sensation," *St. James*, 5 (August– November 1862), p. 343.

p. 138　Stephen Jay Gould, *An Urchin in the Storm* (New York: Norton, 1987), p. 9.

p. 139　Daniel Bell, *The Cultural Contradictions of Capitalism* (New York: Basic Books, 1976), p. 9.

p. 139　A. H. Japp (H. A. Page), "The Morality of Literary Art," *Contemporary Review*, II (June 1867), pp. 164–77.

Chapter 14: The Fishy Extremities of *Lady Audley's Secret*

p. 146　On Braddon: Winifred Hughes, *The Maniac in the Cellar: Sensation Novels of the 1860's* (Princeton: Princeton University Press, 1980), p. 122.

p. 146　Constance Kent: Hartman, *Victorian Murderesses*, p. 117.

p. 146　Charles Reade to *The Daily Telegraph*: This letter is reprinted in the endpapers of the 1898 Chatto & Windus edition of *Hard Cash*.

p. 147　The seventeenth-century Lady Audley: Her sensational story is recounted in the volume called *Crim. Con.* cited in the notes for Chapter One.

p. 150　"We hear every day": *Lady Audley's Secret* (New York: Dover, 1974), pp. 19–20.

p. 151　"This northern road": *Ibid.*, p. 159.

p. 151　Mr. Maldon's household goods: *Ibid.*, pp. 105–06.

p. 152　"In those troublesome dreams": *Ibid.*, p. 162.

p. 152　"Villain-finder": Review of *Lady Audley's Secret*, *The Times*, London, November 18, 1862, p. 4.

p. 153　"Opened the outer door": *Lady Audley's Secret*, p. 254.

p. 154　"An unnatural lustre": *Ibid.*, p. 205.

p. 154   "Hanging on his arm": *Ibid.*, p. 65.

p. 155   "The lovely woman with the fishy extremities": Review of *Lady Audley's Secret, The Times*, p. 4.

p. 155   Conclusion of *Lady Audley's Secret*: pp. 285–86.

p. 156   Psalm 37:25: W. M. Thackeray, *The Newcomes* (London: Bradbury & Evans, 1855), II, 336.

p. 157   G. A. Sala, "On the 'Sensational' in Literature and Art," *Belgravia*, 4 (February 1868), p. 449.

Chapter 15: *Armadale:* "A Sensation Novel with a Vengeance"

p. 159   Sensation novel "with a vengeance": H. F. Chorley, review of *Armadale, Athenaeum*, 70 (1866), p. 732.

p. 160   "So complex and tortuous": Robert Ashley, *Wilkie Collins* (London: Arthur Barker, 1950), p. 85.

p. 160   "Labyrinthine": Kenneth Robinson, *Wilkie Collins: A Biography* (London: The Bodley Head, 1951), p. 191.

p. 160   "Material enough for a whole sensation novel": *Ibid.*, p. 192.

p. 160   Getting the plot wrong: Robinson on p. 191 makes no distinction between the two Allan Armadales (see below), while William Marshall (in *Wilkie Collins* [New York: Twayne, 1970]) makes a similar error on p. 73.

p. 160   Prefatory note to *Armadale*. Wilkie Collins, *Armadale* (1900; New York: AMS, 1970), I, 74.

p. 165   "Fairweather Vale": *Ibid.*, II, 425.

p. 166   "Read your newspapers": *Ibid*, II, 47.

p. 167   *Trials*, IV, 358.

p. 167   "Punish her a little": *Armadale*, II, 331.

p. 168   "Healthy Anglo-Saxon flesh": *Ibid.*, I, 100.

p. 168   "Christian kindness": *Ibid.*, I, 102.

p. 169   Robert MacLeod, *The Persistent Problems of Psychology* (Pittsburgh: Duquesne University Press, 1975), pp. 180–82.

p. 169   "The one object": *Armadale*, II, 298–99.

p. 170   "A woman fouler than the refuse of the streets": Review of *Armadale, The Spectator*, 39 (1866), pp. 638–39.

p. 171   "Everything was right": *Armadale*, II, 319.

p. 171   Miss Gwilt's figure: *Ibid.*, I, 470–71.

p. 171   Gwilt's story: Review of *Armadale, The Spectator*, 39 (1866), p. 639.

p. 172   "I shall write no more today": *Armadale*, II, 363.

p. 172   Mother Oldershaw on the stage: *Ibid.*, II, 568–69.

p. 173   Dr. Downward rising: *Ibid.*, II, 565.

Chapter 16: "Green Tea": A Forerunner of *Dr. Jekyll and Mr. Hyde*

p. 175   Elizabeth Bowen, "Introduction," J. S. LeFanu, *Uncle Silas* (London: The Cresset Press, 1947), p. 11.

p. 175   Hesselius on medicine: "Green Tea," *Best Ghost Stories of J. S. LeFanu*, ed. E. F. Bleiler (New York: Dover, 1964), p. 181.

p. 177   On Dr. Harley: *Ibid.*, p. 188.

p. 178   Buckle on murder: Henry Thomas Buckle, *History of Civilization in England*, I (London: Parker, 1858), 20–23.

p. 179   "Law of uniform and periodic repetitions": *Ibid.*, 24.

p. 179   Buckle on suicide: *Ibid.*, 25.

p. 180   Buckle on "cultivators of physical science": *Ibid.*, 32.

p. 180   The monkey on the book: "Green Tea," p. 198.

p. 181   Arnold on periodicals: Matthew Arnold, "The Function of Criticism at the Present Time," *Prose of the Victorian Period*, ed. William Buckler (Boston: Houghton Mifflin, 1958), p. 430. See also *The Wellesley Index to Victorian Periodicals*, ed. Walter Houghton, I (Toronto: University of Toronto Press, 1966), 8.

p. 182   Arnold on Wragg: *Ibid.*, pp. 431–33.

Chapter 17: A "Mysterious Something Between Sensation and Thought"

p. 185   Complacency of orthodox respectability: "Introductory and Critical Preface," *The Spectator* (London: Routledge, Warne, & Routledge, 1860), p. vii.

p. 187   "Northumberland Street encounter": W. M. Thackeray, "On Two Roundabout Papers Which I Intended to Write," in *Roundabout Papers*, ed. J. E. Wells (New York: Harcourt Brace, 1925), pp. 178–80.

p. 187   First use of "sensation" in news reports: "The Lighter Reading of the Eighteen-Sixties," in Wilkie Collins, *The Woman in White*, ed. Kathleen Tillotson and Andrea Trodd (Boston: Houghton Mifflin, 1969), p. xii.

p. 187   Excrement-eating: *Trials*, V, 188.

p. 188   On Collins's early work: Margaret Oliphant, "Modern Novelists—Great and Small," *Blackwood's Edinburgh Magazine* (May 1855), pp. 566–67.

p. 190   Braddon on Brodie: M. E. Braddon, *The Trail of the Serpent* (London: Ward, Lock, & Tyler, 1866), p. 267.

p. 190   "When we describe an organ": Margaret Oliphant, "Psychological Inquiries," *Blackwood's Edinburgh Magazine* (April 1855), p. 402.

p. 191   Dualism: *Ibid.*, pp. 402–03.

p. 191   "Being intimately connected": *Ibid.*, p. 404.

p. 192   Dreams: *Ibid.*, pp. 407–08.

p. 192   "Happily, in our waking hours": *Ibid.*, p. 408.

p. 193   Marcus in *The Other Victorians*, p. 31.

p. 193   "We indeed hope": *Ibid.*, p. 409.

p. 193   Animals and the mysterious something: *Ibid.*, p. 412.

p. 194   Simpler and higher types of animal: *Ibid.*, p. 417.

p. 194   "The great Author of nature": *Ibid.*, p. 412.

p. 194   "Infringing on the prerogatives": *Ibid.*, p. 419.

p. 195   On Darwinism and psychology: Robert M. Young, "The Role of Psychology in the Nineteenth Century Evolutionary Debate," in *Historical Concepts of Psychology*, eds. M. Henle, J. Jaynes, and J. J. Sullivan (New York: Springer, 1973), pp. 82–83.

p. 196   New study of Victorian news: Lucy Brown, *Victorian News and Newspapers* (Oxford: Clarendon Press, 1985).

p. 197   "An appeal to nerves rather than to the heart": "Our Female Sensation Novelists," *The Christian Remembrancer*, 46 (July 1863), p. 210.

p. 197   On *East Lynne*: *Ibid.*, p. 215.

p. 197   "Possession by one idea": *Ibid.*, p. 214.

p. 198   "A whole new set of words": *Ibid.*, p. 212.

p. 198   "Female Yahoo": *Trials*, V, 188.

p. 198   *Lady Audley's Secret*, p. 187.

p. 198   *The Woman in White*, p. 76.

p. 198   *Armadale*, II, 299.

p. 198   Charles Dickens, *Our Mutual Friend* (Baltimore: Penguin, 1971), p. 609.

p. 198   Bulwer's letter is quoted by Robert Lee Wolff in *Strange Stories* (Boston: Gambit, 1971), p. 293.

p. 198   *Hard Cash*, p. 197.

p. 198   Lionel Trilling, "Victorian Prose," in *Victorian Prose and Poetry*, eds. L. Trilling and H. Bloom (New York: Oxford University Press, 1973), p. 8.

p. 199   On *Hard Cash*: "Reade's 'Very Hard Cash,'" *Brownson's Quarterly Review* (April 1864), p. 223.

p. 199   *In Memoriam* as "characteristic": Harold Bloom, Headnote to "In Memoriam," in *Victorian Prose and Poetry*, p. 440.

p. 200   Freud's psychoanalytic theories: Shirley Staton, *Literary Theories in Praxis* (Philadelphia: University of Pennsylvania Press, 1987), p. 7.

p. 200   Decentered universe: *Ibid.*, p. 10.

Chapter 18: Black Swine in the Sewers of Hampstead

p. 203   Surreptitious disposal of illegitimate child: *Trials*, IV, 370–71, 379–82. The "Black Swine" editorial appears on pp. 381–82. As I have indicated, it was clipped from *The Daily Telegraph*, October 10, 1859, p. 4, cols. 5–6.

p. 206   Need for someone to explain code of respectability: Neil McKendrick, "Sex and the Married Victorians," Review of Peter Gay, *The Bourgeois Experience*: Vol. 1, *Education of the Senses. New York Times Book Review*, January 8, 1984, p. 35.

p. 208   Macaulay's claims: Quoted in Asa Briggs, *A Social History of England* (New York: Viking, 1984), p. 229.

p. 209   Self-gratification of readers of mystery stories: Geraldine Pederson-Krag, "Detective Stories and the Primal Scene," in *The Poetics of Murder*, eds. Glenn W. Most and William W. Stowe (New York: Harcourt Brace, 1983), p. 20.

p. 209   The whodonut: Geoffrey H. Hartman, "Literature High and Low: The Case of the Mystery Story," *The Poetics of Murder*, p. 214.

p. 209   The countertext: See my list of sources, most particularly those works published after 1970.

p. 209   Men in pubs dressed as women: This detail appears in a number of social histories. An interesting contemporary account of pubs and criminal business is Baron Nicholson, *Rogue's Progress*, ed. R. Bradley (Boston: Houghton Mifflin, 1965).

p. 209   Fear of disease: Bruce Haley, *The Healthy Body in Victorian Culture* (Cambridge: Harvard University Press, 1978).

p. 210   On photography: G. H. Martin and David Francis, "The Camera's Eye," *The Victorian City*, eds. H. J. Dyos and Michael Wolff, pp. 227–46).

p. 211   Roads to Kensington: Briggs, *A Social History of England*, p. 207.

p. 212   Incoherent city: H. J. Dyos, *Exploring the Urban Past*, eds. David Cannandine and David Reader (Cambridge: Cambridge University Press), pp. 25–26.

p. 213   On F. M. Browne's *Work*: Christopher Wood, *Victorian Panorama: Paintings of Victorian Life* (London: Faber & Faber, 1976), pp. 115–16.

p. 217   The "true verbal and graphic equivalent of urbanism": Dyos, *Essays in Urban History*, p. 10.

Chapter 19: Happy Endings

p. 219   "If we move from Austen to Conrad": George Levine, *The Realistic Imagination* (Chicago: University of Chicago Press, 1983), p. 42.

p. 219   On Eliot: *Ibid.*, pp. 46–47.

p. 220   The external in Conrad: *Ibid.*, p. 50.

p. 220   A "wild and gorgeous apparition of a woman": Joseph Conrad, *Heart of Darkness* (New York: Norton, 1988), ed. Robert Kimbrough, p. 60.

p. 220   Kurtz as all Europe: *Ibid.*, p. 50.

p. 220   "The horror!": *Ibid.*, p. 68.

p. 221   "The last word": *Ibid.*, p. 75.

p. 221   "Rendered Kurtz that justice": *Ibid.*, p. 76.

p. 221   Savagery in England: *Ibid.*, p. 10.

p. 221   " 'Mistah Kurtz' ": *Ibid.*, p. 69.

p. 222   "Unravelling of the threads of civilization": Peter Brooks, *Reading for the Plot: Design and Intention in Narrative* (New York: Knopf, 1984), p. 243.

p. 222   "A very lack of the possibility of order": *Ibid.*, p. 242.

p. 222   "Minimal language": *Ibid.*, p. 250.

p. 222   "The very start of Marlow's narrative": *Ibid.*, p. 336.

p. 223   Tanselle: In his 1987 Rosenbach Lecture, "A Rationale of Textual Criticism."

p. 225   "Bigamy has been Miss Braddon's big black baboon": "Belles Lettres," *Westminster Review* (October 1866), p. 269.

p. 226   On the Crystal Palace Exhibition: George W. Stocking, Jr., *Victorian Anthropology* (New York: The Free Press, 1987), p. 3.

p. 227   Stocking on Buckle: *Ibid.*, p. 115.

p. 228   Hara-kiri as diplomacy: Laurence Oliphant, "Sensation Diplomacy in Japan," *Blackwood's Edinburgh Magazine*, 93 (April 1863), pp. 397–413.

p. 229   On Stocking: George Levine, "Happy Ending," Review of *Victorian Anthropology*, *New York Times Book Review*, March 1, 1987, p. 24.

Bibliography: A Selected List of References for Victorian Sensationalism

Section I: Nineteenth-Century Sources

Amos, Sheldon. "Civilization and Crime." *Fortnightly Review*, 2 (Sept. 15, 1868), 319–28.

Anon. *Crim. Con.: Actions and Trials and Other Legal Proceedings Relating to Marriage before the Passing of the Present Divorce Act.* London, 1887?

———. "Dickens' and Wilkie's *No Thoroughfare*." *The Times*, London, December 27, 1867, p. 9.

———. "Execution of William Palmer." *The Leader*, 7 (June 21, 1856), 582–83.

———. "Griffith Gaunt." *Every Saturday*, 7 (April 10, 1869), 477–79. (Reprinted from *The Daily Telegraph*.)

———. "A Group of New Novels." *Dublin University Magazine*, 65 (March 1865), 348–50.

———. "The License of Modern Novelists." *Edinburgh Review*, 106 (July 1857), 124–56.

———. "Miss Braddon's Novels." *Dublin University Magazine*, 75 (April 1870), 436–45.

———. "Mr. Dickens' Last Novel." *Dublin University Magazine*, 58 (December 1861), 685–93.

———. "On Readers in 1760 and 1860." *Macmillan's Magazine*, 1 (April 1860), 487–89.

———. "On Sleep and Dreams." *Macmillan's Magazine*, 9 (April 1864), 473–81.

———. "Our Civilization." *The Saturday Review*, II (June 28, 1856), 195–96.

———. "Our Female Sensation Novelists." *The Christian Remembrancer*, 46 (July 1863), 209–37.

———. "Palmer at Stafford." *The Leader*, 7 (June 14, 1856), 557.

————. "Philosophy of Sensation." *St. James*, 5 (August–November 1862), 340–46.

————. "Reade's Very Hard Cash." *Brownson's Quarterly Review*, 1 (April 1864), 223–37.

————. Review of *Armadale* by Wilkie Collins. *The Westminster Review*, XXXVI (October 1866), 269–71.

————. Review of *Aurora Floyd* by M. E. Braddon. *The Times*, London, February 4, 1863, p. 5.

————. Review of *The Doctor's Wife* by M. E. Braddon. *The Times*, London, December 30, 1864, p. 8.

————. Review of *East Lynne* by Mrs. Henry Wood. *The Times*, London, January 25, 1862, p. 6.

————. Review of *Great Expectations* by Charles Dickens. *The Times*, London, October 17, 1861, p. 6.

————. Review of *Guy Deverell* by J. S. LeFanu. *The Times*, London, January 18, 1866, p. 7.

————. Review of *Halliburton's Troubles* by Mrs. Henry Wood. *The Times*, London, January 22, 1863, p. 7.

————. Review of *Hard Cash* by Charles Reade. *The Times*, London, January 2, 1864, p. 6.

————. Review of *Lady Audley's Secret* by M. E. Braddon. *The Times*, London, November 18, 1862, p. 4.

————. Review of *Limits of Religious Thought Examined* by H. L. Mansel. *The Times*, London, January 10, 1859, p. 10.

————. Review of *Lost Name* by J. S. LeFanu. *The Times*, London, September 21, 1868, p. 4.

————. Review of *The Moonstone* by Wilkie Collins. *The Times*, London, October 3, 1868, p. 4.

————. Review of *No Name* by Wilkie Collins. *The Times*, London, January 22, 1863, p. 7.

————. Review of *Origin of Species* by Charles Darwin. *The Times*, London, December 26, 1859, p. 8.

————. Review of *Orley Farm* by Anthony Trollope. *National Review*, 16 (January 1863), 27–40.

————. Review of *Our Mutual Friend* by Charles Dickens. *The Times*, London, November 29, 1865, p. 6.

————. Review of *The Ring and the Book* by Robert Browning. *The Times*, London, June 11, 1869, p. 4.

————. Review of *Sensation Trials; or Causes Célèbres in High Life* by "Civilian." *Athenaeum*, 46 (July 1, 1865), 18. Reply: 46 (July 8, 1865), 53–54.

————. Review of *A Strange Story* by Edward Bulwer Lytton. *The Christian Remembrancer*, 43 (April 1862), 448–67.

————. Review of *Transformation (The Marble Faun)* by Nathaniel Hawthorne. *The Times*, London, April 7, 1860, p. 5.

————. Review of *Uncle Silas* by J. S. LeFanu. *The Times*, London, April 14, 1863, p. 4.

————. Review of *The Woman in White* by Wilkie Collins. *The Times*, London, October 30, 1860, p. 6.

————. "The British Press: Its Growth, Liberty, and Power." *North British Review*, 30 (May 1859), 367–402.

————. "The Popular Novels of the Year." *Fraser's Magazine*, 68 (August 1863), 253–69.

————. "The Purity of the Press." *The Saturday Review*, V (June 26, 1858), 656–57.

————. "The Rugeley Poisonings." *The Leader*, 7 (Jan. 19, 1856), 52–55.

————. "The Rugeley Poisonings." *The Leader*, 7 (Jan. 26, 1856), 78–80.

————. "The Sensational Williams," *All the Year Round*, XI (Feb. 13, 1864), 14–17.

————. "Trial of Palmer." *Littell's Living Age*, 50 (1856), 270–73.

————. "What Is Sensational?" *All the Year Round*, 17 (March 2, 1862), 221–24.

Arnold, Matthew. *Culture and Anarchy*, ed. J. Dover Wilson. Cambridge: Cambridge University Press, 1966.

Austin, Francis E. "The Medical Evidence of Crime." *Cornhill Magazine*, 7 (March 1863), 338–48.

Bell, Robert. "Stranger Than Fiction." *Cornhill Magazine*, 2 (August 1860), 211–24.

Blandford, George F. " 'Acquitted on the Ground of Insanity'; from a 'mad doctor's' point of view." *Cornhill Magazine*, 12 (October 1865), 426–40.

Bourne, H. R. Fox. *English Newspapers: Chapters in the History of Journalism*. London: Chatto & Windus, 1887.

Braddon, M. E. "Lord Lytton." *Belgravia*, 20 (March 1873), 73–81.

Brodie, Sir Benjamin C. *Mind and Matter, or, Psychological Inquiries*. New York: Putnam's, 1857.

Buchanan, Robert. "Immorality in Authorship." *Fortnightly Review*, 6 (Sept. 15, 1866), 289–300.

Buckle, Henry T. *History of Civilization in England*. 2 vols. London: Parker & Son, 1858–61.

Campbell, G. D. "The Supernatural." *Edinburgh Review*, 116 (October 1862), 378–97.

Capes, Frederick. "Scientific Evidence: The Trials of Palmer, Dove, etc." *The Rambler*, 18 O.S. (September–October 1856), 226–31, 308–14.

Carpenter, Mary. "On the Treatment of Female Convicts." *Fraser's Magazine*, 67 (January 1863), 31–46.

Chorley, H. M. Review of *Armadale*. *Athenaeum*, 70 (1866), 32.

Coble, Frances Power. " 'Criminals, Idiots, Women, and Minors.' " *Fraser's Magazine*, 78 (December 1868), 777–94.

Dallas, E. S. "Popular Literature—The Periodical Press." *Blackwood's Edinburgh Magazine*, 85 (February 1859), 180–95.

Darwin, Charles. *On the Origin of Species*. Cambridge: Harvard University Press, 1964.

De Quincey, Thomas. *The Ecstasies of Thomas De Quincy*, chosen by Thomas Burke. New York: Doubleday Doran & Co., n.d.

Dibblee, G. Binney. *The Newspaper*. New York: Home University Library of Modern Knowledge, No. 58, Henry Holt & Company, n.d.

Doherty, John. "The Ring and the Book." *Dublin Review*, 65 (July 1869), 48–62.

Donnelly, Thomas. "Crime and Its Detection." *Dublin Review*, 50 (May 1861), 150–94.

Engels, Frederick. *The Condition of the Working Class in England in 1844*. Translated and edited by W. D. Henderson and U. H. Chaloner. New York: Macmillan, 1958.

Finlason, W. F. "Madeline Smith and Scottish Jurisprudence." *Dublin Review*, 43 (September 1857), 128–71.

———. "The Plea of Insanity in Trials for Murder." *Dublin Review*, 46 (March 1859), 58–92.

Forgues, E. D. "Dégénérascence du Roman." *Revue des Deux Mondes*, 40 (August 1862), 688–706.

Gainsforce, R. J. "English and Irish Crime." *Dublin Review*, 42 (March 1857), 142–56.

Gleig, G. R. "Spiritual Destitution in the Metropolis." *Quarterly Review*, 109 (April 1861), 414–63.

Hannay, James. "Great Britain: From Our Own Correspondent." *New York Daily Tribune* (June 21, 1856), p. 6; (June 24, 1856), p. 6; (June 28, 1856), p. 6; (July 8, 1856), p. 8.

Holmes, Timothy. *Sir Benjamin Collins Brodie*. London: T. Fisher Unwin, 1898.

Hunt, F. Knight. *The Fourth Estate*. London: D. Rogue, 1850.

Hunt, William. *Then and Now, or Fifty Years of Newspaper Work*. London: Hamilton, Adams & Co., 1887.

Hutton, Lawrence, ed. *Letters of Charles Dickens to Wilkie Collins*. New York: Kraus Reprint Co., 1939.

James, Henry. "Miss Braddon." *The Nation*, 1 (Nov. 9, 1865), 593–94.

———. Review of *Our Mutual Friend*. *The Nation*, 1 (Dec. 21, 1865), 786–87.

Knapp, Andrew, and William Baldwin, eds. *The Newgate Calendar.* Vols. I–IV. London: J. Robins & Co., 1824, 1825.

Lewes, George Henry. "Criticism in Relation to Novels." *Fortnightly Review,* 3 (Dec. 15, 1865), 352–61.
———. "Our Survey of Literature and Science." *Cornhill Magazine,* 7 (January 1863), 135.
———. "Physicians and Quacks." *Blackwood's Edinburgh Magazine,* 91 (February 1862), 165–78.
———. "Spontaneous Combustion." *Blackwood's Edinburgh Magazine,* 89 (April 1861), 385–402.

Macaulay, Thomas Babington. *History of England.* 3 vols. New York: Dutton, 1910–13.
Macintosh, Charles A. *Popular Outlines of the Press, Ancient and Modern.* London: Wertheim, Macintosh, & Hunt, 1859.
Mansel, H. L. "Sensation Novels." *Quarterly Review,* 114 (April 1863), 251–68.
———. *The Limits of Religious Thought.* Boston: Gould & Lincoln, 1860.
Martineau, Harriet. "Life in the Criminal Class." *Edinburgh Review,* 122 (October 1865), 337–71.
Mayhew, Augustus, et al. "Rugeley Number" of *Illustrated London Times,* February 2, 1856.
Mayhew, Henry. *London's Underworld.* Ed. Peter Quennell. New York: Spring Books, 1969.
———. *Mayhew's Characters.* Ed. Peter Quennell. London: Spring Books, n.d.
Mazo, Thomas. "On the Relations of the Public to the Science and Practice of Medicine." *Fraser's Magazine,* 62 (August 1860), 179–90.
Murray, P. A. "Spiritism and Modern Devil Worship." *Dublin Review,* 61 (October 1867), 253–80.
My Secret Life. New York: Grove Press, 1966.

The Newgate Calendar. Eds. Andrew Knapp and William Baldwin. Vols. I–IV. London: J. Robins & Co., 1824, 1825.
Nicholson, "Lord Chief Baron." *Rogue's Progress.* Ed. R. Bradley. Boston: Houghton Mifflin, 1965.

Oliphant, Laurence. "Sensation Diplomacy in Japan." *Blackwood's Edinburgh Magazine,* 93 (April 1863), 397–413.
Oliphant, Margaret. "Bulwer." *Blackwood's Edinburgh Magazine,* 77 (February 1855), 222–33.
———. "Charles Reade's Novels." *Blackwood's Edinburgh Magazine,* 106 (October 1869), 488–514.
———. "Modern Novelists, Great and Small." *Blackwood's Edinburgh Magazine,* 77 (May 1855), 554–68.

————. "New Books." *Blackwood's Edinburgh Magazine*, 107 (May 1870), 628–51.

————. "Sensation Novels." *Blackwood's Edinburgh Magazine*, 91 (May 1862), 564–84.

Owen, Mrs. M. E. "Criminal Women." *Cornhill Magazine*, 14 (August 1866), 152–60.

Page, H. A. "The Morality of Literary Art." *Contemporary Review*, 5 (June 1867), 161–89. Signed: A. H. Japp.

Rae, W. Fraser. "Sensation Novelists: Miss Braddon." *North British Review*, 43 (September 1865), 180–204.

Sala, George A. *Life and Adventures of George Augustus Sala*. New York: Scribner's, 1895.

————. "On the 'Sensational' in Literature and Art." *Belgravia*, 4 (February 1868), 449–58.

Smile, Samuel. "The Police of London." *Quarterly Review*, 129 (July 1870), 87–129.

Stephen, Fitzjames. "Anti-Respectability." *Cornhill Magazine*, 8 (September 1863), 282–94.

————. "The Criminal Law and the Detection of Crime." *Cornhill Magazine*, 2 (December 1860), 697–708.

Stephen, Leslie. "The Decay of Murder." *Cornhill Magazine*, 20 (December 1869), 722–33.

Swinburne, A. C. "Wilkie Collins." *Fortnightly Review*, 52, O.S. (November 1889), 589–99.

Thackeray, William Makepeace. *Roundabout Papers*. Ed. John Edwin Wells. New York: Harcourt, Brace, 1925.

Wellsman, Walter. *Fleet Street 1846–90*. London: privately printed, 1890.

Whitty, E. M. *St. Stephen's in the Fifties*. Ed. Justin McCarthy. London: T. F. Unwin, 1906.

Yates, Edmund. *Fifty Years of London Life*. New York: Harper, 1885.

Section II: Twentieth-Century Studies

Altick, Richard D. *The English Common Reader*. Chicago: University of Chicago Press, 1957.

————. *Victorian Studies in Scarlet*. New York: Norton, 1970.

Appleman, P., W. Madden, and M. Wolff, eds. *1859: Entering an Age of Crisis.* Bloomington: University of Indiana Press, 1959.

Ashley, Robert. *Wilkie Collins.* London: Arthur Barker, 1952.

———. "Wilkie Collins and the Detective Story." *Nineteenth Century Fiction*, 6 (1951), 47–60.

Auerbach, Nina. *Woman and the Demon.* Cambridge: Harvard University Press, 1982.

Bell, Daniel. *The Cultural Contradictions of Capitalism.* New York: Basic Books, 1976.

Bloom, Harold, Paul de Man, Jacques Derrida, Geoffrey Hartman, and J. Hillis Miller. *Deconstruction and Criticism.* New York: Seabury, 1979.

Boll, Ernest. "The Plottings of *Our Mutual Friend.*" *Modern Philology*, XLII (1944), 96–122.

Bowers, R. H. "The Canceled 'Song of Solomon' Passage in Reade's *Hard Cash.*" *Nineteenth Century Fiction*, 6 (1951), 225–33.

Boyce, George, James Curran, and Pauline Wingate. *Newspaper History: From the Seventeenth Century to the Present.* Beverly Hills: Sage, 1978.

Briggs, Asa. *A Social History of England.* New York: Viking Press, 1984.

Brill, Alex. "On Murder and Detection: New Articles by Dickens." *Dickens Studies*, 5 (1969), 45–61.

Brooks, Peter. *Reading for the Plot.* New York: Knopf, 1984.

Brown, Lucy. *Victorian News and Newspapers.* Oxford: Clarendon Press, 1985.

Browne, Nelson. *Sheridan LeFanu.* London: Arthur Barker, 1951.

Buckley, Jerome. *The Victorian Temper.* Cambridge: Harvard University Press, 1969.

———, ed. *The Worlds of Victorian Fiction.* Cambridge: Harvard University Press, 1976.

Burns, Wayne. "Charles Reade and the Collinses." *Modern Language Notes*, LXII (1974), 392–99.

———. *Charles Reade: A Study in Victorian Authorship.* New York: Bookman Associates, 1961.

Butt, John, and Kathleen Tillotson. *Dickens at Work.* Fair Lawn, N.J.: Essential Books, 1958.

Chertok, Leon, and Raymond deSaussure. *The Therapeutic Revolution: From Mesmer to Freud.* New York: Brunner Mazel, 1979.

Clareson, Thomas D. "Wilkie Collins to Charles Reade: Some Unpublished Letters," in *Victorian Essays, A Symposium.* Eds. W. Anderson and T. Clareson. Kent, Ohio: Kent State University Press, 1967.

Collins, Philip. *Dickens and Crime.* London: Macmillan, 1965.

Colp, Ralph, Jr. "Charles Darwin, Dr. Edward Lane, and the 'Singular Trial' of *Robinson* v. *Robinson and Lane.*" *Journal of the History of Medicine and Allied Sciences*, XXXVI, no. 2 (April 1981), 205–13.

Cox, Don Richard, ed. *Sexuality and Victorian Literature*. Knoxville: University of Tennessee Press, 1984.

Davis, Nuel Pharr. *The Life of Wilkie Collins*. Introduction by Gordon N. Ray. Urbana: University of Illinois Press, 1956.

Dijkstra, Bram. *Idols of Perversity: Fantasies of Feminine Evil in Fin de Siècle Culture*. New York: Oxford University Press, 1986.

Drinkwater, John, ed. *The Eighteen Sixties*. New York: Macmillan, 1932.

Dyos, H. J. *Exploring the Urban Past*. Cambridge: Cambridge University Press, 1982.

———, and M. Wolff. *The Victorian City*. 2 vols. London: Routledge & Kegan Paul, 1973.

Eagleton, Terry. *Literary Theory: An Introduction*. Minneapolis: University of Minnesota Press, 1983.

Ellis, S. M. *Wilkie Collins, LeFanu and Others*. London: Constable, 1931.

Escott, T. H. S. *Masters of English Journalism*. London: T. F. Unwin, 1911.

Fradin, Joseph I. " 'The Absorbing Tyranny of Everyday Life': Bulwer-Lytton's *A Strange Story*." *Nineteenth Century Fiction*, 16 (1961), 1–16.

Ford, George H. *Dickens and His Readers; Aspects of Novel Criticisms Since 1836*. Princeton: Princeton University Press, 1955.

Gay, Peter. *The Bourgeois Experience: Victoria to Freud*. 2 vols. (*The Education of the Senses* and *The Tender Passion*). New York: Oxford University Press, 1984–86.

George, M. Dorothy. *London Life in the Eighteenth Century*. New York: Harper & Row, 1965.

Gilbert, Sandra, and Susan Gubar. *The Madwoman in the Attic*. New Haven: Yale University Press, 1980.

Glugel, J. C. *A Hundred Years of Psychology, 1833–1933*. New York: Macmillan, 1934.

Gordon, Andrew. "Dickens and the Moral Scheme of *Great Expectations*." *Dickensian*, 65 (1969), 3–11.

Gould, Stephen Jay. *An Urchin in the Storm*. New York: Norton, 1987.

———. *Ever Since Darwin*. New York: Norton, 1972.

Graves, Robert. *They Hanged My Saintly Billy*. Garden City, N.Y.: Doubleday, 1957.

Gregory, Marshall. "Values and Meaning in *Great Expectations:* The Two Endings Revisited." *Essays in Criticism*, 19 (1969), 402–09.

Grubb, G. G. "The Personal and Literary Relationships of Dickens and Poe." *Nineteenth Century Fiction*, 5 (1950), 1–22, 101–20, 209–21.

Haley, Bruce. *The Healthy Body and Victorian Culture*, Cambridge: Harvard University Press, 1978.

Harris, Frank. *Presentation of Crime in Newspapers*. Hanover, N.H.: Sociological Press, 1932.

Hartman, Mary S. *Victorian Murderesses*. New York: Schocken Books, 1977.

Henkin, Leo J. *Darwinism in the English Novel, 1860–1910*. New York: Russell & Russell, 1963.

Heywood, C. "Miss Braddon's *The Doctor's Wife:* An Intermediary between *Madame Bovary* and *The Return of the Native.*" *Revue de Littérature Comparée*, 38 (1964), 255–61.

———. "*The Return of the Native* and Miss Braddon's *The Doctor's Wife:* A Probable Source." *Nineteenth Century Fiction*, 18 (1963), 91–94.

———. "A Source for *Middlemarch*: Miss Braddon's *The Doctor's Wife* and *Madame Bovary.*" *Revue de Littérature Comparée*, 44 (1970), 184–94.

Hibbert, Christopher. *The English: A Social History 1066–1945*. New York: Norton, 1987.

Himmelfarb, Gertrude. *Marriage and Morals Among the Victorians*. New York: Knopf, 1986.

Hollingsworth, Keith. *The Newgate Novel, 1830–1847*. Detroit: Wayne State University Press, 1963.

Houghton, Walter. *The Victorian Frame of Mind, 1830–70*. New Haven: Yale University Press, 1957.

House, Humphrey. *The Dickens World*. 2nd ed. London: Oxford University Press, 1960.

Hughes, Winifred. *The Maniac in the Cellar: Sensation Novels of the 1860's*. Princeton: Princeton University Press, 1980.

Humpherys, Anne. "The Geometry of the Modern City: G. M. W. Reynolds and *The Mysteries of London.*" *Browning Institute Studies*, II (1983), 69–80.

Johnson, Diane. *Lesser Lives*. New York: Knopf, 1972.

Johnson, Edgar. *Charles Dickens: His Tragedy and Triumph*. 2 vols. New York: Simon & Schuster, 1952.

Jones, Lawrence. "Desperate Remedies and the Victorian Sensation Novel." *Nineteenth Century Fiction*, 20 (1965), 35–50.

Jordan, Henry. "The Daily and Weekly Press in England in 1861." *South Atlantic Quarterly*, 28 (1929), 302–17.

Jump, J. D. "Weekly Reviewing in the Eighteen-fifties." *Review of English Studies*, 24 (1948), 42–57.

Kendrick, Walter M. "The Sensationalism of *The Woman in White.*" *Nineteenth Century Fiction*, 32 (1977), 18–35.

Lasch, Christopher. Review of *The Making of Modern Society* by Edward Shorter. *The New York Review of Books*, December 11, 1975, pp. 50–54.

Levine, George. *The Realistic Imagination: English Fiction from Frankenstein to Lady Chatterley*. Chicago: University of Chicago Press, 1981.

———. Review of *Victorian Anthropology* by G. W. Stocking, Jr., in *The New York Times Book Review*, March 1, 1987, p. 24.

Macdonald, William Bell. *Various Trials Cut from Newspapers.* 5 vols. Lockerbie, Scotland, 1839–62.

MacLeod, Robert B. *The Persistent Problems of Psychology.* Pittsburgh: Duquesne University Press, 1975.

Malcolm, Janet. "Reflections: *J'Appelle Un Chat Un Chat.*" *The New Yorker* (April 20, 1987), 84–102.

Marcus, Steven. *The Other Victorians.* 2nd ed. New York: New American Library, 1974.

Marshall, William H. *Wilkie Collins.* New York: Twayne Publishers, 1970.

Maurer, Oscar. "Anonymity vs. Signature in Victorian Reviewing." *Studies in English*, 27 (1948), 1–27.

Maxwell, W. B. *Time Gathered.* London: Hutchinson, 1937.

Miller, J. Hillis. *Charles Dickens: The World of His Novels.* Bloomington: Indiana University Press, 1969.

———. *The Disappearance of God.* Cambridge: Harvard University Press, 1975.

Milley, Henry J. "The Eustace Diamonds and the Moonstone." *Studies in Philology*, 36 (1939), 651–63.

Most, Glenn W., and William W. Stowe. *The Poetics of Murder: Detective Fiction and Literary Theory.* New York: Harcourt Brace Jovanovich, 1983.

Muller, C. J. "Charles Reade's *Hard Cash.*" *Unisa English Studies*, 94 (1971), 7–20.

Nelson, Harland. "Dickens' *Our Mutual Friend* and Henry Mayhew's *London Labour and the London Poor.*" *Nineteenth Century Fiction*, 20 (1965), 207–23.

Olsen, Donald. *The City as a Work of Art.* New Haven: Yale University Press, 1986.

Ousby, Ian. *Bloodhounds of Heaven: The Detective in English Fiction from Godwin to Doyle.* Cambridge: Harvard University Press, 1976.

Pearsall, Ronald. *The Worm in the Bud.* London: Weidenfeld & Nicolson, 1969.

Phillips, Walter C. *Dickens, Reade, and Collins.* New York: Columbia University Press, 1919.

Plumb, J. H. "The Victorians Unbuttoned," *In the Light of History.* Boston: Houghton Mifflin, 1973.

Praz, Mario. *The Hero in Eclipse in Victorian Fiction.* London: Oxford University Press, 1956.

———. *The Romantic Agony.* Trans. Angus Davidson. Cleveland: World Publishing Company, 1967.

Ray, Gordon. Review of *The Hero in Eclipse in Victorian Fiction* by Mario Praz. *Nineteenth Century Fiction*, 11 (1955), 152–55.

Robinson, Kenneth. *Wilkie Collins: A Biography*. London: The Bodley Head, 1951.

Rose, Phyllis. *Parallel Lives: Five Victorian Marriages*. New York: Knopf, 1983.

Sadleir, Michael. *Dublin University Magazine, Its History, Contents, and Bibliography*. Dublin: Bibliographical Society of Ireland, 1938.

———. "Miss Braddon." *Times Literary Supplement*, 41 (Oct. 10, 1942), 504.

———. "Notes on *Lady Audley's Secret*." *Times Literary Supplement*, 39 (May 11, 1940), 236.

———. *Things Past*. London: Constable, 1944.

Salmon, Lucy M. *The Newspaper and the Historian*. New York: Oxford University Press, 1923.

Schaeffer, William D. Review of *The Other Victorians* by Steven Marcus. *Nineteenth Century Fiction*, 21 (March 1967), 386.

Showalter, Elaine. "Subverting the Feminine Novel: Sensation and Feminine Protest," *A Literature of Their Own: British Woman Novelists from Brontë to Lessing*. Princeton: Princeton University Press, 1977, 153–82.

Smith, Anthony. *The Newspaper: An International History*. 1979.

Somervell, D. C. *English Thought in the 19th Century*. London: Methuen, 1936.

Squires, Paul C. "Charles Dickens as Criminologist." *Journal of the American Institute of Criminal Law and Criminology*, XXIX (1938–39).

Staton, Shirley, ed. *Literary Theories in Praxis*. Philadelphia: University of Pennsylvania Press, 1987.

Stocking, George W. *Victorian Anthropology*. New York: The Free Press, 1987.

Straus, Ralph. *Sala, The Portrait of an Eminent Victorian*. London: Constable, 1942.

Summers, Montague. "Miss Braddon." *Times Literary Supplement*, 41 (Aug. 29, 1942), 432.

———. "Miss Braddon's Black Band." *Times Literary Supplement*, 42 (April 24, 1943), 204.

Treuherz, Julian. *Hard Times: Social Realism in Victorian Art*. Mt. Kisco, N.Y.: Moyer Bell, 1987.

Twitchell, James B. *Dreadful Pleasures: An Anatomy of Modern Horror*. New York: Oxford University Press, 1985.

Williams, Raymond. *Culture and Society: 1780–1950*. New York: Columbia University Press, 1958.

———. *The Long Revolution*. London: Chatto & Windus, 1961.

Wolfe, Peter. "Point of View and Characterization in Wilkie Collins' *The Moonstone*." *Forum H*, 4 (1965), 27–29.

Wolff, Robert Lee. *Sensational Victorian: The Life and Fiction of Mary Elizabeth Braddon*. New York: Garland, 1979.

———. *Strange Stories*. Boston: Gambit, 1971.

Wood, Christopher. *Victorian Panorama: Paintings of Victorian Life*. London: Faber & Faber, 1976.

Yeo, Eileen, and E. P. Thompson. *The Unknown Mayhew*. New York: Pantheon Books, 1971.

Young, G. M. *Victorian England: Portrait of an Age*. London: Oxford University Press, 1963.

Young, Robert M. "The Role of Psychology in the Nineteenth Century Evolutionary Debate," in M. Henle, J. Jaynes, and J. J. Sullivan, eds. *Historical Concepts of Psychology*. New York: Springer, 1973.

Index

INDEX

FOR THE BEST IN PAPERBACKS, LOOK FOR THE

In every corner of the world, on every subject under the sun, Penguin represents quality and variety—the very best in publishing today.

For complete information about books available from Penguin—including Pelicans, Puffins, Peregrines, and Penguin Classics—and how to order them, write to us at the appropriate address below. Please note that for copyright reasons the selection of books varies from country to country.

In the United Kingdom: For a complete list of books available from Penguin in the U.K., please write to *Dept E.P., Penguin Books Ltd, Harmondsworth, Middlesex, UB7 0DA*.

In the United States: For a complete list of books available from Penguin in the U.S., please write to *Dept BA, Penguin, Box 120, Bergenfield, New Jersey 07621-0120*.

In Canada: For a complete list of books available from Penguin in Canada, please write to *Penguin Books Ltd, 2801 John Street, Markham, Ontario L3R 1B4*.

In Australia: For a complete list of books available from Penguin in Australia, please write to the *Marketing Department, Penguin Books Ltd, P.O. Box 257, Ringwood, Victoria 3134*.

In New Zealand: For a complete list of books available from Penguin in New Zealand, please write to the *Marketing Department, Penguin Books (NZ) Ltd, Private Bag, Takapuna, Auckland 9*.

In India: For a complete list of books available from Penguin, please write to *Penguin Overseas Ltd, 706 Eros Apartments, 56 Nehru Place, New Delhi, 110019*.

In Holland: For a complete list of books available from Penguin in Holland, please write to *Penguin Books Nederland B.V., Postbus 195, NL-1380AD Weesp, Netherlands*.

In Germany: For a complete list of books available from Penguin, please write to *Penguin Books Ltd, Friedrichstrasse 10-12, D-6000 Frankfurt Main I, Federal Republic of Germany*.

In Spain: For a complete list of books available from Penguin in Spain, please write to *Longman, Penguin España, Calle San Nicolas 15, E-28013 Madrid, Spain*.

In Japan: For a complete list of books available from Penguin in Japan, please write to *Longman Penguin Japan Co Ltd, Yamaguchi Building, 2-12-9 Kanda Jimbocho, Chiyoda-Ku, Tokyo 101, Japan*.

FOR THE BEST IN LITERARY CRITICISM, LOOK FOR THE

☐ **THE MORONIC INFERNO**
And Other Visits to America
Martin Amis

With mixed feelings of wonder and trepidation, British writer Martin Amis examines America in an insightful, thoroughly stimulating collection of pieces.

"As surefooted in its march across cultural boundaries as it is enviably, infuriatingly fluent"—*The Boston Globe*

208 pages   *ISBN: 0-14-009647-7*   **$6.95**

☐ **THE WRITER'S QUOTATION BOOK** (Revised Edition)
A Literary Companion
Edited by James Charlton

Updated to include more than 400 witticisms, confessions, opinions, and observations, this charming compendium covers every aspect of books and the writing life.

"Full of sparkle and wit"—*Cleveland Plain Dealer*

108 pages   *ISBN: 0-14-008970-5*   **$4.95**

☐ **WRITERS AT WORK**
The *Paris Review* Interviews: Seventh Series
Edited by George Plimpton

As John Updike writes in the introduction to this volume, these interviews of Milan Kundera, John Barth, Eugene Ionesco, and ten others, are "testimonials to the intrinsic worth and beauty of the writers' activity."

"Even 300 years from now these conversations will be invaluable to students of 20th-century literature."—*Time*

332 pages   *ISBN: 0-14-008500-9*   **$7.95**

You can find all these books at your local bookstore, or use this handy coupon for ordering:

Penguin Books By Mail
Dept. BA Box 999
Bergenfield, NJ 07621-0999

Please send me the above title(s). I am enclosing _____
(please add sales tax if appropriate and $1.50 to cover postage and handling). Send check or money order—no CODs. Please allow four weeks for shipping. We cannot ship to post office boxes or addresses outside the USA. *Prices subject to change without notice.*

Ms./Mrs./Mr. _____

Address _____

City/State _____ Zip _____

Sales tax: CA: 6.5%   NY: 8.25%   NJ: 6%   PA: 6%   TN: 5.5%

FOR THE BEST IN LITERARY CRITICISM, LOOK FOR THE

☐ **WRITERS AT WORK**
The *Paris Review* Interviews: Eighth Series
Edited by George Plimpton

These thirteen interviews of Elie Wiesel, John Irving, E. B. White, and translator Robert Fitzgerald, among others, reveal definitively that all writers are, in fact, creative writers.

"Long may this splendid series thrive."—*People*
446 pages   ISBN: 0-14-010761-4   **$8.95**

☐ **THE SECRET MUSEUM**
Pornography in Modern Culture
Walter Kendrick

From the secret museums where the obscene frescoes of Pompeii were kept to the Meese Commission's report, Walter Kendrick drolly explores society's changing conceptions of pornography.

"Highly illuminating . . . Kendrick writes crisply and amusingly."
—*The New York Times*
288 pages   ISBN: 0-14-010947-1   **$7.95**

☐ **THE FLOWER AND THE LEAF**
A Contemporary Record of American Writing Since 1941
Malcolm Cowley

Since the early 1920s, Malcolm Cowley has been reading, writing, and reflecting on literature; this collection of his work presents a fascinating portrait of our times and our literature.

"The creative logic of his connections make him a writer's writer and a reader's critic."—*Saturday Review*   390 pages   ISBN: 0-14-007733-2   **$7.95**

☐ **THE WAY OF THE STORYTELLER**
Ruth Sawyer

In this unique volume, a great storyteller reveals the secrets of her art—then goes on to tell eleven of her best stories.

"As invigorating as a wind blowing over the Spring meadows"
—*The New York Times Book Review*
356 pages   ISBN: 0-14-004436-1   **$6.95**